This book is a

the arrival

of a Jewish baby

This book was read by

Name of parents, grandparents, relatives, friend

To prepare for the arrival of

Child's Name

Birth Date

Celebration Dates(s)

This book was a gift from

Also by Anita Diamant

Nonfiction

The New Jewish Wedding

Living a Jewish Life: Jewish Traditions, Customs and Values for Today's Families

Bible Baby Names: Spiritual Choices from Judeo-Christian Tradition

Choosing a Jewish Life: A Handbook for People Converting to Judaism and for Their Family and Friends

Saying Kaddish: How to Comfort the Dying, Bury the Dead, and Mourn as a Jew

How to Raise a Jewish Child: A Practical Handbook for Family Life

Fiction

The Red Tent

Good Harbor

The Last Days of Dogtown

Day After Night

Essays

Pitching My Tent: On Marriage, Motherhood, Friendship, and Other Leaps of Faith

The New Jewish Baby Book

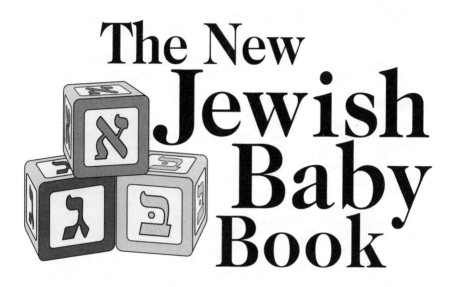

2nd Edition

Names, Ceremonies & Customs— A Guide for Today's Families

ANITA DIAMANT

JEWISH LIGHTS Publishing
Woodstock, Vermont

The New Jewish Baby Book, 2nd Edition:
Names, Ceremonies & Customs—A Guide for Today's Families
2014 Second Edition, Quality Paperback, Fourth Printing

For information regarding permission to reprint material from this book, please mail or fax your request in writing to Jewish Lights Publishing, Permissions Department, at the address / fax number listed below, or e-mail your request to permissions@jewishlights.com.

Grateful acknowledgment is given to the following sources for permission to use material: "Kensuke Solomon" and "Eve Askin" birth announcements © Elaine Adler. Selections by Rabbi Debra Cantor and Rebbeca Jacobs on *simhat bat* adapted from *Moreh Derekh,* the Rabbinical Assembly's Rabbi's Manual, edited by Rabbis Perry R. Rank and Gordon M. Freeman, © 1998 by the Rabbinical Assembly, page 228. "Noah's Ark" print © Mickie Caspi and Caspi Cards & Art. All rights reserved. Used by permission. "Daniel" birth announcement © 1999 Peggy H. Davis; "Double Rings" © 2002 Peggy H. Davis; "Markowitz" birth announcement © 2002 Peggy H. Davis. "Blessing of the Children," excerpted from Marcia Falk, *The Book of Blessings: New Jewish Prayers for Daily Life, the Sabbath, and the New Moon Festival* (Harper, 1996; paperback edition, Beacon Press, 1999). Copyright © 1996 by Marcia Lee Falk. Used by permission of the author. www.marciafalk.com. "Rachel Batya Stein" and "Daniel Alexander Wolf" birth announcements © 2004 Jonathan Kremer. Additional permissions statements can be found in the Notes section beginning on page 254. Every effort has been made to trace and acknowledge copyright holders of all material used in this book. The publisher apologizes for any errors or omissions that may remain, and asks that any omission be brought to their attention so they may be corrected in future editions.

Library of Congress Cataloging-in-Publication Data
Diamant, Anita.
The new Jewish baby book : names, ceremonies & customs : a guide for today's families / Anita Diamant.—2nd ed.
p. cm.
Includes bibliographical references and index.
ISBN-13: 978-1-58023-251-7 (quality pbk.)
ISBN-10: 1-58023-251-5 (quality pbk.)
1. Jewish children—Religious life. 2. Baby books. 3. Names, Personal—Jewish. 4. Berit milah. 5. Brit bat. 6. Judaism—Customs and practices. I. Title.
BM727.D53 2005
296.4'4—dc22
2004029323

10 9 8 7 6 5 4

Manufactured in the United States of America
Cover and Interior design: Tim Holtz

Published by Jewish Lights Publishing
A Division of LongHill Partners, Inc.
Sunset Farm Offices, Route 4, P.O. Box 237
Woodstock, VT 05091
Tel: (802) 457-4000   Fax: (802) 457-4004
www.jewishlights.com

The New Jewish Baby Book is for:

- People who are about to have a baby or who have just become parents.

- People who are looking for a Jewish name for their baby.

- New parents who wish to understand fully what it means to circumcise a baby boy with Jewish rituals and ceremonies.

- New parents who wish to celebrate the arrival of a baby girl in a meaningful Jewish way.

- New adoptive parents who are looking to express their joy in Jewish terms.

- Professionals and lay-leaders in the Jewish community—rabbis, cantors, *mohalim,* educators, and synagogue leaders—who have contact with new parents.

- Family members and friends who may not be entirely familiar with the ceremonies being planned by the new parents.

- Non-Jewish family members and friends who wish to learn more about Jewish traditions and customs.

Contents

for my parents
Hélène Diamant
and
Maurice Diamant, whose memory is a blessing

Foreword

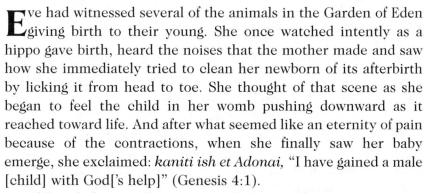

Eve had witnessed several of the animals in the Garden of Eden giving birth to their young. She once watched intently as a hippo gave birth, heard the noises that the mother made and saw how she immediately tried to clean her newborn of its afterbirth by licking it from head to toe. She thought of that scene as she began to feel the child in her womb pushing downward as it reached toward life. And after what seemed like an eternity of pain because of the contractions, when she finally saw her baby emerge, she exclaimed: *kaniti ish et Adonai,* "I have gained a male [child] with God['s help]" (Genesis 4:1).

Although her words are somewhat amorphous, anyone who has been blessed with the birth of a child can understand something of what this first mother felt. The verb *kanah* in Hebrew can mean to purchase or to gain, but has the clear connotation of "in perpetuity." In bringing Cain into the world, Eve sensed that birthing a child had as much to do with the future as with the present. It was through this little child that both she and Adam were guaranteed a future beyond themselves.

But there was more. As they acted upon the spark of divinity in both of them, having been created in God's image, they solidified their relationship with the Divine. It was as if Eve might have actually said: *Kaniti et Adonai,* "[through the birthing of their child] I gained a greater sense of God." *Kanah* also has the connotation of "create," and in their creative act, Adam and Eve experienced the presence of God as never before. In the Garden of Eden, everything was provided for them; nothing demanded their responsibility. Outside the paradisal Garden in the struggle in the real world, Adam and Eve came to know the exaltation of the creating of life as well as the responsibility that it entails.

The world outside the Garden of Eden into which Cain was thrust was much more complex and difficult than that in which his parents grew. If Adam and Eve had only to choose between eating or not eating the fruit of the Tree of Knowledge, Cain surely had choices to make at every turn.

All the more so are our children, who are born into a world in which the complexities of life and relationships can be overwhelming. We know this all too well even as Jews. The high rate of intermarriage, the increasing incidence of single parent families, the equality of men and women; all have had an impact on the way we must view the rites and rituals surrounding the birth, naming, and entry of children into the covenantal relationship between God and the Jewish people. New Jewish parents or prospective parents are confronted with a host of difficult questions, ranging from possible welcoming and naming ceremonies for a baby girl to how to include non-Jewish family members in an appropriate way in the *brit milah* of their newborn son. Jewish professionals, rabbis, cantors, educators, and *mohalim* also are forced to help single or gay parents who have adopted a child create meaningful ceremonies as well as assist non-Jewish relatives in understanding the significance of bringing a child to the Jewish people.

Anita Diamant's *The New Jewish Baby Book* is an invaluable resource and guide for Jewish parents and their families as they deal with the birth of their child. It will help educate them as to the origin, meaning, and importance of all the rituals and customs associated with the birth of a new child, while presenting them with any number of possible alternative ceremonies for *brit milah* and *brit bat,* an extensive list of male and female Hebrew names, and guideposts for how to handle these events.

For liberal Jews today, the issues and choices surrounding the birth of a child are manifold, and most Jewish adults need much help in educating themselves so as to know how to respond in personally meaningful ways. Anita Diamant will assist new Jewish parents in making intelligent choices that can enhance the spiritual significance of this most important moment in their lives and in the lives of their families.

In dealing sensitively with the oftentimes painful realities of Jewish family life today, especially as they surface when a child is born and in raising and responding to the myriad questions new parents always have, Anita Diamant has presented them with perhaps their first baby gift. *The New Jewish Baby Book* will enable them not only to experience the authentically Jewish way, while being respectful of the traditions of other family members, but also to grow in knowledge and commitment themselves as Jews.

Rabbi Norman J. Cohen
Provost, Hebrew Union College–
Jewish Institute of Religion

Preface

The Rabbis taught that mother, father, and the Blessed Holy One are partners in the creation of new life. Yet, for too long, the spirituality of childbirth has been a well-kept secret in the contemporary American Jewish community. Ask any mother (and often, fathers, too) the story of her child's birth, and you invite a flood of sacred stories, intense feelings, indescribable joy, and a sense of closeness to God. Everyone knows that the time of childbirth is a time when parents come very close to God, but the secret is closely guarded because so few Jews are able to speak of this truth out loud. Here is a book that is willing to do just that.

As a young rabbi serving a large, traditional congregation some years ago, I often wove stories about my young daughter into my sermons. I talked about her as my own first fruit, as a teacher who brought me the most valuable lessons about living—about gratitude, about wonder, about patience, about laughter, about God's presence in the everyday miracles of life. And yes, I told stories about her birth—an occasion so sacred to me that it compares in my own experience to my people's experience of Sinai—the day the gateway to God opened wide before my eyes. I consistently received the most heartfelt responses to these sermons, from both women and men. People were moved and grateful to hear their own experience of the extraordinary holiness of childbirth affirmed.

Anita Diamant's work is a beautiful expression of the profound spirituality of the experience of pregnancy and childbirth. This book is an invaluable contribution to any Jewish bookshelf, as it nourishes and gives voice to parents' sense of overpowering wonder at the process of preparing for and responding to the birth of a child. The book pulsates with the awe and joy and fear that are the real stuff of this time of life for parents. It eloquently voices what goes on in the heart and spirit of new parents, and gives parents easy access to the many ways in which Jewish tradition expresses those very same sentiments in its ancient rituals.

As in *The New Jewish Wedding,* Anita uses her clear and delightful journalist's style to open the door to the many meanings and practices of Jewish traditions around the birth of a baby. The book brims over with usable suggestions on how to celebrate and sanctify the experience of childbirth, giving even newcomers to Jewish tradition an enticing invitation to enter into the dynamics of Jewish teachings, allowing their own hearts to speak through time-honored Jewish idiom.

In doing this, Anita not only gives parents ways to express the inexpressible, but invites all kinds of Jews to enter into a partnership with Jewish tradition. In Anita's account, Judaism becomes a friend, a partner, as parents are empowered to link their own needs and longings with tradition's teachings to create ceremonies and spiritual responses that are both personally powerful and Jewishly meaningful.

Laced with Anita's characteristic lightness and good humor, the book offers a menu of possibilities, a plethora of opportunities for responding to childbirth with creativity, spiritual awareness, and Jewish authenticity. The book brims over with tantalizing tidbits—interpretations, suggestions, reminders, exquisite touches to sanctify and beautify childbirth rituals. This is all done with deep respect for the diversity of our Jewish community as well as the needs of individuals, and particular awareness of the changing character of the Jewish family in our community (hence valuable sections on adoption and the interfaith family).

This book is not a *halachic* encyclopedia. In fact, it contains an occasional item that may be problematic for traditional Jews, and so they may wish to discuss the key elements of their own ceremonies with a rabbi. But the book is of enormous value even to the most traditional of Jews, for its comprehensiveness, its liturgical creativity, its good humor, and its spiritual depth.

To new and expectant parents using this book, may it help nourish your joy and wonder as you bring a child into your life, and may it invite you to fully claim your partnership with God, as you create your new family. Mazal Tov!

Rabbi Amy Eilberg
Codirector, Yedidya Center
for Jewish Spiritual Direction

Acknowledgments

You may not see them, but Rabbi Lawrence Kushner's finger-prints are all over this book. I first met Rabbi Kushner while researching an article for the *Boston Phoenix*. He became what journalists call "a source," and although the years have made us into friends as well, he remains for me, always, a source.

A great many people provided insight, information, and wonderful creative ideas as I worked on this book. Rabbi Barbara Penzner is a constant source of guidance and loving support; Dr. Robert Levenson helped with both medical and spiritual insights about circumcision; Jane Redmont added sensitive input about non-Jewish readers.

Thanks also to Rabbi Susan Abramson, Elaine Adler, Dr. Joseph Adolph, Fern Amper and Eli Schaap, Rabbi Al Axelrad, Toni Bader, Naomi Bar-Yam, Judith Baskin, Janet Buchwald, Debra Cash, Betsy Cohen, Howard Cooper, Rabbi Ilana Garber, Ora Gladstone, Roni Handler, Dr. Victor Himber, Marga Kamm, Carol Katzman and Michael Katzman, Aliza Kline, Rabbi David Kline, Rabbi Neil Kominsky, Jonathan Kremer, Karen Kushner, Gila Langner, Amy Mates and Billy Mencow, Phyllis Nissen, Saul E. Perlmutter, Rabbi Jeffrey Perry-Marx, Cantor Sam Pesserof, Betsy Platkin Teutsch, Nina Price, Stephanie Ritari, Joel Rosenberg, Brian Rosman, Arthur Samuelson, Rabbi Dennis Sasso, Cantor Robert Scherr, Alvin Schultzberg, Rabbi Daniel Shevitz, Susan Shevitz, Danny Siegel, Hanna Tiferet Siegel and Rabbi Daniel Siegel, Rabbi Rifat Sonsino,

Ella Taylor, Rabbi Edward S. Treister and Rochelle Treister, Moshe Waldoks, Louisa Williams, and Shoshana Zonderman.

Special thanks to the artists and poets whose words and images grace these pages and to Stuart M. Matlins, Lauren Seidman, and the staff of Jewish Lights Publishing.

And of course, I would never have written this book were it not for my beloved husband, Jim Ball, and our daughter, Emilia. It was Emilia's birth that showed me the gap on the bookshelf where this book needed to be. She has been, from the moment of her birth, a joy and a wonder.

Introduction

As a first-time expectant mother, I was excited, nervous, nauseated, ravenous for information, and worried. I asked my friends who already had children hundreds of questions—about car seats, about diapers, about breast-feeding, about labor, about changes in relationships with spouses, about coping with sleeplessness, about patience. I read the books my friends recommended, and even more important, I watched them cope and their children thrive.

Although the ultrasound suggested that my baby would be a girl, my husband and I had a boy's as well as a girl's name ready. The baby would be Emilia or Eliot, in memory of my maternal grandmother, Esther Leah. But apart from the tradition of naming to honor the memory of a loved one, my husband and I spent almost no time thinking about the Jewish dimensions of our child's impending birth. Nor did we have any inkling of the overpowering, inarticulate awe we felt at the miracle of her birth—feelings we instantly felt required the blessings of our tradition and our community.

As soon as we became the proud and exhausted parents of Emilia, we scrambled to put together some sort of welcoming ritual that would coincide with my parents' visit from out of town. But it's not easy to write a ceremony that expresses the inexpressible when you are totally sleep-deprived.

The resources available to us at the time were few and scattered. On the night before Emilia's *brit bat* (covenant for a daughter), we found ourselves shuffling through a sheaf of papers from the synagogue's files, trying to cobble together a ritual that would feel right to us. The ceremony was held after Shabbat morning services at Congregation Beth El of the Sudbury River Valley. It was beautiful and moving, and apparently no one knew how breathless we were about the whole thing.

When I talked with Jewish friends who'd given birth to boys at about the same time, they expressed even more bewilderment. Although most did not hesitate to have their sons circumcised, their lack of understanding about the religious significance of the ritual—and about how they might participate in it—left them feeling dazed, out of control, and something less than joyful at their sons' circumcisions.

I wrote *The New Jewish Baby Book* in response to these feelings of awe and bewilderment, to help parents feel inspired and empowered to use Jewish tradition as a means for expressing their own great joy. This new edition reflects the changes in society and in the Jewish community—including the evolving and expanding nature of our families, medical advances, and Internet resources. But the basics remain the same, and the basics are beautiful.

Jewish tradition has always considered parenthood a sacred joy. "Be fruitful and multiply" is counted as the first mitzvah—the first commandment listed in the Bible. Having children is celebrated and honored as the crown of human experience, the source of the greatest possible happiness. The arrival of a new Jewish baby has always been greeted with ceremonial rejoicing and a wealth of customs and traditions. *The New Jewish Baby Book* will guide you as you find your place in this history of delight and gladness.

From the moment you discover—or decide—that you are going to become the parent of a Jewish child, you face a particular set of choices, starting with the selection of a name, and continuing through all the ways of welcoming your baby into the covenant and community of Judaism. *The New Jewish Baby Book* is here to help. This is not a book of religious prescriptions and prohibitions. You will find precious few "shoulds" in these pages. *The New Jewish Baby Book* provides the information you'll need to make authentic, meaningful, and memorable choices.

Drawn from the wealth of mythic, historic, religious, culinary, and literary traditions that surround the arrival of a new Jewish baby, and informed by contemporary insight and practice, *The New Jewish Baby Book* describes the many ways that new parents can celebrate the arrival of a child, the newest member of your extended families, and a unique and precious chapter in the on-going saga of the Jewish people.

In the close-knit Jewish communities of the past, almost everyone knew something about these customs and traditions since long before anyone became a parent; nearly everyone had attended *brisses* and namings. For a variety of reasons, many of us lack that kind of firsthand experience and find ourselves rediscovering and reinventing Jewish practice as we move from one milestone and rite of passage to the next. *The New Jewish Baby Book* is the perfect resource for this wonderful time in your life.

Part 1, *"Chai*—Life," touches briefly upon the mystery and awe of pregnancy and birth. From private moments alone with your spouse to baby showers, this chapter will help you acknowledge the changes in your body and in your family in distinctively Jewish ways.

Part 2, "A Jewish Name," provides guidelines for a key decision as a Jewish parent—what to call your baby. The lists of names for boys and girls contain suggestions from around the world, some as old as the Bible, some as new as the Land of Israel.

Part 3, *"Brit*—Covenant" begins with an explanation of the core Jewish concept of covenant. Whatever your circumstances—whether you know the sex of your unborn child, whether your baby is already here, or whether you are adopting—this part of the book provides historical context for your family's celebration and includes readings and translations that can be used in a variety of settings. Part 3 proceeds with a discussion of circumcision, including everything parents need to know about its laws, rituals, and customs, as well as its historical, biblical, and theological underpinnings. You will also find a frank discussion of the fears and emotional debate surrounding circumcision, advice on how to find and talk to a *mohel* (a person trained in the practice of ritual circumcision), and information about circumcision for adopted sons.

Part 3 continues with a guide to Jewish ceremonies that celebrate the birth of a daughter, with sample *brit bat* ceremonies, as well as a description of the common structure, prayers, and rituals.

Part 3 ends with ways to tailor your celebration. "*Hiddur Mitzvah*—Beautiful Touches" includes suggestions for ways to enhance any covenant celebration with written guides, ritual objects, music, and words.

Part 4, "*Simcha*—Joy," describes the ways to celebrate and share the blessings, from suggestions for birth/adoption announcements to the full round of parties and practices that surround the arrival of a baby, including the ancient practice of *pidyon haben*— redemption of the firstborn.

Part 5, "The Changing Jewish Family," presents a Jewish perspective on issues that are, for the most part, unique to our times. The Jewish family comes in more shapes, sizes, and constellations than ever before: multiracial, single-parent, gay and lesbian, non-Jews committed to raising Jewish children, and non-Jewish grandparents and other relatives. "The Changing Jewish Family" outlines some of the issues and emotions that may arise in these "new-tradition" families. Acknowledging the fact that an increasing number of Jews are fulfilling the commandment to "be fruitful and multiply" by means of adoption, Part 5 also includes information about resources for Jewish adoptive families and adoption ceremonies.

Finally, Part 6, "The First Year," describes some of the ways to celebrate the first twelve months with a new baby, from the first Shabbat at home together to parties that celebrate a child's weaning.

Every Jewish baby is a link in a chain that extends back to Sinai, when, according to Midrash (the Jewish literature of biblical interpretation), the souls of all Jews—even those yet unborn— were present for the giving of the Torah, the first five books of the Hebrew Bible.

Every Jewish baby is a triumph of life over death, especially in the wake of the Holocaust, which annihilated so many Jewish children.

And every Jewish baby embodies the universal human longing for redemption, for a world as innocent and peaceful as a newborn's face.

A story is told: God commands us to perform countless acts of love. How can we begin to obey such a difficult commandment? The answer lies (or soon will lie) in your arms. In every smile, every diaper change, every sleepless night, every lullaby, every wordless prayer of thanks, in the unending ways we care for and teach and protect our children, we perform countless acts of love. And the world is made holier. And so are we.

Part 1

Chai—Life

Conception

When the Baal Shem Tov, the great Jewish mystic and founder of Hasidism, was asked why people love children so much, he answered that a child is still very close to his or her conception. And because there was so much ecstasy at the conception, it still shows in the child.

Judaism, which sanctifies so many of life's passages with *brachot* (blessings) and mitzvot (sacred obligations), is comparatively silent about the awe-inspiring experiences of conception, pregnancy, and birth. Until recently, however, every Jewish wedding implicitly announced a family's hope that conception would take place as quickly as possible. Thus, a bride's immersion in a ritual bath *(mikveh)* was an expression of her decision to become a mother as well as a wife.[1]

Today, of course, many couples postpone parenthood, waiting months or years before trying to start a family. Whenever it is made, the decision to begin a family—or add to it—is the most life-altering of all choices. So couples have created rituals—some based on traditional sources, some entirely their own—to mark this turning point.

Deciding to have a child alters a couple's sexual relationship. Physical intimacy, which is celebrated as a great blessing in and of

itself by Jewish tradition, becomes a means to a sacred end: the
creation of a new life. A choice so momentous suggests the need
for a self-conscious act of separation—in Hebrew, *havdalah*—
between one stage of life and another.

Some couples choose to acknowledge their decision to become
Jewish parents by making use of *mikveh*. Although the ritual bath
is most commonly associated with *taharat hamishpahah* (the
laws regulating women's sexual availability vis-à-vis menstrua-
tion), that is by no means its only use. Some Jews—both men and
women—visit the *mikveh* before Shabbat and/or in preparation for
the High Holy Days of Rosh Hashanah and Yom Kippur. Ritual
immersion can also be used to prepare spiritually for a major life
transition—to mark the distance between a private "before" and
"after." *Mikveh* in anticipation of conceiving is an option for both
partners, either in a natural body of water or in a traditional ritual bath.

The traditional blessing for immersion is:

בָּרוּךְ אַתָּה יְיָ, אֱלֹהֵינוּ מֶלֶךְ הָעוֹלָם,
אֲשֶׁר קִדְּשָׁנוּ בְּמִצְוֹתָיו, וְצִוָּנוּ עַל הַטְּבִילָה.

*Ba-ruch a-ta Adonai, Eh-lo-hei-nu meh-lech
ha-o-lam, a-sher ki-d'sha-nu b'mitz-vo-tav,
v'tzi-va-nu al ha-t'vi-lah.*

Holy One of Blessing, Your Presence fills creation,
You sanctify us with Your commandments and
command us concerning immersion.

An alternative blessing is:[2]

בָּרוּךְ אַתָּה יְיָ
אֱלֹהֵינוּ מֶלֶךְ הָעוֹלָם,
אֲשֶׁר טוֹבְלֵנוּ בְּמַיִם חַיִּים.

*Ba-ruch a-ta Adonai, Eh-lo-hei-nu meh-lech
ha-o-lam, a-sher tov-lei-nu b'ma-yim hay-yim.*

Blessed are You, God, Majestic Spirit of the universe, who embraces us within Your living waters.

Here is a personal prayer for conception:

> Now as I immerse myself, I begin a new cycle, a
> cycle of rebirth and renewal in Your world and Your
> people Israel. I prepare in hopes of creating new life
> according to the mitzvah of *pe'ru ur'vu* (be fruitful
> and multiply), and for the sanctification of that life
> in *huppah* (the marriage canopy), *Torah* (Jewish
> learning), and *v'maasim tovim* (acts of loving kind-
> ness).[3]

Setting apart your lovemaking in a new way can begin anytime, of course. However, Jewish tradition encourages lovemaking
on Shabbat, particularly on Friday night, when husbands and
brides traditionally offer one another blessings.[4] According to
Midrash (Judaism's imaginative literature of biblical interpretation), the Sabbath reunites God's male and female aspects. The
joy, peace, and relaxation associated with Friday evening was
thought to make for a particularly auspicious time for conception.[5]

Friday night also happens to be a perfect time to make a separation between one way of doing things and another. For many
people, the workweek is done. Shabbat, with its intimations of
Edenic peace, begins. It's time to concentrate on each other.

There are no rules for such a private moment, so choose what
you feel comfortable with: a special, leisurely meal lit by Shabbat
candles, your favorite songs, a luxurious bath, love poetry. You
might read your *ketubah* (the Jewish marriage contract) and look
at wedding pictures to remind yourselves of the joy you felt on that
special day. You can recite or sing *Sheheheyanu,* the prayer of
thanksgiving that marks all manner of beginnings (see page 11).

As you light candles, consider this lovely notion, based in
gematria, the numerical system attached to Hebrew letters: *aleph,*
the first letter, equals one, *bet* is two, and so on. The Hebrew word
for candle, *ner,* adds up to 250. Two candles equals 500, which
happens to be the total of the Hebrew phrase *pe'ru ur'vu,* "be
fruitful and multiply." In some weddings, the parents of both bride
and groom walk down the aisle carrying candles for just this
reason.[6]

Pregnancy

Pregnant women have always evoked respect, affection, and excitement in the Jewish community. In the life of the shtetl (Jewish villages of eastern Europe), pregnant women were pampered and protected in the belief that unpleasantness might hurt the baby. In many communities, pains were taken not to let the evil spirits—especially Lilith—know that a baby was due at all.[7]

Whether or not you think of yourself as religious, pregnancy makes virtually everyone a supplicant. Most of the prayers of expectant parents are the pure promptings of the heart: Dear God, please make it a healthy baby. (Also, please make these hemorrhoids go away.) Prayers like these are as old as memory.

But there are also formal acknowledgments of this liminal time in Jewish tradition. In some communities, men recite additional prayers during their wives' pregnancies, during the daily synagogue service.[8] In the eighteenth century, women's petitionary prayers, called *tehinnot,* were published in the vernacular (mostly Yiddish), as in the following excerpt, translated by Rabbi Nina Beth Cardin:

> Just as You remembered Sarah, heeded Rebekah,
> saw Leah's sorrow, and did not forget Rachel, just as
> You listened to the voice of all the righteous women
> when they turned to You, so may You hear the sound

of my plea and send the redeeming angel to protect
me and to help me throughout my pregnancy.[9]

The life cycle of the family and the passages that women's bodies go through have been given new expression in contemporary voices, as in this prayer by Rabbi Judy Shanks, written during her pregnancy:

With all my heart, with all my soul, with all my might,
I pray for the health of this child.
I pray for it to be perfect in mind and body,
To issue safely and easily from me
At the proper time,
To grow steadily and sturdily
In a home filled with joy at its presence,
To be nurtured into a person who greets the world
with passion, enthusiasm, dance, love, humility, faith.

With all my heart, with all my soul, with all my might,
I pray for the health of this world.
I beg its leaders to temper their insanity with reason,
So that my child may be born into a world that seeks longevity,
not annihilation.
Let the world join in the thrill of creation,
And turn its back on the lust for destruction.
Let my child never know the pain and absurdity of warfare.
Let it take part in the dances of peace.

With all my heart, with all my soul, with all my might,
I pray for God to watch over me and my family,
I pray for strength and courage when I labor to bring forth this child,
I pray for the capacity to return my husband's love for me,
I pray for the ability to love and nurture this child,
I pray to feel God's presence now and always.[10]

Celebrating Pregnancy

Fear of the evil eye is a deeply embedded legacy of Jewish folklore. The idea that a party for an unborn child might tempt fate and somehow "cause" something bad to happen to a mother or baby lingers to this day. However, given the larger culture's embrace of the baby shower as a rite of passage, there is a diversity of opinion and practice among Jews. This is an entirely personal call.

With the addition of distinctive Jewish elements, a baby shower can become a memorable milestone on the road to becoming a Jewish parent.

Here are some ideas for ways to make your baby shower unique:

- Ask the guests who are mothers to contribute photographs of themselves when they were pregnant along with photographs of their babies, to be collected into a friendship album for the new mother. Put a picture of the mother-to-be on the cover and leave room for her own baby pictures on the last few pages of the book.

- Ask each guest to bring a fruit that symbolizes her wish for the mother-to-be: an apple for wisdom, a pineapple for generosity, figs for strength, and so forth.[11]

- After everyone is assembled, ask every woman to recite her Hebrew name and her matrilineage—the name of her mother, grandmothers, great-grandmothers, and other female relatives as far back as she can.

- Ask guests to bring presents that are specifically Jewish, such as gift certificates for home-cooked Shabbat meals, Jewish children's books, and Jewish ritual items. You can even register at a Judaica shop, listing such items as a *tzedakah* (charity) box for the baby's room, a colorful mezuzah to hang on the nursery doorpost, a Hanukkah *draydl* (top).

- There is no reason to make your baby shower an all-female celebration. Invite the father and his friends, and ask those that are fathers to share their stories about becoming parents, too.

- Consider melding the ancient tradition of Rosh Hodesh (literally, "head of the month") into your celebration. Rosh Hodesh is a semi-holiday that falls on the first day of every lunar month, marked by special prayers during the synagogue service. According to tradition, women were exempt from all work on Rosh Hodesh—a reward, says the Midrash—for refusing to donate their jewelry to the building of the Golden Calf. Today, small groups of American and Israeli women meet monthly to study, pray, eat, socialize, and celebrate the unique qualities of Jewish women's spirituality. Established Rosh Hodesh groups sometimes create ceremonies of preparation for their pregnant members and rituals of passage for women who are newly delivered.[12]

- Turn on the video camera and ask guests to offer a blessing to the unborn child. This can be a priceless heirloom—and a real treasure-trove for a bar or bat mitzvah movie.

Your "celebration" of pregnancy need not be limited to parties and public observances. Shabbat can provide a way to mark the momentous milestones of pregnancy. After the bustle of the week (and after older children are asleep), Friday night can be the perfect time to recall the "events" of the week: the end of morning sickness, the first kick, the first meeting of your childbirth class. Taking time to reflect upon these developments—being mindful of the miracles within—is a precious gift.

Birth

Agony, joy, wonder, terror, laughter, anger, tears, remember to breathe, crying out, despair, courage, profanity, prayer, the wonderful nurses, awe, a miracle.

The struggle, pain, power, and triumph of giving birth is the most intense encounter with the Holy that most of us will ever know. After the baby is born—held, kissed, studied, cradled, nursed, admired—language is inadequate. At this moment when there are no words, Jewish tradition provides two timeless prayers.

בָּרוּךְ אַתָּה יְיָ, אֱלֹהֵינוּ מֶלֶךְ הָעוֹלָם,
הַטּוֹב וְהַמֵּטִיב.

*Ba-ruch a-ta Adonai, Eh-lo-hei-nu meh-lech
ha-o-lam, ha-tov v'ha-mei-tiv.*

Blessed are You Adonai, Ruler of Creation, who is
good and does good.

and

בָּרוּךְ אַתָּה יְיָ, אֱלֹהֵינוּ מֶלֶךְ הָעוֹלָם,
שֶׁהֶחֱיָנוּ וְקִיְּמָנוּ וְהִגִּיעָנוּ לַזְּמַן הַזֶּה.

*Ba-ruch a-ta Adonai, Eh-lo-hei-nu meh-lech
ha-o-lam, sheh-heh-cheh-ya-nu v'ki-y'ma-nu
v'hi-gi-a-nu la-z'man ha-zeh.*

Blessed are You Adonai, Ruler of Creation, who
has kept us alive, sustained us, and enabled us to
reach this moment.

The other traditional words that seem appropriate at the birth
of a child are the opening lines of *brit milah* and *brit bat*:

בָּרוּךְ הַבָּא.

Ba-ruch ha-ba.

Blessed is he who comes.

or

בְּרוּכָה הַבָּאָה.

B'ru-cha ha-ba-a.

Blessed is she who comes.

This blessing was written by Seth Riemer, Betsy Platkin
Teutsch, and David Teutsch expressly for the moment when parents hold their child for the first time:

בָּרוּךְ אַתָּה יְיָ, אֱלֹהֵינוּ מֶלֶךְ הָעוֹלָם,
מְשַׂמֵּחַ הָאֵם בִּפְרִי בִטְנָה
וּמֵגִיל הָאָב בְּיוֹצֵא חֲלָצָיו.

*Ba-ruch a-ta Adonai, Eh-lo-hei-nu meh-lech
ha-o-lam, m'sa-mei-ach ha-eim bif-ri vit-nah
u-mei-gil ha-av b'yo-tzei cha-la-tzav.*

Blessed are You, the incomparable our God, the
Sovereign of all worlds, who lets the mother
rejoice in the fruit of her womb, and the father
with his offspring.[13]

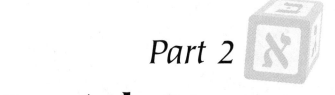

Part 2

A Jewish Name

Naming

All parents are passionate about the choice of their child's name, but everyone handles the decision-making process differently. Some people have names in mind long before they conceive or begin the adoption process and refer to the mother's belly by its soon-to-be name. Others pour over lists and hold off on the final decision until the baby is born. Some ask friends and relatives for reactions to the top contenders, while others keep their chosen names a secret. Whatever your style, this section provides history, practical advice, and a list of contemporary Jewish names to help you choose.

What's in a Name?

Choosing your baby's name is a second conception that begins the process of shaping the human being—the mensch—your child will become. With a name, you begin giving your child an identity, a community, and a way of understanding the world and his or her place in it.

For Jews, a name is a complicated gift. A baby named Daniel or Rebecca may recall a loved relative who has died, but it is also a link to every Daniel or Rebecca back to biblical times. Your child's name places him or her squarely in the unfolding story of your family and of the Jewish people.

Names have always had powerful associations in Jewish tradition. *Hashem,* "the Name," is one of the many indirect ways of referring to God. The dozens of alternatives—including *Adonai* (Lord) and *Eloheinu* (Our God)—stem from a belief that God's real name is unpronounceable and unknowable because, somehow, God's *real* name, the Name of Names, contains the essence, power, and unity that *is* God. The founder of Hasidism, Israel ben Eliezer, was called the Baal Shem Tov, "master of the good name," not simply because he enjoyed a reputation for goodness. His name also implies that he possessed great insight into the power and wisdom of God's name.

The Bible portrays naming as the first independent human act. Adam's job in Eden was to name the beasts of the field, the birds of the air, and every living thing. This was not a make-work project. The Hebrew for "word," *davar,* also means "thing," suggesting a close connection between names and natures. There is something about human names that seems to confirm this insight. Naming a baby feels like a self-fulfilling prophecy: a beautiful name will predict a beautiful soul, a strong name prefigures endurance. Like Adam's task in the Garden of Eden, giving the "right" name to your baby is a wonder-filled exercise of creative power.

The Torah highlights dramatic name changes that occur at moments of profound and far-reaching spiritual transformation that define the Jewish people. Abram and Sarai become Abraham and Sarah after they accept the covenant and become the symbolic parents of the Jewish people. The transformation involves the addition of the Hebrew letter *hay,* which is considered especially significant because it appears twice in the unpronounceable name of God.

Equally striking is the name change of Jacob, which means "supplanter" and refers to his victorious struggles with Esau, his brother. But after Jacob wrestles with an angel, he is given a completely new name, Israel, "wrestler with God," and becomes the patriarch of the twelve tribes.

Proverbs 22 says, "A good name is rather to be chosen than good oil," oil being a measure of wealth. "A good name" here probably refers to reputation, but the tradition stresses the idea that names have inherent value and power. According to the rabbis of the Talmud, the Jews enslaved in Egypt had all but forgotten God, but because they held fast to their language, to the practice of circumcision, and to their Hebrew names, they were saved from total assimilation.

Acknowledging the importance of naming, the Midrash advises, "One should examine names carefully in order to give his son a name that is worthy so that a son may become a righteous person, for sometimes the name is a contributing factor for good as for evil." Still, the power attributed to a "good" name is only as strong as the person who bears it. The tradition also stresses that each person earns his or her name. The Mishnah, the first part of the Talmud, says, "The crown of a good name excels all other crowns, including the crown of learning, of priesthood, and even of royalty."[1]

Giving your child a name that is unambiguously connected to Jewish tradition is an announcement of identity and commitment. While a rose by any other name might well smell as sweet, people are more complicated than roses. Human beings are a mixture of nature and nurture, of education and environment: people who are loved tend to be loving; children who hear English spoken at home learn to speak English. A child named Tiffany is given a legacy of beauty and elegance, but Tiffany is an explicitly material legacy. A baby named Rachel, on the other hand, receives an altogether different kind of inheritance—one that will eventually lead her to the Bible to look up her namesake, and perhaps to other books and stories about the biblical Rachel. She will, most likely, become curious about other interesting and inspiring women who bore the name before her. Rachel is a gift of many dimensions.

Names in the Bible

During biblical times, people had one name, and every child was given a name that was more or less unique. Over the thousand years described in the Bible, there is only one Abraham, one Sarah, one Miriam, and one Solomon. None of the twenty-one kings of Judah was named after David, the founder of the dynasty.

There are 2,800 personal names in the Hebrew Bible.[2] The relatively few biblical names still in use (about 5 percent) have a wide range of origins. Many are theophoric, which means that they exalt God. Names with the common prefix or suffix *el, eli, ya,* or *yahu* all refer to the Holy One: Elisha—my God is salvation; Raphael—God has healed.

Other biblical names describe the circumstances of birth. Moses comes from Pharaoh's daughter's explanation, "Because I drew him out of the water" (Exod. 2:10). And when Leah, Jacob's unloved wife, bears her first child, she calls him Reuben and explains her meaning: "Surely the Lord has looked upon my affliction; now, therefore, my husband will love me" (Gen. 29:32). Chava, Eve's Hebrew name, comes from the word for life, *chai*.

The Bible is also filled with names taken from nature, which to North American ears resonate with Native American associations: Deborah—bee; Jonah—dove; Barak—lightning, Tamar—palm tree. This tradition has been revived with a passion in modern Israel, where popular names include Tal and Tali (dew), Elon and Elana (oak), Oren (fir tree), and Vered (Rose).

Sacred and Secular

Despite their importance and durability, biblical Hebrew names have always competed with names from other languages and cultures. Even during the Talmudic period, Aramaic, Greek, and Roman names outnumbered biblical names among Jews. During the Middle Ages in eastern Europe, boys were usually given a secular name, called a *kinnui,* and a religious name, a *shem kodesh.* Eventually, the secular name became so dominant that some parents didn't bother giving a Hebrew name at all, a development that so alarmed the rabbis of the time that they decreed it mandatory.[3]

Still, it remained common for men to have two names, one for use in the secular world and the other for religious purposes, including being called to read the Torah in the synagogue, signing documents, and serving as a witness.

In many cases there was no apparent connection between the two names, though there were some translations. Thus, in France, men called Chayim (life) in synagogue were often known as Vive (life) on the street. In Germany, the use of the first name Wolf was probably based on the biblical Benjamin, whose tribe was associated with that animal. However, it was just as common for people to choose a secular name because it sounded like or shared the initial consonant of a Hebrew name or simply because it was popular in the surrounding culture.

Customs differed somewhat in the Sephardic world. Syrian boys were never called by an Arabic name only. Equivalents in Hebrew and Arabic were hyphenated, as in Shelomo-Shelem (peace) or Yehudah-Aslan (lion).[4]

Girls were rarely given two names. The one that sufficed was sometimes Hebrew, as in Hannah or Esther, but many Yiddish or Ladino names took hold as authentically Jewish in their own right, despite uncertain etymology. For example, Feigel, which was a popular name among Polish Jews of the nineteenth century, may have been based on words for violet, bird, or even fig.[5] On the other hand, Vida was a direct translation from the Hebrew *chai,* or Eve.

This disparity between boys' and girls' names is based on traditional roles in Jewish communal life. Since women were not called to read from the Torah or permitted to serve as witnesses in Jewish courts, a Hebrew name was not considered necessary for them. As the status of Jewish women changed to include these and other public roles and responsibilities, Hebrew names have become nearly universal for both sexes.

With the opening of the ghettos in Europe, it became increasingly common for Jews to select names from the larger society. This practice met with resistance from traditionalists, who saw it as an act of accommodation and assimilation, blurring outward distinctions between Jews and gentiles. However, by the end of the nineteenth century in northern Europe and in early twentieth-century America, a new category of Jewish-gentile names emerged. Jews seemed drawn to certain names. In pre–World War I Germany, for example, Ludwig, Morritz, and Siegfried were so popular among Jews that non-Jews began to avoid them. Isadore and Izzy (which means "gift of Isis") were so often used as alternatives to Isaac and Israel that they became Nazi epithets. In the United States, Hymie, a nickname for Hyman, which was a popular Americanization of Chayim, became an anti-Semitic slur as well.[6]

Jewish immigrants to America often selected new names when they arrived. Although traditional names never completely disappeared, many Yiddish names seemed too foreign for the new country. So the Yiddish Bluma (flower) blossomed into Rose, Lily, and Iris. The old-country Tzvi (deer), who was known in Yiddish as Hersch (deer), became Harry. America also inspired many Jews to provide children with "middle" names.

Naming After Relatives

Although the custom of naming children after parents and grand-parents is not found in the Bible, it is a very ancient practice, common among the Egyptian Jews of the sixth century B.C.E., who most likely borrowed the idea from their non-Jewish neighbors, and continued by Jews of Ashkenazic, or eastern European, descent, who name their children only after relatives who have passed away.

The tradition is different among Sephardic Jews, those from Spain and northern Africa, who name children after living relations. In some Sephardic communities the practice follows a precise pattern: the first son is named after the father's father, the second son is named after the mother's father, the first daughter is named after the father's mother, the second daughter after the mother's mother. Beyond that, names may be selected to honor any family member or friend.[7]

Because the majority of North American Jews are Ashkenazic, the custom of naming after a deceased relative is most common in the English-speaking world. In many cases, parents give the baby the same Hebrew name as the person honored and then select a secular name on the basis of the initial letter or sound of the Hebrew, which is how it came to pass that Baruch (blessed) became Barry and Bradley, and that Naomi became Norma and Natalie—or "Christmas child."

Superstition

Names have been associated with witchcraft since the beginning of human speech, probably due to the global suspicion that a soul can be identified, and thus made vulnerable, through its name. In some cultures, babies receive a secret name as well as a public name, to guard the soul against enemies and evil forces. Superstitions about the power of names abound in Jewish life, too, and are even acknowledged in the Talmud, which states, "Four things can abrogate the fate of man, and they are charity, supplication, change of name, and change of action." Jews often employed name changes to fool the angel of death.

Considering the high infant mortality rates of earlier times, it's easy to understand why death and demonic powers were thought to be drawn to babies. In Poland, newborn boys who were ill or somehow at risk were given names like Alte or Alter (which mean, respectively, "another" and "old one") or Zaide (grandpa) to confuse the evil spirits. Not only would such a name confound death, who would be looking for a baby and instead find an old man, but it also implied that the child would live long enough to grow old and become a grandfather. Similarly, a name like Chayim (life) was given as a talisman.

Ashkenazic Jews also shunned the practice of naming children after living relatives to prevent the Grim Reaper from making a mistake and taking a child instead of a grandparent. Sephardic Jews, on the other hand, assumed the angel of death might err in favor of longevity for both generations if they bore the same name.

In our day, even Jews who mock all forms of superstition tend to follow the advice of the medieval rabbi Judah Hechasid, who wrote, "Although one should not believe in superstitions, it is better to be careful." Thus many Jewish parents eschew baby showers and would no sooner consider naming their child after a living grandparent as they would think of leaving the baby outside in a snowstorm.

Fashion

Throughout history, rabbis and scholars have railed against the demise of authentic Jewish names and warned against the assimilation that results from choosing secular names for children. But the mishmash of Jewish naming customs is at least as old as the Babylonian exile (586 B.C.E.).

Names are as vulnerable to fashion as hemlines. Jewish names were not handed down from Sinai; they have been hammered out of history. The Talmudic period saw a burst of new Hebrew names (Meir, Nachman, Ahavah) as well as a revival of obscure ones

(Hillel and Gamliel). But even then, many Jews were giving their babies distinctly non-Jewish names from the vernacular, which for many generations was Aramaic.

The name Esther, for example, is Persian in origin and shares a root with Ishtar, the great fertility goddess of the ancient Near East. Although the Hebrew equivalent of Esther is Hadassah, no one argues the Jewish pedigree of Esther. Likewise, Mordecai, the other hero of the Purim story, has a Persian name—and an idolatrous one at that, meaning "devotee of the god Marduk."

Despite all the historic precedents, Jewish use of non-Jewish names has been a constant source of irritation to those who consider themselves conservators of tradition. The Hellenization of Jewish names (Jason for Joshua) dismayed the rabbis of late antiquity. Alexander, a name with no Jewish lineage, has enjoyed a loyal following since biblical times and continues to be popular.

New generations adopt a new set of names that reflect the customs and fashions of the times. In America, for example, Sam and Molly and Nettie and Ike gave birth to Sylvia and Charles, Rosalyn and Leonard. They in turn named their children Ellen and Alan, Gail and Larry, who named their kids Jennifer and Josh.

When it comes to naming, the return to Jewish roots is enjoying a very long renaissance. Biblical names like Rebecca and Aaron are enormously popular. There has also been a run on certain "ethnic" immigrant names—including Emma and Jake. Another enduring trend is the adoption of modern Hebrew names.

Some parents choose unambiguously Jewish names for several reasons. For one thing, names like Isaac and Aviva may help children develop a Jewish identity from early on. Ruth and David also make life easier in that such names work equally well in the various settings modern Jews are likely to inhabit: in secular situations, including school and work; in religious life, as when one is called to the Torah; and as a visitor to, or resident of, the State of Israel.

Modern Hebrew Names

With the founding of the State of Israel in 1948, Hebrew was revived and reconstructed as a modern language. In the process, the lexicon of Jewish names exploded. Many who went to Palestine after the Holocaust were eager to cast off all reminders of the Diaspora, including their names. Some chose to translate Yiddish names to Hebrew: Shayna (pretty one) became Yaffa; Gittle (good one) became Tova. Others simply chose a Hebrew name, so that Mendel and Morritz became Menachem and Meir.

The first generation of sabras, children born in Israel, inspired a host of new names such as Aliyah (wave of immigration), Or-Tzion (light of Zion), and even Balfour (for the British foreign secretary who in 1917 issued a declaration of England's approval for the establishment of a Jewish state in Palestine). There was also a resurrection of ancient biblical names that had not been heard for generations, such as Amnon, Yoram, Avital, and Tamar. Even names of evil biblical characters resurfaced, such as Aviram, who was swallowed by the earth in retribution for his instigation of the rebellion against Moses.

As the people gave life to the land, the land inspired names such as Kineret (sea), Arnon (stream bed), and Ora (light). Boys' names inspired a generation of new girls' names, too: Ariella from Ariel, Gabriella from Gabriel. And some names serve both boys and girls: Yona (dove), Ayala and Ayal (deer), Leor and Leora (my light), Liron and Lirona (my song).

Israeli names have a music and a life all their own, with diminutives and abbreviations applied to even the most ancient Hebrew names. Yosef becomes Yossi, Avraham becomes Avi, Rachel yields Racheli, Esther becomes Esti. Adding a final "t" to the end of girls' names has transformed even as venerable a name as Leah to Le'at.

The Israeli lexicon is flexible and open to international influences. For example, "Liane" is basically a French name with a vaguely plausible but somewhat improbable Hebrew etymology yielding "my joy."[8]

Your Family, Your Names

Setting off in search of the perfect name for your Jewish baby may lead to interesting genealogical territory as you mine for the Hebrew names of parents, grandparents, uncles, and aunts after whom you wish to name your child. The process may also send you to your bar or bat mitzvah certificate to find your own. And if you don't happen to have a Hebrew name now, becoming a parent is the perfect time to select one for yourself.

Traditionally, a child's full Hebrew name includes his or her parents' names as well. No Jew is simply Solomon or Abigail. Solomon's *ketubah,* or marriage contract, will read *Shlomo ben Moshe v'Rivka,* Solomon, the son of Moses and Rebecca. When Abby is called to read from the Torah, she will be called *Avigail bat Raphael v'Miriam,* Abigail, the daughter of Raphael and Miriam.

The choice of a baby's name can give rise to intergenerational and/or inter-*machatunim* (in-law) conflict. The easiest way to make a child's name a tool for knitting families together is to give the baby lots of them. Sharona-Avahah-Rivkah-Bella can honor four relatives or friends. And think how impressive it will sound when she is called to the Torah!

How and why you chose a particular name will eventually be of enormous interest to your child. Children love to hear stories about themselves, and the origin of a name can make a fascinating tale. Someday, you can tell your Dalia or Simon about the names you considered and rejected, about the day you found their name in this very book, about Great-Grandmother Dora and Uncle Sy. The more numerous and meaning-filled your stories, the better. You will be asked to tell them again and again as your child grows up.

Finally, if your child's Hebrew name differs from his or her secular name, make sure you keep a record of it in either a baby keepsake box or a book,[9] or have it inscribed on a lovely commemorative naming certificate (like the ones on pages 198–201).

Names for an Adopted/Converted Child

Adoption and conversion are increasingly common in the Jewish world. Although statistics on adoption and conversion in the Jewish community are sketchy at best, it is a growing phenomenon and a source of strength, blessing, and great joy.

In general, parents of adopted and/or converted children tend to use the same criteria as Jewish birthparents in selecting first names. The same customs, superstitions, and arguments apply no matter how your baby finds his or her way into your arms. However, in the case of international adoption, some families choose to acknowledge a baby's country and culture of origin by including a second or third name that reflects the child's unique journey—for example, Judith Seong (Korean for "beauty") Bernstein.

In terms of family names, it was once the custom to give all adopted children the "generic" name still used by most adult Jews-by-choice, which hearkens back to the very first Jewish parents, *Avraham Avinu* (Abraham our father) and *Sarah Imenu* (Sarah our mother).[10] This nomenclature makes spiritual sense in that every convert can claim a special kinship to the progenitors of the entire Jewish people, who themselves were Jews-by-choice. To be identified as a child of Abraham and Sarah is to receive "the crown of a good name," a name to be borne with pride and deserving of honor.

Nevertheless, this practice is not commonly used for children, who generally carry their adoptive parents' Hebrew names—thus, *Yehudit Seong bat Mordecai v'Shira.*

Family names are more complicated when one of the child's parents is Jewish and the other is not. Custom varies in such cases. Often, only the Jewish parent's name is used (e.g., *Rachel bat Moshe*). Sometimes the non-Jewish parent's name is stated in English *(Rachel bat Moshe v'Ellen)*. This is a choice best made with input from your rabbi.

The List and How to Use It

No list of names is complete. The compilation that follows is not a scholarly work or a definitive dictionary, but a guide for naming a Jewish child in the English-speaking world today. You will not find all of 2,800 names that appear in the Hebrew Bible, which means that choices were made. For example, the long-suffering Job is not included, nor are such evildoers as Amalek, Haman, and Jezebel. Many, though by no means all, modern Hebrew/Israeli names are listed, as part of the author's best effort to catalog names that conform to current English-language tastes and trends. This list is unabashedly idiosyncratic.

Although you may find all the help you need on the following pages, there are other places to turn. A rabbi, cantor, or *mohel* (one who performs ritual circumcision) can be a great help. If you want advice in selecting a modern Hebrew name, talk to an Israeli or someone who has lived in Israel.

One of the most comprehensive resources on Jewish names is *The Complete Dictionary of English and Hebrew Names* by Alfred J. Kolatch (Middle Village, NY: Jonathan David Publishers, 1996). Kolatch's large book includes a remarkable Hebrew vocabulary index, so if you wish your baby's name to reflect a quality, such as compassion, you will find suggestions under that heading.

All the names on the lists included here have some sort of Jewish "pedigree." (Though it must be said that, with a little effort, you can find a Jewish precedent for the use of almost any name. Legend has it that some Danish Jews were named Christian after King Christian X, who wore a yellow Star of David when the Nazis ordered his Jewish subjects to wear them.)

In addition to biblical and Israeli names, you will find some Yiddish and Sephardic ones, as well as some associated with the American Jewish community that have experienced a renaissance in the past few years (Max, Jake, Sadie).

Many Israeli names are beautiful in both sound and meaning: Eliora (God is my light), Gila (joy), Rimona (pomegranate). Then again, some are simply melodic. For example, Aderet, which sounds lovely, means "cloak." On the other hand, the timeless and lovely Leah can be translated as "weariness."

Finally, it's important to remember that fashion will change. For many generations, a child born on a Jewish holiday was given a name that reflected the celebration; it was a safe bet that anyone called Mordecai or Esther arrived during Purim. While this custom still has currency in some traditional communities, it has fallen out of favor in most of the English-speaking Jewish world. However, there are names that were considered unthinkably old-fashioned for much of the twentieth century that have been reclaimed with a vengeance; just count the Nathans and Hannahs in the synagogue nursery school.

Speaking of Hannah, there are far fewer biblical names for girls than for boys. This reflects a Jewish past in which women's names were often lost and a tradition with few female prophets, queens, and warriors. The poverty of the historical record about women scholars, leaders, and public figures compounds the problem.

However there is another form of *yichus* (hereditary status) attached to women's names from the more recent past. "Emma" recalls modern Jewish heroines like the political activist Emma Goldman and the poet Emma Lazarus. And there may well be heroines in your own family saga. Great-Grandma Pearl, who put her children through college by working in a sweatshop where she was a union organizer, is no less inspiring a namesake than, say, Avital, known only as a wife of King David. Naming a daughter Penina or Margalit is a fitting way to honor the valorous Pearl.

As you use the lists, remember:

- All names appear in English first. The most common spelling is given first, followed by alternatives, followed by a transliteration of the Hebrew pronunciation if it differs significantly from the English.

- All translations are from Hebrew, unless otherwise noted.

- All English versions of Hebrew names are transliterations, which means there are no exact correlations. Choose the spelling you prefer. Dina, Deena, Dena, and Dinah are all correct.

- The final "h" on names ending with a vowel (Malkah) can be dropped (Malka).

- In Hebrew pronunciation, the emphasis is generally on the last syllable. Adam, for instance, is Ah-*dahm*. Sarah is Sah-*rah*. There are exceptions—for example, Ye*ho*shua. If you are unsure, ask your rabbi or someone more familiar with spoken Hebrew.

- A number of names are given with variations that change the meaning somewhat. Most common are the suffixes -*i*, -*li*, and -*iel*. For example, Ron, which means "joy" or "song," can become Roni (my joy), Ronli (joy is mine), or Roniel (joy of God).

- There is no "J" sound in Hebrew. Where a "J" appears, the Hebrew sound is "Y." Thus, Jonina is Yonina. In most cases, and especially where there is no common English J-sound version, such names are listed under "Y." However, where an English version is possible (Jasmine or Yasmin), both are given under the listing for "J."

A Son! Boys' Names

A

AARON, ARON, AHARON אהרן
> Teaching, singing, shining, or mountain. The Aramaic root means "messenger." Aaron was the older brother of Moses and Miriam, the first Israelite high priest and progenitor of all priests. Rabbinic tradition stresses his love of peace.

ABBA אבא
> Father. It might seem odd to name your son "Daddy," but then, Israeli statesman Abba Eban wore it well.

ABEL הבל
> Breath. The son of Adam and Eve, and the ill-fated brother of Cain.

ABIR אביר
> Strong.

ABNER, AVNER אבנר
> Literally, father of light. Avner ben Ner was King Saul's uncle and the commander of his army.

ABRAHAM, AVRAHAM אברהם
> Father of a mighty nation. Abraham, the first Hebrew, began life as Abram, but when he accepted the covenant, by circumcising himself and establishing the practice among his

people, the Hebrew letter *hay*, which appears twice in the unpronounceable name of God *(yud hay vav hay)*, was added to his name. The Arabic equivalent is Ali Baba.

Abram, Avram אברם

Exalted father. Abraham's original name.

Absalom, Avshalom אבשלום

Father of peace. King David's third son. A later Absalom played a prominent part in the defense of Jerusalem against the emperor Pompey.

Achiya אחיה

God is my brother. One of King David's warriors. Achi means "brother."

Adam אדם

Earth. In Phoenician and Babylonian, it means "mankind." The first man. Not a popular name among Jews until modern times.

Adin עדין

Beautiful, pleasant, gentle. A biblical name, its variations include Adi, Adina, Adino, Adiv.

Adlai עדלי

Aramaic, refuge of God. The biblical Adlai was a shepherd.

Admon אדמון

The name of a red peony that grows in the upper Galilee.

Akiba, Akiva עקיבא

Akiva is derived from the same root as Jacob, Ya'akov, which means "supplanter," or "held by the heel." Rabbi Akiva was a first-century scholar and teacher, and the founder of a famous academy. Common nicknames include Koby and Kivi.

Alexander אלכסנדר

Protector of men. Ever since the third century B.C.E., when Alexander the Great spared Jerusalem from harm, Jewish boys have been named in his honor. As the story goes, the high priest of Jerusalem was so grateful for Alexander's

largesse that he proclaimed that all Jewish males born in
the city for a year would bear the conquerer's name, and it
has remained popular ever since, in many forms, including
Sander (Yiddish) and Sasha (a Russian diminutive).
Nicknames include Alex and Sandy.

ALON אלון
Oak tree. One of the sons of Shimeon. A very popular name
in Israel.

ALYAN עלין
Heights. One of the sons of Seir in the Bible.

AMAL עמל
Work. A member of the tribe of Asher.

AMATZ, AMAZIAH אמץ, אמציה
Strong, courageous.

AMI עמי
My people. A popular Israeli name. The root is found in many
other names, a few of which follow.

AMICHAI עמיחי
My people is alive.

AMIEL עמיאל
God of my people.

AMIKAM עמיקם
Nation arisen.

AMIN אמין
Trustworthy.

AMIR אמיר
Mighty, strong.

AMIRAM עמירם
My people is lofty.

AMITAI אמיתי
True, faithful. Amitai was the father of Jonah.

AMNON אמנון
Faithful. Amnon was the oldest son of David.

AMOS עמוס
Burdened. A prophet who preached social morality in the Northern Kingdom of Israel during the eighth century B.C.E. A popular Israeli name.

AMRAM עמרם
A mighty nation. Amram was the father of Moses, Miriam, and Aaron.

ANSHEL אנשעל
Yiddish for Asher.

ARI ארי
A shortened form of Aryeh, but a popular name in its own right.

ARIEL אריאל
Lion of God. Also a poetic name for the city of Jerusalem. Ari and Arik are diminutives.

ARNON ארנון
Roaring stream. In the Bible, the Arnon was a stream in the frontier of the Moab, a kingdom east of the Dead Sea.

ARYEH אריה
Lion. The biblical Aryeh was an army officer.

ASA אסא
Healer. A king of Judea.

ASHER אשר
Blessed, fortunate. Asher was the son of Jacob and Zilpah and the leader of one of the twelve tribes of Israel.

AVI אבי
Father. A diminutive of Avraham, but also used as a name on its own, this is the prefix/root for many names, some of which follow.

AVICHAI אביחי
My father lives.

AVIDAN אבידן
Father of justice, or God is just.

AVIEL אביאל
God is my father.

AVIEZER אביעזר
Father helper.

AVIGDOR אביגדור
Father protector. Popular in Israel.

AVIMELECH אבימלך
Father king.

AVINOAM אבינעם
Father of delight.

AVISHAI אבישי
Aramaic, gift of God. A grandson of the biblical Jesse.

AVISHALOM אבישלום
Father of peace.

AVIV אביב
Spring.

AVROM אברם
Yiddish for Abraham.

AZI עזי
Strong.

AZRIEL עזריאל
God is my help.

B

BARAK ברק
Lightning. A biblical soldier during the reign of Deborah.

BARAM ברעם
Son of the nation.

BARUCH ברוך
Blessed. Baruch was a friend to the prophet Jeremiah. The Yiddish version, Bendit, is probably based on the name Benedict.

BEN-AMI בן־עמי
Son of my people. The prefix/root *ben,* or "son," gives rise to many names.

BENJAMIN, BINYAMIN בנימין
Son of my right hand. Benjamin was the younger of Rachel's sons and Jacob's favorite. As the only one of the twelve brothers who did not participate in Joseph's sale into slavery, Benjamin was honored by having the Holy Temple built on territory allotted to his tribe.

BEN-ZION בן־ציון
Son of Zion. Benzi is a popular nickname.

BERYL בעריל
A Yiddish diminutive for "bear," which is sometimes further shortened to Ber. The Hebrew equivalent is Dov.

BOAZ בעז
Strength and swiftness. The great-grandfather of King David, Boaz was a wealthy, land-owning Bethlehemite who married Ruth.

C

CALEB, CALEV כלב
Heart, also dog. Of the twelve spies sent by Moses to Canaan, only Caleb and Joshua brought back a favorable report, for which they were allowed to enter the Promised Land.

CHAIM, CHAYIM, HAYYIM חיים
Life.

D

DAN דן

Judge. Dan was the fifth son of Jacob, and firstborn of Bilhah, Rachel's maidservant. Dani is a variant.

DANIEL דניאל

God is my judge. The hero of the Book of Daniel was an interpreter of visions who predicted the future triumph of a messianic kingdom.

DAVID דוד

Beloved. David, the shepherd who killed Goliath, became king first of Judah and later of Israel. According to legend, the Messiah will be a descendant of David. The name has been a favorite since Talmudic times.

DEROR, DERORI, DROR דרור, דרורי

Freedom. Also, a bird. A popular Israeli name.

DEVIR דביר

Holy place. In the Bible, Devir was a king of Eglon.

DOR דור

A generation.

DORAN, DORON דורן, דורון

Gift.

DOTAN דותן

Law. In the Bible, Dotan was a place in Palestine, north of Samaria.

DOV דב

Bear.

E

EFRAYIM, EPHREM, EPHRAIM אפרים

Fruitful. Efrayim was one of Joseph's sons—Jacob's grandson. His name is mentioned in the traditional Friday night blessing for sons.

EFRON עפרון
A bird.

ELAZAR אלעזר
God has helped. Aaron's third son, Elazar, became the high priest after him. There have been many famous Elazars throughout history, including Elazar ben Jair, a commander at Masada, whose eloquence persuaded the city's defenders that suicide was preferable to surrender or defeat.

ELI, ELY עלי
Ascend. In the Bible, Eli was a high priest and the last of the judges in the days of Samuel.

ELIAKIM אליקים
God established.

ELIEZER אליזער
My God has helped. Eliezer was the name of Abraham's steward, Moses's son, and a prophet in the time of Jehosaphat. Three great Talmudic scholars and many great German rabbis were called Eliezer.

ELIHU אליהוא
He is my God. Elihu appears in the Bible as a young friend of Job.

ELIJAH, ELIAHU אליהו
The Lord is my God. Elijah the prophet lived during the ninth century B.C.E. and led the fight against the cult of Baal. According to tradition, he ascended to heaven in a chariot of fire but did not die. Elijah became a figure in Jewish folklore, appearing to common folk disguised as a beggar. Elijah is viewed as a herald of the Messiah, and his presence is invoked during Passover and at circumcisions. The name is translated into Elie in French, Elia in Italian. English versions include Eliot, Ellis, and Elias. Elya is a common Israeli nickname.

ELISHA אלישע
God is my salvation. Elisha the prophet succeeded Elijah. In Second Kings, there are miraculous stories about his long life.

ELKANAH אלקנה
God bought.

EMANUEL, EMMANUEL עמנואל
God is with us.

ENOCH חנוך
Dedicated. Enoch was Cain's son, born after Abel died.

ESHKOL אשכול
A cluster of grapes. In Hebrew letters, Eshkol signifies a gathering of scholars. Levi Eshkol (1895–1969) was Israeli prime minister from 1963 to 1969.

ETAN, EYTAN איתן
Strong.

EVEN אבן
Stone. Eben and Eban are common English versions.

EYAL איל
A stag.

EZEKIEL יחזקאל
God will strengthen. Ezekiel was a prophet who lived during the sixth century B.C.E., during the last days of the First Temple. Ezekiel's description of the divine throne was the major text for Jewish mysticism (*Ma'aseh Merkavah*).

EZRA, EZRI עזרא, עזרי
Help. A priest and scribe of the fifth century B.C.E. Ezra led the return from Babylon to Jerusalem, where he became a key figure in the reconstruction of the Temple. He is credited with introducing the square Hebrew alphabet.

G

GABRIEL, GAVRIEL גבריאל

God is my strength. Gabriel the angel visited Daniel in the biblical tale. In Israel, the diminutive Gabi is also used as a full name. Gavirol is a Sephardic variation, with Gavri as a nickname.

GAD גד

Happy. Gad was one of Jacob's sons.

GAL, GALI גל, גלי

A wave or a mountain. Also, Galya.

GAMALIEL, GAMLIEL גמליאל

God is my reward. The name of many Talmudic scholars.

GAN גן

Garden.

GARON גרון

A threshing floor.

GEDALIA, GEDALIAH, GEDALIAHU גדליה, גדליהו

God is great. Gedaliah was a governor of Judea.

GERSHOM, GERSHON, GERSON גרשום, גרשון

I was a stranger there. Moses named his older son Gershom, referring to the Egyptian captivity. The name has served many teachers, including Gershom Scholem, the great twentieth-century scholar of Jewish mysticism.

GIBOR גבור

Strong, hero.

GIDEON גדעון

A mighty warrior. A biblical warrior, reputed to have fathered seventy sons. Gidi is a popular nickname.

GIL, GILL, GILI, GILLI גיל, גילי

Joy. Gili means "my joy."

GILAD, GILEAD, GILADI גלעד, גלעדי

A place name that refers to a mountain range east of the Jordan River.

GUR, GURI, GURIEL גור, גורי, גוריאל

Respectively, young lion, my young lion, and God is my lion. Guryon is another variation.

H

HADAR הדר

Adornment. A biblical king of Edom.

HANAN חנן

Grace or gracious. A shortened form of Yohanan.

HAREL הראל

Mountain of God. A biblical place name.

HASKEL, HASKELL השכל

Wise.

HASKEL, HASKELL חזקעל

Yiddish form of Ezekiel.

HERSCH, HERSH הערש

Yiddish, a deer. The diminutives and variations of Hersch are numerous: Herschel, Hesh, Heshel, Herzl, Hirsh, Hirsch. Tzvi is the Hebrew equivalent.

HILLEL הלל

Praised. The name was often given in honor of the great scholar Hillel, who was born in Babylon in 75 B.C.E.

HIRAM חירם

Noble-born. Hiram was king of Tyre, circa 969–936 B.C.E. He helped plan, build, and equip the Temple in Jerusalem.

HOD הוד

Splendor, vigor. Hod was a member of the tribe of Asher. Popular in Israel.

I

ILAN אילן
Tree. An alternative transliteration for Alon.

IRA עירא
Arabic, swiftness.

ISAAC, ITZAK, YITZHAK יצחק
Laughter. Isaac was the son of Abraham and Sarah, and the first Jew to be circumcised on the eighth day of life. The name has remained popular throughout Jewish history. Isaac Luria, the Safed mystic, established Lurianic Kabbalah. Nicknames include Ike, Issa, and Yitz.

ISAIAH, YISHAYAHU ישעיה, ישעיהו
God is salvation. Isaiah was a prophet in Jerusalem in the eighth century B.C.E. Isa is a popular nickname.

ISRAEL, YISRAEL, YISROEL ישראל
Wrestler with God. The name given to Jacob after he wrestled with the angel. Israel is a synonym for the Jewish people.

ISSACHAR יששכר
There is a reward. Issachar was the son of Jacob and Leah, and one of the leaders of the twelve tribes of Israel.

ITAI, ITTAI אתי
Friendly. Itai was one of David's warriors.

ITIEL איתיאל
God is with me. Itiel was a member of the tribe of Benjamin.

ITTAMAR איתמר
Island of palm. Ittamar, whose name signifies gracefulness, was one of Aaron's sons. Ismar is an Ashkenazic transliteration of the name.

J

JACOB, YACOV, YA'ACOV יעקב
Held by the heel, supplanter. The third of the patriarchs, Jacob fathered the twelve tribes. His name was changed to Israel after his wrestling match with an angel. There are many nicknames and derivatives of Jacob, from James to Jack to Jake to Yankele.

JARED, YARED ירד
To descend.

JEDEDIAH, YEDADIAH ידידיה
The name of priestly ancestral houses, mentioned in the Book of Nehemiah.

JEREMIAH, JEREMY, YIR'MIAHU ירמיה, ירמיהו
God will uplift. Jeremiah the prophet lived around 625 B.C.E. His gloomy forecasts aroused resentment, and he spent many years in jail.

JESSE, YISHAI ישי
Wealthy. Ruth's grandson Jesse was the father of King David.

JETHRO, YITRO יתרו
Abundance, riches. Father of Zipporah and Moses's father-in-law, Jethro was a Midianite priest.

JOEL, YOEL יואל
God is willing. Joel was one of the twelve minor prophets who preached in Judea.

JONAH, YONAH יונה
Dove. Jonah was the prophet of whale fame.

JONATHAN, YONATAN יונתן
God has given. Jonathan, the son of Saul, is remembered for his friendship with David. Yoni is a popular Israeli nickname.

JORDAN, YARDEN ירדן

Descend. Jori is a popular Israeli nickname.

JOSEPH, YOSEF יוסף

God will increase. Almost 25 percent of Genesis is devoted to Joseph's story. A dreamer as well as a shrewd politician, his name has been a favorite throughout Jewish history. Jose, the Aramaic form of the name, was popular in Talmudic times.

JOSHUA, YEHOSHUA יהושע

God is my salvation. Joshua succeeded Moses and led the Hebrews into the Land of Israel. Moses changed his successor's name from Hoshua by adding a *yud,* one of the letters of God's name; thus, Yehoshua.

JOSIAH, YOSHIAHU יאשיהו

God has protected. Son of Amnon, Josiah became a king of Judah when he was eight years old.

JUDAH, YEHUDA יהודה

Praise. Judah was the fourth son of Jacob and Leah and received special blessings from his father. Yehuda is the source of the words "Judaism," "Jewish," and "Jew." There have been many famous Judahs, including Judah Halevi, a great Hebrew poet.

K

KADMIEL קדמיאל

God is the ancient one.

KALIL כליל

Crown or wreath.

KANIEL קניאל

A reed or stalk. In Aramaic, spear.

KATRIEL כתריאל

Crown of the Lord.

KENAN קינן
> To acquire. A nephew of Abraham in the Bible.

KOBY קובי
> A nickname for Jacob.

KOCHAV כוכב
> Star.

KORE, KOREI קורא
> Quail, or to call.

L

LABAN לבן
> White. Laban was Rebecca's brother, father of matriarchs Rachel and Leah, and grandfather of the twelve tribes of Israel.

LAVI לביא
> Lion.

LAZAR לאזאר
> A Greek form of Eliezer and a popular Yiddish name.

LEOR ליאור
> I have light.

LEV לב, לייב
> Heart in Hebrew. In Yiddish, lion. Label is a Yiddish nickname.

LEVI לוי
> Attendant. The name signifies devotion. In the Bible, Levi was the third of Jacob's sons born to Leah. His descendants became the Levites, the priests of the Temple.

LIRON לירון
> Song is mine.

LOTAN לוטן
> To envelope or protect. Popular in Israel.

M

MAIMON מימון

Aramaic, luck or good fortune. The philosopher, Moses ben Maimon, known as Maimonides, is the most illustrious bearer of the name.

MALACHI מלאכי

Messenger or angel. The last of the prophets.

MALKAM מלכם

God is their king.

MATTATHIAS, MATTITYAHU מתתיהו

Gift from God. Mattathias, a name linked with Hanukkah, was the father of Judah Maccabee, the patriarch of the Hasmonean dynasty. Common nicknames include Matt, Matti, Matia.

MAX

Once common among Jewish immigrants to America, Max has recently become popular again. A contraction of Maxmilian, Latin for "great" or "famous," this is not a Hebrew name.

MEGED מגד

Goodness, sweetness.

MEIR, MEYER מאיר

One who shines.

MENACHEM מנחם

Comforter. Menachem was a biblical king known for his cruelty. This was the name given to boys born on the ninth of Av, the day of mourning for the destruction of the Temple. Yiddish derivatives include Mendel and Mannes.

MENASSEH, MANASSEH, MENASHE מנשה

Causing to forget. The older of Joseph's sons, Menasseh and his brother Ephraim are mentioned in the Shabbat blessing for sons.

MERON מרון

Troops. Also a town in Israel. A popular Israeli name.

MICAH מיכה

Who is like God. Micah was a prophet in Judah during the eighth century B.C.E.; he denounced oppression by the ruling classes.

MICHAEL מיכאל

Who is like God. Michael was the angel closest to God, and God's messenger who carried out divine judgments. Variations on Michael include Mike, Mickey, Mitchell, and the Russian, Misha.

MIRON מירן

A holy place.

MORDECHAI, MORDECAI מרדכי

Persian, warrior or warlike. Mordechai, Queen Esther's cousin, helped save the Jews of Shushan. A name commonly given to boys born during Purim. Its Yiddish nicknames include Mottel, Motke, and Mordke. Motti is the Israeli diminutive.

MORI מורי

My teacher.

MOSES, MOSE, MOSHE משה

Saved from the water. Also Egyptian, son or child. The leader and teacher who brought the Israelites out of bondage in Egypt. Variations on the name include Moss, Moise (French), and Moishe (Yiddish).

N

NAAMAN נעמן

Sweet, beautiful. A general in the army of Aram.

NACHMAN נחמן

Comforter.

NACHUM, NAHUM נחום
Comforted. A prophet in the seventh century B.C.E.

NADAV נדב
Benefactor.

NAMIR נמיר
Leopard.

NAOR נאור
Light.

NAPHTALI, NAFTALI נפתלי
To wrestle. Jacob's sixth son by Bilhah.

NATHAN נתן
He gave. Nathan was one of the minor prophets, who, together with Zadok the priest, anointed Solomon king. In Yiddish, the name is Nusan.

NATHANIEL נתנאל, נתניאל
Gift of God. Nathaniel was David's brother.

NAVON נבון
Wise.

NEHEMIAH, NECHEMYA נחמיה
Comforted of the Lord. Nehemiah served as a governor of Judea and was involved in rebuilding the walls of Jerusalem.

NIMROD נמרוד
Rebel.

NIR, NIREL, NIRIA, NIRIEL ניר, ניראל, ניריה, ניריאל
Plow or plowed field. Niriel means the tilled field of the Lord.

NISSAN ניסן
Flight, also emblem. Nissan is also the name of the lunar month in which Passover falls. Nisi is a popular nickname.

NISSIM נסים
Miracles. A name associated with Hanukkah, popular among Sephardic Jews in Israel.

NITZAN ניצן
Bud.

NIV ניב
Aramaic and Arabic, speech.

NOAH נח
Rest, quiet, or peace. Noah, the only righteous man of his time, was selected to survive the great flood sent by God to punish an evil world. In Hebrew, it is pronounced Noach.

NOAM נעם
Sweetness, friendship.

NUR, NURI נור, נורי
Aramaic, fire. Also Nuria, Nurieh, and Nuriel, which means "fire of the Lord."

O

OBEDIAH, OVADIAH, OVED עובדיה, עובד
Servant of God. Obadiah was one of the twelve minor prophets and the author of the Bible's shortest book. Oved was King David's grandfather.

OFER עפר
A young deer.

OMRI אמרי
Arabic, to live long. Omri was a king in Israel during the ninth century B.C.E.

OREN, ORIN, ORRIN, ORON ארן
Fir tree, cedar. A popular Israeli name.

OZ, OZNI עז, אזני
Strength, hearing. Ozni was a grandson of Jacob.

P

PALTI, PALTIEL, PILTAI פלטי, פלטיאל, פלטי
My deliverance. Palti was Michal's second husband. Piltai was a member of a priestly family.

PERETZ פרץ
>
> Burst forth.

PESACH פסח
>
> Pass over. A name given to boys born during Passover.

PINCHAS, PINCUS פנחס
>
> Dark-complexioned. The priest Pinchas (Phineas in Greek) was a grandson of Aaron.

R

RAANAN רענן
>
> Fresh, luxuriant.

RACHIM, RACHAMIM רחים, רחמים
>
> Compassion. A common name among Sephardic Jews.

RANEN, RANON רנן, רנון
>
> To sing.

RAPHAEL רפאל
>
> God has healed. Raphael is one of the four archangels and, according to the Talmud, one of the three messengers who visited Abraham and Sarah and told them they would have a son. Also spelled Rafael and Refael; Rafi is a popular nickname.

RAVID רביד
>
> Ornament.

RAVIV רביב
>
> Rain or dew.

RAZ, RAZI, RAZIEL רז, רזי, רזיאל
>
> Aramaic, secret.

REUBEN, REUVEN ראובן
>
> Behold, a son. Jacob and Leah's first son.

RIMON רימון
>
> Pomegranate.

RON, RONEL, RONEN, RONI, RONLI רון, רונאל, רוני, רונלי
>
> Song or joy, in various settings.

S

SAADIAH, SAADYA סעדיה
Aramaic for Ezra, meaning "God's help." Saadiah ben Joseph was a great Egyptian-born scholar of the ninth century. A popular Sephardic name.

SAGI סגי
Strong.

SAMSON, SHIMSHON שמשון
Sun, signifying strength. Strong-man Samson, most famous for his betrayal by Delilah, was from the tribe of Dan.

SAMUEL, SH'MUEL שמואל
God has heard. Samuel, the son of Hannah, helped create a centralized monarchy in the eleventh century B.C.E., and, as prophet and judge, anointed King Saul and later King David. Samuel was the last of the judges.

SANDER סנדר
Yiddish for Alexander. (See above.)

SASHA
A Russian diminutive for Alexander. Also a girl's name.

SAUL, SHA'UL שאול
Borrowed. Saul was the first king of Israel, from the tribe of Benjamin.

SELIG סעליג
Yiddish, blessed. Also spelled Zelig.

SETH, SHET שת
Appointed. Seth was Adam's son, born after Abel's death.

SHAI שי
Gift.

SHALOM, SHLOMO, SHOLOM, SHLOMI שלום, שלמה, שלומי
Peace.

SHAMIR שמיר
Strong.

SHRAGA שרגא
Aramaic, light.

SIMCHA שמחה
Joy. Also a girl's name.

SIMON, SIMEON, SHIMON, SHIMEON שמעון
To hear or be heard. Shimon was the second son born to Jacob and Leah. (Simon is the Greek version.) Simi is a popular Israeli nickname for Shimon.

SIVAN סיון
The seventh month of the Hebrew calendar.

SOLOMON שלמה
Peace. Solomon, the son of David and Bathsheba, built the Second Temple and wrote Song of Songs, Proverbs, and Ecclesiastes. His reputation for wisdom is enshrined in the word Solomonic. In Yiddish, Shlomo.

T

TABBAI טבאי
Aramaic, good. Names like Tov, Tovi, and Tavi share the root and the meaning.

TAL, TALOR טל, טליאור
Dew, dew of light. Also a girl's name.

TAMIR, TIMUR תמיר, תמור
Tall, like the tamar or palm tree.

TIVON טבעון
Student of nature.

TOBIAH, TUV'YA טוביה
God is good. Toby is the popular nickname.

TZEVI צבי
Deer. Also spelled Tzvi and Zevi. Popular in Israel.

U

URI, URIEL אורי, אוריאל

From the root for light. Uriel is one of the four angels who resides around God's throne.

UZI, UZIEL עזי, עזיאל

From the root for strength. Uzi means "my strength." Uziel means "God is my strength."

W

WOLF, WOLFE וואלף

Yiddish, wolf. Variants include Vulf and Velvel. The Hebrew is Ze'ev.

Y

YAKIR יקיר

Beloved, honorable.

YALON ילון

He will rest. A son of Caleb.

YAMIR ימיר

To change.

YANIR יניר

He will plow.

YARON ירון

To sing.

YAVNIEL יבניאל

God will build.

YEFET יפת

Beautiful. Also spelled Yafet, Yaphet. Yefet was one of Noah's sons.

YEHIEL יחיאל

May God live. Yehiel was chief musician in the court of King David.

YIFTACH יפתח
Open.

YIGAL יגאל
He will redeem. Popular in Israel.

YOAV יואב
God is father. King David's nephew and an officer in his army.

YOCHANAN יוחנן
God is gracious. There are more than fifty rabbis named Yochanon quoted in the Talmud.

YORAM יורם
God is exalted.

YORAN יורן
To sing.

YOTAM יותם
One of Gideon's sons.

Z

ZACH זך
Pure or clean.

ZACHARY, ZACHARIAH זכריה
Remembering the Lord. The name of one of the minor prophets, and of a king of Judah and a king of Israel. Nicknames include Zack and Zeke.

ZALMAN זמלן, צלמון
Yiddish for Shlomo.

ZAMIR זמיר
Song, also nightingale.

ZAVDI, ZAVDIEL זבדי, זבדיאל
My gift, gift of God. An officer in David's army.

ZEBULON, ZEVULON זבולון
To exalt or honor. Zevulon was the sixth son of Jacob and Leah.

ZEDEKIAH צדקיה
God is righteousness. A king of Judah.

ZE-EV, ZEV, ZEVI, ZEVIEL זאב, זאבי, זאביאל
Hebrew, wolf (see Wolf). Very popular in Israel.

ZEPHANIAH צפניה
God has treasured. A seventh-century prophet, Zephaniah belonged to the family of Judah.

ZERACH זרח
Light rising.

ZION, TZION ציון
Excellent, a sign. A name for the Jewish people; also a mountain in Jerusalem.

ZIV, ZIVI זיו, זיוי
To shine.

ZOHAR זהר
Light, brilliance.

ZUSHYE, ZUSYA זושע, זוסע
Yiddish, sweet.

A Daughter!
Girls' Names

A

ABIGAIL, AVIGAIL אביגיל
> Father's joy. Abigail was an early supporter of King David, even before she became his wife. She was known for her beauty, wisdom, and powers of prophecy.

ABIRA אבירה
> Strong.

ABRA אברה
> From the Hebrew root Abba, father. A diminutive of Abraham.

ADA, ADI עדה, עדי
> Ornament.

ADARA אדרה
> Adar is the twelfth month in the Hebrew calendar.

ADENA, ADINA עדינה
> Noble or adorned, gentle.

ADERET אדרת
> A cape or outer garment.

ADIRA אדירה
> Strong or mighty.

ADIVA אדיבה
Gracious, pleasant.

ADRA אדרה
Aramaic, glory or majesty.

ADVA אדוה
Aramaic, wave or ripple.

AHARONA אהרנה
Feminine version of Aaron, teaching or singing. Variations include Arona, Arni, Arnina, Arnit, Arninit.

AHAVA אהבה
Love, beloved.

ALEEZA, ALIZA, ALITZA עליזה, עליצה
Joy or joyous one.

ALEXANDRA אלכסנדרה
Feminine version of Alexander. For a full explanation of the name, see Alexander. Queen Salome Alexandra was a ruler of Judea from 76–67 B.C.E.

ALIYA, ALIYAH עליה
To go up. Being called to the Torah during a synagogue service is known as being given an *aliyah*. Also, moving to Israel is called making *aliyah*.

ALMA עלמה
Maiden. In Spanish, soul.

ALONA אלונה
Oak tree. Alon is a popular boy's name.

ALUMA, ALUMIT עלומה, עלומית
Girl or maiden.

AMALIA עמליה
The work of the Lord.

AMIRA אמירה
Speech. Ear of corn.

ANAT ענת
> To sing.

ANNA, ANN חנה
> These and many more (Annette, Annie, Anita, Anya) are all forms of the biblical name Hannah. Anna is the Hellenized version that inspired so many diminutives.

ARAVA ערבה
> Willow.

ARELLA אראלה
> Angel, messenger.

ARIELLA אריאלה
> Lioness of god.

ARMONA, ARMONIT ארמונה, ארמונית
> Castle or palace.

ARNA, ARNIT ארנה, ארנית
> Cedar.

ARNONA, ARNONIT ארנונה, ארנונית
> Feminine version of Arnon, a roaring stream.

ARZA, ARZIT ארזה, ארזית
> Cedar beams.

ASHIRA עשירה
> Wealthy.

ATALIA, ATALYA עתליה
> God is exalted.

ATARA, ATARET עטרה, עטרת
> Crown.

ATIRA עתירה
> Prayer.

AVIELA, AVIELLA אביאלה
> God is my father.

AVITAL אביטל
Dew of my father. Avital was one of King David's wives.

AVIVA אביבה
Spring. A popular Israeli name. Avivit and Avivi mean springlike. Avivit also means lilac.

AVODA עבודה
Work.

AYALA אילה
Deer or gazelle.

AZA, AZAH, AZIZA עזה, עזיזה
Strong.

AZRIELLA עזריאלה
God is my strength.

B

BAILA, BAYLE ביילע
Yiddish form of Bilhah, one of the four women who gave birth to the tribes of Israel.

BASHA באשע
A diminutive of Batsheva.

BAT-AMI בת־עמי
Daughter of my people.

BATSHEVA בת־שבע
Daughter of the oath. The beautiful Batsheva was one of King David's wives and the mother of King Solomon.

BATYA בתיה
Daughter of God.

BELLA, BELLE
Americanized Yiddish derivatives of Bilhah.

BENYAMINA בנימינה
The feminine form of Benjamin.

BERIT, B'ERIT בארית
Well, a source of water.

BERURIA, BERURYAH ברוריה
Pure or clean. Beruriah, the daughter of Rabbi Haninah ben Teradyon and the wife of Rabbi Meir, lived in the second century C.E. and was the only woman in Talmudic literature whose views were taken seriously by her contemporaries.

BINA בינה
Understanding, intelligence.

BIRA בירה
Capital.

BLUMA, BLUME בלומע
Yiddish, flower.

BONA בונה
Builder.

BRACHA ברכה
Blessing.

B'RINA, BREENA ברנה
With joy.

BRINA ברײנה
Based on the Yiddish for "brown."

C

CARMEL, CARMELLE, CARMELA, CARMELIT כרמל, כרמלה, כרמלית
Vineyard. A popular Israeli name with many variations: Carma, Carmit, Carmia.

CARNA, CARNIT קרנה, קרנית
Horn. Carniella means "horn of God."

CHAVA חוה
Eve. Mother of life. A variant English spelling is Hava.

CHAYA חיה
Life.

CLARA כלרה
Yiddish for clean.

D

DAFNA דפנה
Laurel.

DALIA, DALIT דליה, דלית
Branch.

DANIELLA, DANIELLE דניאלה
God is my judge. The feminine version of Daniel has many
derivatives: Dania, Dani, Danya, Danit.

DANYA דניה
Feminine version of Dan.

DAVIDA, DAVITA דוידה
Feminine version of David, beloved or friend. Nickname: Davi.

DEBORAH, DEBRA, DEVORAH, DEVRA דבורה
To speak kind words or a swarm of bees. Devorah was a
prophetess and judge who led a revolt against a Canaanite
king. Her composition, the "Song of Deborah," is one of the
oldest known Hebrew poems.

DEENA, DENA, DINA, DINAH דינה
Judgment. Deena was the daughter of Leah and Jacob, the
only girl among his eleven children.

DEGANIA דגניה
Corn. Also the name of the first kibbutz.

DELILA דלילה
Poor or hair. Samson's mistress Delila was a Philistine.

DERORA, DRORA דרורה
Freedom.

DIZA, DITZA דיזה, דיצה
Joy.

DODI דודי
Beloved, friend.

DORIT דורית
A modern name, popular in Israel.

DORONA, DORONIT דורונה, דורונית
Aramaic for gift.

DORYA דוריה
Generation of God.

DOVA, DOVEVA, DOVIT דובה, דובבה, דובית
Bear.

E

EDNA עדנה
Delight, pleasure. Edna appears in the Book of Tobit, which is part of the Apocrypha.

EFRAT אפרת
Honored, distinguished. The wife of Caleb.

EFRONA עפרונה
A songbird.

ELANA אילנה
Oak tree. Also spelled Ilana.

ELIANA אליענה
God has answered me.

ELINOAR אלינער
God of my youth.

ELIORA אליאורה
God is my light.

ELISHEVA אלישבע
God is my oath. Elisheva was Aaron's wife and thus the matriarch of the priestly caste. The Hellenized form is

Elizabeth, which has many popular nicknames: Ella, Elisa, Eliza, Elise, Elsie, Betsy, Liz, Libby, Bet, Beth, Betty, Elyssa. Elisheva Bikhowsky (1888–1949) was a Russian-born poet who settled in Israel in 1925, where she wrote and published in Hebrew.

EMANUELLA עמנואלה
God is with us.

EMMA עמה
Originally from the Teutonic for "grandmother" or "big one," the name was popular among Jewish immigrants to America at the turn of the century. Famous Emmas include the Russian-born anarchist writer and organizer Emma Goldman and the poet Emma Lazarus, who penned the verse on the Statue of Liberty.

EMUNA אמונה
Faith.

ESTHER אסתר
Persian, star. Esther is the heroine of the story of Purim. She, with help from her cousin Mordecai, averted the annihilation of the Jews in her community. The Hebrew name for Esther is Hadassah, which means "myrtle." Variations include Esta, Essie, Estelle, and Estella. Etti is an Israeli nickname.

EVA, EVE חוה
Life. According to Genesis, Eve was the first woman, the mother of all human life. The Hebrew is Chava.

EZRAELA עזראלה
God is my help. The feminine version of Ezra.

F

FREIDA, FRAYDE, FREYDEL פריידע, פריידעל
Yiddish, joy.

G

GABRIELLA, GAVRIELLA גבריאלה
God is my strength. The feminine version of Gabriel. Nicknames include Gabi and Gavi.

GALI, GALIT גלי, גלית
Fountain or spring.

GALYA גליה
God has redeemed.

GAMLIELA, GAMLIELLE גמליאלה
Feminine versions of Gamliel, a name common among Talmudic scholars.

GANIT גנית
Garden.

GARNIT גרנית
Granary.

GAVRILLA גברילה
Heroine, strong.

GAYORA גיאורה
Valley of light.

GAZIT גזית
Hewn stone.

GILA גילה
Joy. Gilana and Gilat also mean "joy." Gilia, a variant, means "my joy is in God."

GILADA גלעדה
My joy is forever.

GINA, GINAT גנה, גינת
Garden.

GITTA, GITTLE גיטע, גיטל
Yiddish, good one. (See Tova.)

GIVA, GIVONA גבעה, גבעונה
Hill.

GOLDA, GOLDE גולדה
Yiddish, golden. The Hebrew is Zehava.

GURIT גורית
Cub.

H

HADARA, HADURA הדרה, הדורה
Splendid.

HADASS, HADASSAH הדס, הדסה
Myrtle tree, a symbol of victory. This is the Hebrew form of
the name Esther. Nicknames include Dass and Dasi.

HAGIT חגית
Festive, joyous.

HAMUDA חמודה
Precious.

HANNAH חנה
Gracious, merciful. In the Bible, Hannah was the wife of
Elkanan, the mother of Samuel, and the subject of a heart-
breaking tale of infertility and faith rewarded. (Samuel
means "God has heard.") The Christian Bible refers to
Hannah as Anna, which means that all its variations—
Annie, Annette, Anita—are rooted in Hannah.

HASIA חסיה
Protected of the Lord.

HASIDA חסידה
Pious one. Also, stork.

HAVIVA חביבה
Beloved.

HEDVA חדוה
Joy.

HEDYA הדיה
Voice of the Lord.

HEFZIBA חפצי־בה
My desire.

HEMDA חמדה
Precious.

HERZLIA הרצליה
Yiddish, deer. The feminine version of a masculine name, this is also the name of an Israeli city.

HILLA הלה
Praise.

HINDA הינדע
Yiddish, deer.

I

IDIT עדית
Choicest.

ILANA, ILANIT אילנה, אילנית
Oak tree. Also spelled Elana.

IRIT עירית
Daffodil. Popular in Israel.

ISAACA יצחקה
Laughter. The feminine version of Isaac.

ISRAELA, ISA ישראלה, ישה
The name of the people, almost always used in the diminutive, Isa.

ITI, ITTI אתי
With me.

J

JACOBA, YACOVA יעקבה
To supplant. The feminine version of Yacov.

JASMINE, YASMIN יסמין
Persian flower name.

JEMINA, YEMINA ימינה
Righthanded.

JESSIE, JESSICA, YISKA יסכה
God's grace.

JOHANNA, YOCHANA יוחנה
God is gracious. The feminine version of Yochanon.

JONINA, YONINA יונינה
A dove.

JOSEPHA, YOSEFA יוספה
God will increase. The feminine version of Joseph.

JUDITH, YEHUDIT יהודית
Praise. In the Apocryphal story, Judith was the heroine who saved Jerusalem by pretending to defect to General Holofernes's camp, where she beheaded him while he slept.

K

KADIA, KADYA כדיה
Pitcher.

KALANIT כלנית
Anemone.

KANARIT, KANIT כנרית, כנית
Songbird.

KARNA, KARNIT קרנה, קרנית
Horn, as in ram's horn.

KAYLA קיילע
Yiddish form of Kelila.

KELILA כלילה
A crown of laurel, symbolizing victory.

KEREN קרן
Horn. Related to Karna. A popular Israeli name.

KETURAH קטורה
Perfumed.

KETZIA, KEZIA קציעה
Fragrant. One of Job's daughters.

KINNERET כנרת
Hebrew name of the Sea of Galilee. Also, harp.

KIRYA קריה
Village.

KOCHAVA כוכבה
Star.

L

LAILA, LEILA, LILA לילה
Night.

LEAH, LEA לאה
In Hebrew, weariness; in Assyrian, mistress or ruler. Leah, the daughter of Laban, was Jacob's first wife and one of the four matriarchs of Judaism. She gave birth to six sons: Reuben, Simeon, Levi, Judah, Issachar, and Zebulun, and one daughter, Deena.

LEEBA, LIBA ליבע
Yiddish, beloved. In Israel, the name also refers to the Hebrew root *lev*, which means "heart."

LEORA, LIORA ליאורה
My light.

LEVANA, LIVANA לבנה
Moon or white. Popular among Sephardic Israelis.

LEVONA לבונה
Spice or incense.

LIAN ליאן
My joy.

LIAT ליאת
You are mine.

LILY לילי
A favorite among Jewish-American immigrants in the early twentieth century.

LIMOR לימור
My myrrh.

LIRON, LIRONA לירון
My song.

LIVIA, LIVYA לויה
A crown. When the accent falls on the last syllable, Livia means "lioness."

LUZA לוזה
Almond tree.

M

MAGDA מגדא
A high tower.

MAHIRA, MEHIRA מהירה
Energetic.

MALKA מלכה
Queen. A popular Sephardic name. (See Regina.)

MARA מרה
Bitter.

MARGALIT מרגלית
Pearl. (See Peninah.)

MARNI, MARNINA מרני, מרנינה
Rejoice.

Marva מרוה
Plant in the mint family.

Maxima מקסימה
Enchanter.

Maya מיה
Modern Hebrew name based on a Roman mythological goddess.

Meri מרי
Rebellious.

Michaela מיכאלה
Who is like God. The feminine version of Michael, one of the archangels. Mia is a nickname.

Michal מיכל
A contraction of Michaela. Michal was King Saul's youngest daughter and one of King David's wives.

Mili מילי
Who is for me?

Mira מירה
Light. The feminine version of Meir.

Miriam, Miryam מרים
In Hebrew, sorrow or bitterness; in Chaldean, mistress of the sea. Miriam was a prophetess, singer, and dancer, the sister of Moses and Aaron. Nicknames include Mim, Mindy, Minna, Mira, Mirel, Miri, Mirit, and Mollie.

Mirit מירית
Sweet wine.

Moriah, Morit מוריה, מורית
Teacher.

N

Naamah, Naamit נעמה, נעמית
Pleasant, beautiful.

NAAVA נאוה
Beautiful.

NADYA נדיה
From the word for dowry. A common name in Israel.

NAOMI נעמי
Beautiful, pleasant. In the Book of Ruth, Naomi was Elimelech's wife and Ruth's loving mother-in-law.

NASIA, NASYA נסיה
Miracle of God.

NATANIA, NETANYA נתניה
Gift of God.

NEDIVA נדיבה
Generous, noble.

NEHAMA נחמה
Comfort.

NEIMA נעימה
Pleasant.

NESYA נסיה
Yiddish for Nissan, the month of flowers.

NETTA, NETIA נטע, נטיעה
A plant.

NILI נילי
A plant.

NINA נינה
Great-granddaughter.

NIRA נירה
Light.

NIRIT נירית
A flowering plant.

NITZA נצה
Bud.

Noa נועה
Tremble, shake. A biblical name popular in Israel today.

Nurit נורית
Buttercup.

O

Odelia אודליה
I will praise God.

Odera עודרה
Plow.

Ophira אופירה
Gold.

Ophrah, Ofra עפרה
Young deer.

Ora אורה
Light.

Orli, Orlit אורלי, אורלית
My light.

Orna, Ornit ארנה, ארנית
Cedar.

P

Pazit פזית
Gold.

Peninah, Peninit פנינה, פנינית
Pearl or coral. Elkanah's second wife. (See Margalit.)

Peri פרי
Fruit.

Puah פועה
A midwife during the Egyptian captivity, Puah and her colleague Shifra disobeyed Pharoah's order to kill all male Hebrews at birth.

R

RACHEL רחל

A ewe, symbol of gentleness and purity. Rachel was the best-loved wife of Jacob and gave birth to Joseph and Benjamin. There have been many renowned Rachels, among them a wealthy woman who, against her father's wishes, married a poor and unlearned man named Akiva. He became the great Rabbi Akiva.

RAISA, RAIZEL רייזא, רייזעל

Yiddish for Rose.

RAKEFET רקפת

Cyclamen, a flower common in Israel.

RANANA רעננה

Fresh.

RANIT, RANITA רנית, רניתה

Joy or song.

RAPHAELA רפאלה

God has healed. The feminine version of Raphael.

RAYNA, REYNA ריינע

Yiddish, pure or clean.

RAZI, RAZIA, RAZIELLA רזי, רזיה, רזאלה

Aramaic, secret. Razili means "my secret."

REBECCA, REBEKAH רבקה

Beautiful, or to tie or bind. Rebekah, the wife of Isaac, is the strong-willed matriarch who masterminded her son Jacob's deception of his father to gain the family blessing. Nicknames include Becky and Rikki.

REGINA

Sephardic name meaning "queen." Malka in Hebrew.

RIMONA רמונה

Pomegranate.

Rina רנה
Joy or song.

Riva ריבה
Young girl. Also a diminutive of Rebecca.

Rivka רבקה
The Hebrew form of Rebecca.

Rona, Roni, Ronit, Ronia רונה, רונית, רוניה
Joy or song.

Rose, Rosa רוזה
The English translation of the Hebrew name Shoshana. Rose has been a popular name in many languages, including English, Yiddish, Ladino, and Hebrew. (See Raisa, Susan, Varda, Vered.) Rose Schneiderman (1882–1972) was an American labor organizer and president of the Women's Trade Union League from 1918 to 1949.

Ruth רות
Friendship. The daughter-in-law of Naomi, who chose to stay with Naomi and the Jewish people after the death of her husband. Ruth, considered the model of the righteous Jew-by-choice, is an ancestor of King David, from whose line—says the tradition—the Messiah will come. Ruti is a popular nickname in Israel.

S

Saada סעדה
Support or help.

Sadie
A diminutive of Sarah, Sadie was a popular name among Jewish immigrants to the United States.

Samantha
The name Samantha is often given in memory of a grandfather Samuel, although there is no connection between the two names. It is not a Hebrew name.

SARA, SARAH שרה

Princess. Sarah was the first Jewish woman, the wife of Abraham, and, at the age of ninety, the mother of Isaac. Nicknames include Sari, Sarene, Sarina, and Sarit. Yiddish versions include Sorale and Soralie.

SASHA

Variation on Alexandra, used as a proper name in the United States.

SERAFINA שרפינה

To burn. From the same root as the biblical seraphim, the angels surrounding God's throne.

SHALVIA שלויה

Peace, tranquility.

SHARON שרון

In the Bible, Sharon was a plain where roses bloomed, hence King Solomon's songs about the roses of Sharon. Sharona is a variation.

SHAYNA, SHAINA שיינע

Yiddish, beautiful.

SHELI, SHELLI שלי

Mine.

SHIFRA שפרה

Beautiful. Shifra, a midwife, and her colleague Puah disobeyed Pharoah's order to kill all male Hebrews at birth. A popular Israeli name.

SHIRA, SHIRI שירה, שירי

Song. My song.

SHLOMIT שלומית

Peaceful.

SHLOMIYA שלומיה

Peace.

SHOSHANA שושנה
> A lily or a rose.

SHULAMIT שולמית
> Peace. Shula is a nickname.

SIDRA, SIDRAH סדרה
> Torah portion.

SIMA סימה
> Aramaic, gift.

SIMCHA שמחה
> Joy. Also a boy's name.

SIMONA, SIMONE סימונה
> To hear. The feminine version of Simon, Simeon.

SIVANA סיונה
> Sivan is the ninth month of the Hebrew calendar.

SIVIA, SIVYA, TZIVIA צביה
> Deer.

SOPHIE
> A popular name among Jewish immigrants to America.

SUSAN שושנה
> Rose or lily (see Rose, Shoshana, Varda, Vered). Susannah is a variation.

T

TAL, TALIA, TALYA, TALI טל, טליה, טלי
> Dew.

TALMA תלמה
> Hill.

TAMAR, TAMARA תמר, תמרה
> Date palm. Also, righteous and graceful. A Yiddish variation is Tema.

TEMIMA תמימה
Honest.

TIFERET תפארת
Beautiful.

TIKVA תקוה
Hope.

TIRA טירה
Encampment.

TIRZA תרצה
Cypress, also desirable. Tirza was the biblical capital of Samaria.

TORI תורי
My turtledove.

TOVA טובה
Good one. Often Toby in English.

TZAFRIRA צפרירה
Morning breeze.

TZIPORA צפורה
Little bird. Moses's wife. Also spelled Zipporah. Tzipi is a common nickname.

TZURIA צוריה
God is strength.

U

UMA אמה
Nation.

URIT אורית
Light.

V

VARDA ורדה
Rose. (See also Susan).

VERED ורד
> Rose.

VIDA, VITA וידה
> Sephardic name meaning "life." The equivalent of Eve, or the Hebrew Chava.

Y

YAEL, YAELA, YAALIT יעל, יעלה, יעלית
> To ascend.

YAFFA יפה
> Beautiful. Also the name of an Israeli city.

YAKIRA יקירה
> Precious.

YARDENA ירדנה
> Jordan River, to descend.

YARKONA ירקונה
> Green. Also, a bird found in southern Israel and a river in northern Israel.

YECHIELA יחיאלה
> May God live.

YEDIDA ידידה
> Friend, beloved. The mother of Josiah, a king of Judah.

YEIRA יאירה
> Light.

YEMIMA ימימה
> Dove. A daughter of Job. Jemima in English.

YISRAELA ישראלה
> Israeli or Jew.

YOCHEVED יוכבד
> God's glory. Yocheved, an unacknowledged matriarch, was the mother of Moses, Aaron, and Miriam.

YOELLA, YOELIT יואלה, יואלית
God is willing. The feminine version of Yoel or Joel.

YONA, YONINA, YONIT יונה, יונינה, יונית
Dove.

Z

ZAHARA, ZEHARI זהרה, זהרי
Brightness.

ZAHAVA, ZAHAVI, ZEHAVIT זהבה, זהבית
Golden.

ZARA זרה
Variation on Sarah. (See Zora.)

ZE'EVA, ZEVA זאבה
Wolf.

ZIKIT זיקית
Longing.

ZILLA, TZILA צילה
Shadow.

ZIONA ציונה
Excellent, feminine of Zion.

ZIPPORAH צפורה
Little bird. Also spelled Tzipporah or Tzipora.

ZIVA, ZIVIT זיוה, זיוית
Splendid, radiant.

ZIVANIT זיונית
Mayflower.

ZORAH, ZORA זרה
A variation of Sarah. Arabic, dawn.

Part 3

Brit—Covenant

Covenants

*B**rit,* the Hebrew word for covenant, is the way Jews describe and define their relationship to God. A covenant is a contract—a mutual agreement between responsible parties, in other words, a two-way street. According to tradition, the document that spells out the rights and responsibilities for both sides in this agreement between God and the Jewish people is the Torah—the first five books of the Bible.

Four covenants are mentioned in the Torah. The first, Shabbat, is a weekly reminder of the miracle of creation. The second, the rainbow, is the sign of God's promise, made after the great flood, that God would never again destroy the world. The third covenant is the Torah itself, the "tree of life," in which human beings can search for the answers to the most important questions. The fourth covenant is *brit milah,* the covenant of circumcision. *Brit milah,* which the Talmud acknowledges is the most difficult of all the mitzvot, or sacred obligations, is how parents have passed on this contract from one generation to the next.

The covenant of circumcision is the oldest continuous Jewish rite, a ritual that unites Jews throughout the ages and across cultures and signifies the connection between individual human life and the Holy. With this ancient ceremony, parents announce their commitment to taking on the responsibilities and joys of raising a son according to the terms of the contract between God and the

Jews. *Brit bat,* the act of welcoming infant daughters to this historic relationship, does the same with words and rituals.

In many ways, *brit milah* and *brit bat* are as different as two ceremonies can be. Bringing a son into the covenant of Israel is an ancient practice that leaves a permanent physical sign of the bond between each Jewish man and God. Bringing a daughter into the covenant with formal ceremonies that convene family and community has some precedent, but it is, by and large, a modern practice.

The historical absence of a covenant ceremony for daughters was interpreted in two radically different ways: as evidence that women were second-class citizens not fully admitted to the covenant, or as proof that Judaism acknowledges women's spiritual superiority in not needing a physical reminder of God's presence. In the space of a single generation, *brit bat* has become an accepted and, indeed, expected rite of passage that reflects a near-universal acceptance of women's status as full parties to the covenant between God and the Jewish people.

Although there are liturgical similarities between them, *brit bat* is not an imitation of *brit milah.* The two ceremonies are as different as male and female. What they do share, what all Jews share, is the covenant.

Brit Milah—The Covenant of Circumcision

> Such shall be the covenant between Me and you and your off-spring to follow which you shall keep: every male among you shall be circumcised. You shall circumcise the flesh of your foreskin, and that shall be the sign of the covenant between Me and you.
>
> —Genesis 17:10–11

It's a boy!

After the initial rush of happiness and delight comes the realization: we've got to have a *bris*.* The most ancient of all Jewish rituals, a *bris* is traditionally celebrated with feasting and song. And while some Jews approach *brit milah* with more confusion and fear than happiness, it is a *simcha*—a cause for joy and celebration.

Jews have performed the mitzvah of *brit milah* in an unbroken chain for 4,000 years, from the days of Abraham to the present.

---

*The Hebrew word *brit* means covenant, a pledge or obligation. *Brit milah* is the covenant of circumcision, the surgical removal of the foreskin from the penis, a physical sign of the unique relationship between the Jewish people and God. Sephardic Jews sometimes refer to the rite simply as *milah*. In America, the Ashkenazic Hebrew and Yiddish term *bris* is the most familiar name for the religious ritual of circumcision.

During that long history, observant Jews and secular Jews, rabbis and Jews with little or no understanding of the ritual have fulfilled this, perhaps the most difficult of all biblical commandments. Even so, for many liberal Jews, *brit milah* is no longer entirely an automatic response to the arrival of a son, but a decision made after considering a series of questions: Is it safe? Will my baby suffer? What is the best way to have it done?

Deciding to circumcise a son, especially in a traditional manner, announces your identification with Judaism in a powerful, unequivocal way. Most of all, it challenges you to ask, Why? What does this mean to me as an individual and to us as a family? What do we hope it will mean to our son?

This chapter provides information to help you answer these questions. The following pages include an overview of *brit milah,* covering everything from the biblical roots of the ritual to advice about how to hire a *mohel,* a ritual circumciser. (The Yiddish pronunciation is "moil," the Hebrew "mo-*hail.*" The plural is *mohalim.*) The more you know about the history and practice of *brit milah,* the less you will worry about your baby and the more you will be able to understand this ritual as cause for rejoicing and celebration.

Questions and Answers

In the 1960s, 95 percent of all baby boys born in the United States were circumcised in the hospital within days of birth because doctors believed that the procedure was a boon to hygiene and health.[1] This fact allowed many Jewish parents to feel released from the need to "choose" circumcision, and many opted to have it done without ritual by a physician in the hospital.

However, since 1971, the American Academy of Pediatrics has gone on record saying that there are no medical reasons compelling enough to recommend routine surgical removal of the foreskin, the sheath that covers the glans of the penis. By 1985, circumcision declined to 59 percent of newborn boys, and the procedure was no longer automatically covered by all medical insurance plans. Meanwhile, a vocal international anti-circumcision movement, which includes some Jews, has organized to oppose the procedure, describing it as "amputation" and "mutilation," and even comparing the removal of the foreskin to female circumcision, which excises the clitoris and labia.[2]

The debate about circumcision has focused attention on the fact that Jews have never circumcised sons for medical reasons. In the words of Rabbi Moses Maimonides, the great twelfth-century rabbi, philosopher, and physician, "No one should circumcise himself or his sons for any other reasons but for pure faith. Circumcision is the symbol of the covenant which Abraham made in connection with the belief in God's unity."[3] Maimonides' words are remarkably similar to those of the 1999 statement on circumcision by the American Academy of Pediatrics: "Existing scientific evidence demonstrates potential medical benefits of newborn male circumcision; however, these data are not sufficient to recommend routine neonatal circumcision... It is legitimate for parents to take into account cultural, religious, and ethnic traditions, in addition to the medical factors, when making this decision."[4]

The safety and impact of circumcision are certainly legitimate concerns and parents should get answers to all of their medical questions.

Are there medical risks to circumcision?

According to the American Academy of Pediatrics statement, the incidence of complications is not well documented, but studies show an extremely low rate, in one sample of no more than 0.2 to 0.6 percent. The most common complication (less than 0.1 percent) is bleeding. Infections occur even less frequently than that and are minor. *Mohalim* have claimed that their circumcisions, which are never included in the medical literature, result in even fewer problems, but there are no scientific data to substantiate that claim.

Jewish boys have survived circumcision for centuries, and a tradition so meticulous about the sanctity of life and health would not require an act that might jeopardize either. Although anti-circumcision activists cite studies showing that the procedure permanently reduces sexual sensation and satisfaction, other research suggests just the opposite.[5]

Are there any medical benefits to circumcision?

There is some evidence that properly performed newborn circumcision may play a part in preventing some rare mechanical and inflammatory problems of the penis. There may be potential benefits connected to cancer of the penis, which is also rare, and some new research also suggests protection against HIV infection and infection of the kidneys and urinary tract.

Does it hurt?

Yes. Although infants cannot say how much or for how long, increased heart rates and blood pressure indicate physiological distress. And there is no minimizing the discomfort that parents feel on their son's behalf.

The American Academy of Pediatrics report recommends, "If a decision for circumcision is made, procedural analgesia should be provided." *Mohalim* and doctors sometimes numb the area with a nonprescription topical cream, and virtually all infants are given sweet wine, which helps them relax, though it is probably the sugar and not the alcohol that provides the benefit.[6]

Physicians and physician-*mohalim* may choose between a few different kinds of injectible local anesthetic, which probably provides the most effective pain control.

This being said, it must be noted that *brit milah* has been performed without anesthesia for centuries. People who have been to many *brisses* testify that babies tend to start crying when exposed to the discomfort of being naked and placed flat on their backs. The procedure itself takes about thirty seconds and afterward babies are easily comforted, and *mohalim* report that infants rarely cry during the prayers that immediately follow. Babies routinely nurse and fall asleep within minutes of the procedure.

What's the safest, least painful way to have my son circumcised?

Some Jews choose to have their sons circumcised by a physician in the hospital before taking the baby home. Hospitals offer a professional, sterile environment where anesthesia can be provided, and parents are often reluctant to witness the procedure at all.

However, several factors argue against hospital "circs," as they are called. They tend to be performed in stark operating rooms, where the newborn is strapped onto a board and immobilized for as long as ten minutes; in some cases, an intern or resident will do the actual cutting. The baby is not permitted to eat for a few hours before the procedure, and afterward he must be checked by a nurse before he can be returned to his mother.

At home, on the other hand, the room will be warm, the surroundings familiar. Sweet wine or sugar-water are helpful relaxant-anesthetics, given to the baby before the procedure begins. Loving hands hold him, and if a safety restraint is used, he will be immobilized for only a few moments. The circumcision itself is performed quickly, and the baby is swaddled and returned to his mother within minutes.

Another important difference between medical and religious circumcision concerns timing. Medical circumcisions take place any time between the second and sixth day after birth, but *brit milah* is never performed before the eighth day. There is some evidence in favor of waiting the extra few days. In a full-term baby, substances that regulate blood coagulation and facilitate healing are slightly below normal at birth. A further decline in one of these substances occurs between the second and sixth day of life. However, a gradual increase begins after the sixth day, and by the eighth day its presence in the body is at above-normal levels.[7]

Finally, it is important to remember that a medical circumcision is *not a brit milah*. A *bris* is a ritual that includes prayers, is performed by a Jew, and expresses the deliberate intent of bringing a son into the covenant. According to *halachah* (Jewish law), a male who has had a medical circumcision without Jewish ritual is considered a Jew in need of a religious circumcision, called *hatafat dam brit* (see below).

One way to ensure the best of both worlds is to employ a physician who has been trained in the religious and ceremonial traditions of *brit milah*. Both the Reform and Conservative movements have such programs for board-certified doctors (pediatricians, urologists, internists). For information about physician-*mohalim,* speak to your rabbi or cantor, or call a local synagogue and ask for a referral.[8]

What is the psychological impact of circumcision?

If God had asked Abraham to remove a flap of skin from his elbow and the elbows of all males of his household as a permanent sign of the covenant, the *bris* would not be the emotionally loaded commandment it is. Then again, had the request not been so awefull, the sign of the covenant might well have been forgotten.

The fact that the mark of the covenant is surgically imprinted on the penis dramatizes the fundamental importance of the act. Certainly, Judaism ascribes enormous symbolic significance to circumcision. The Talmud, the compendium of traditional rabbinic thought and laws, states that "were it not for the blood of the covenant, heaven and earth would not exist." And the philosopher Spinoza declared that the practice of *brit milah* alone would ensure the survival of the Jewish people.

But ever since Sigmund Freud made the unconscious a subject of popular discussion, circumcision has been interpreted as a symbolic castration. According to Freud, the Jewish father of psychoanalysis, male children are potential competitors for their mothers' affection. Sons thus pose a threat to their fathers, which places boys in danger of paternal hostility. From this perspective, circumcision can be seen as a ritual compromise—a symbolic castration.

It is hard not to see *brit milah* as an essentially male ritual that connects fathers and sons to each other, and to hundreds of generations of Jewish men before them. Observers have noted the relative lack of physical violence between Jewish fathers and sons. It is impossible to say whether the practice of *brit milah* contributes to this pattern, but as the first obligation of Jewish fathers to sons, it has certainly been a constant feature of Jewish family dynamics through the ages.

Evidence of psychological damage from circumcision is a contemporary subject of debate, but there is little science to support the claim. And no infant is carrying the complex cultural and sexual baggage that causes his elders so much discomfort. There is no question that *brit milah* is difficult for adults. The event is, after all, focused on the penis, an exquisitely sensitive organ that also recalls the act that gave him life and is a symbol of the baby's future sexuality.[9]

Why should I circumcise my son?

Parents who circumcise their sons cannot answer this question with strictly rational arguments. Every parent getting ready for a *brit milah* wishes that the Jewish people had abandoned the practice the week before. But the significance and ritual power of *brit milah* is not the stuff of reason, or even of language. This is a radical act of faith, as well as a tangible, physical, visceral connection to our most ancient past.

The simplest, most compelling answer to the question of why we do this to our sons is historical: if we stop doing *brit milah* we stop being Jews as we have been since Abraham. And that is a decision that even the most ambivalent Jew hesitates to make.

In more affirmative terms, the ritual and celebration of *brit milah* demand a communal response to the miracle of every baby's birth. *Brit milah* is a dramatic gesture that makes the community stop and gather to wonder over the miracle of a new baby and the next generation.

The tension, release, and celebration that attend every *bris* reenact the drama of birth: the tension and worry of pregnancy; the life-and-death, bloodstained release of delivery; the wail and acclaim that announce a new life. At the heart of the ritual, *brit milah* is not about the circumcision; it is about the flesh-and-blood miracle of our lives as human beings.

History

Jewish continuity is one of the most compelling reasons Jews continue to perform *brit milah,* but circumcision is not unique to Jews. It has been practiced by people all over the world for centuries. In the ancient world of the Hebrews, the Egyptians, Phoenicians, and Moabites also circumcised their sons. However, non-Jewish circumcision was usually performed at puberty as part of a rite of initiation to manhood and as a test of courage and fortitude. For Jews, infant circumcision is an act of consecration, a sign of identity, and the first step in a lifetime dedicated to religious commitment.

Brit milah is sometimes referred to as the covenant of Abraham, because in the Bible Abram responded to God's command and circumcised himself (at the age of ninety-nine) and all the men of his household, including his thirteen-year-old son Ishmael. In accepting the terms of the covenant, Abram's name was changed to Abraham. (Sarai became Sarah without any ceremony.) The practice of naming a son at a circumcision derives from Abraham's change of name as a result of his *milah.* Isaac, the first son of a circumcised Hebrew, underwent *brit milah* on the eighth day, which is why the ritual has been performed eight days after birth ever since.

The importance of circumcision as a mark of peoplehood is a constant theme in the Bible. When Moses failed to circumcise his son, his wife Zipporah did it herself.[10] After the Exodus from Egypt, the Hebrews who had suspended the practice during their forty years of wandering in the wilderness were circumcised before they entered Canaan.

The covenant of circumcision has been a test of Jewish commitment since biblical times. During the reign of Queen Jezebel, when many Israelites abandoned the covenant of Abraham, the prophet Elijah exhorted the people until they returned to the custom, which earned him the title "Herald of the Covenant."

The fact that Jews consider *brit milah* so important made it a target of anti-Semitic attack throughout history. The first recorded prohibition against circumcision was enacted by Antiochus Epiphanes, the villain of the Hanukkah story, who ordered the execution of mothers along with the sons they had defiantly circumcised. Later, one of the causes of the Bar Kochba rebellion in 132 C.E. was the Roman emperor Hadrian's proscription against *brit milah.*

The Greeks thought circumcision a desecration of the human body, which they revered, and under Hellenistic rule many Jews rejected the practice, too. Some Jews who wanted to participate in nude Greek athletic contests even underwent painful operations to obliterate evidence of the procedure.

During the first century C.E., there was heated debate among early Christians about whether conversion to Christianity required circumcision—in other words, whether a man had to be a Jew before he could become a Christian. When those who opposed circumcision prevailed, the two faiths split irrevocably. Later, Roman law made it illegal to perform circumcisions for the purpose of conversion to Judaism.

In the nineteenth century, some leaders of the early Reform movement suggested that *brit milah* be abolished, but that position gained little support. As Leopold Zunz, a Reform Jew of the era, wrote, "To abrogate circumcision ... is suicide, not reform."[11]

In the twentieth century, stories from the time of the Holocaust and from the former Soviet Union testify to the steadfastness of Jewish practice of *brit milah,* no matter what the consequences. Despite all challenges, *brit milah* has remained a constant feature of the Jewish experience.

Traditional Interpretations

Brit milah was already an ancient custom by the time the rabbis were writing the Talmud and Midrash, the books that explain and expound upon the Torah. The rabbinical literature includes many laws regulating the practice—the who, where, and when of the ritual. There are many commentaries about the *whys* as well.

It was not enough, for example, to explain that *brit milah* be performed on the eighth day simply because that was Isaac's age at his circumcision. The rabbis went on to say that a child who lives for seven full days gains a measure of strength because he has encountered his first Shabbat.

The number eight is associated with things metaphysical. (The number seven is connected to the physical world, as in the seven days of the week and the seven stages of life.) According to the rabbis, the wisdom of the Torah puts *brit milah* on the eighth day to signify that a *bris* is the culmination of creation, the act that makes a baby *tamim* (perfect or complete), in the sense that Abraham was made a whole Jew by his circumcision.[12]

Every aspect of the biblical account of Abraham's circumcision was analyzed by the rabbis. In the Torah, God commands Abram to remove the *orlah,* a word that means not only foreskin but also any barrier standing in the way of a beneficial result. The word *orlah* is also used as a metaphor for obstructions of the heart that prevent a person from hearing or understanding God. Removing the *orlah* of the foreskin is interpreted as a permanent physical sign of dedication to the ongoing task of moving toward the Holy One.

The rabbis wrote that Abraham was selected to be the first man marked by circumcision precisely because he saw and heard God everywhere—because of the lack of barriers between him and the One. *Brit milah* affirms the human ability to change not only our habits but also our very nature, in order to be closer to God. The rabbis wrote that removing the foreskin was a way of sanctifying the act of procreation, but they also viewed it as a way to curb the sexual drive that could draw men away from God.

In the Midrash the story is told that Adam was born without a foreskin, signifying the lack of obstacles between him and God. The appearance of the foreskin in later generations was interpreted as a reminder of Adam's lost purity and the subsequent distance between men and God. Thus, the tradition placed the day of Abraham's circumcision on the tenth of Tishri, the Day of Atonement, when sins are forgiven.

Despite the tradition's reverence for and loyalty to *brit milah,* it also acknowledges it as a bittersweet, ambivalent rite of passage. Rabbi Shimon bar Yochai said, "Behold, a man loves no one better than his son, and yet he circumcises him!" To which Rabbi Nachman bar Shmuel responded, "He rejoices over the mitzvah even though he sees his son's blood being shed."[13]

Planning a *Bris*

Brit milah is regulated and elaborated by the laws of the Talmud, with a liturgy that was already old in the first century C.E. Jewish law clearly spells out the ritual, but the attendant customs vary around the world and change over time. Although the core of the ceremony is nearly universal, no two babies, no two families, and no two *brisses* are quite the same.

You can, if you wish, have a great deal of say about the tone and even the content of the ceremony and celebration of your son's *brit milah.* In this chapter you will find much of the information you need to plan a *bris,* in consultation with your *mohel,* rabbi, and/or cantor. In the event of medical concerns or questions, consult your pediatrician, your *mohel,* or both.

When and Where

Following the birth of a healthy boy, *brit milah* is scheduled eight days later, even if that day falls on Shabbat or a holiday—including Yom Kippur.* When counting, remember that days begin at sundown, so for example, a son born on a Thursday evening will be circumcised on the following Friday.

Despite the emphasis on the eighth day, however, Jewish law *requires* that a *bris* be postponed in case of illness or weakness of any kind. *Brit milah* is performed only when both the pediatrician and the *mohel* agree it's completely safe for the baby.

A *bris* may occur anytime before sundown, but it has long been customary to schedule the ceremony early in the day. The tradition explains the preference for morning *brisses* with the idea that Jews should rush to perform such a happy mitzvah. However, in the days before electricity, the need for bright daylight probably had something to do with the custom, too. Early morning continues to be a favorite time for weekday *brisses* because it allows guests to attend before going to work; breakfast can serve as the *s'udat mitzvah,* the prescribed meal of celebration.

A *bris* may be held anywhere, but most are done in the family home, which is where the ceremony was first performed. From the ninth century and into the twentieth, however, *brit milah* was commonly observed in the synagogue immediately after morning prayers and became a community celebration.[14] This is still the custom among some traditional Jews and is an excellent alternative if your home will not accommodate all the people you expect to attend.

The *Mohel*

A *mohel* is someone trained to perform *brit milah*—which means both the covenantal prayers *(brit)* and the surgical procedure *(milah)*. *Mohalim* are not ordained as rabbis are. Traditionally, one becomes a *mohel* by apprenticeship with an accomplished and established practitioner.

---

*A *bris* may not be scheduled on a Shabbat or holiday, however, for the purpose of conversion, for babies born by cesarean section, or if the *bris* was delayed for health reasons.

The skills of *mohalim* are legendary. It is said that non-Jewish doctors hire non-medically trained *mohalim* to circumcise their sons, and there is a long-standing rumor that the British royal family entrusts its sons to the hands of London's most skilled *mohel.*

The status of the *mohel* as an important Jewish functionary has been acknowledged since at least the first century C.E.[15] But in fact, anyone can hang out a shingle and proclaim himself a *mohel.* There is virtually no regulation or registration for American *mohalim,* as there is in Great Britain.[16] In the United States, word-of-mouth recommendation is actually the only form of control or regulation.

There are very few full-time *mohalim.* Most perform ritual circumcisions "on the side," both as a mitzvah and as an additional source of income. Jewish law permits *brit milah* to be performed by virtually any Jew, though the tradition is firm in its preference for pious men, which is why, until recently, so many rabbis and cantors filled the role.[17] Since the late 1980s, the Reform and Conservative movements have recruited, trained, and certified licensed physicians—women as well as men—to serve as *mohalim* for the liberal Jewish community. (See "Resources for New Parents.")

Finding and Choosing a *Mohel*

In addition to technical skills, the choice of a *mohel* is important for many reasons. Although he may share the honors with a rabbi, the *mohel* usually acts as the master of ceremonies at a *bris,* so he or she will set the tone of the ceremony. A *mohel*'s style can be abrupt and businesslike, gently spiritual, musical, or Borsht-belt funny. The *mohel* can put people at ease, foster a spirit of celebration, inspire, and teach. Many do a fair amount of informal teaching about the history and religious significance of *brit milah* to ensure that everyone present—Jews and non-Jews alike—understands the profound importance of the ritual.

In communities that support several *mohalim,* people tend to make their choice based on the recommendations of rabbis and cantors, who have the most experience attending *brisses.* Feel free to call local rabbis, even if you are not affiliated with a particular synagogue, to ask for names and phone numbers. Some *mohalim* place advertisements in Jewish newspapers, though if you contact one through such an ad, be sure to get some references. And contact more than one *mohel*. Given the busy schedules of physician-*mohalim* in particular, it's a good idea to have at least one backup.

Conversations with the *Mohel*

Your first contact with the *mohel* will probably be over the telephone. In the not-so-distant past, parents would contact the *mohel* only after the baby was born, but it is increasingly common for parents to call much earlier in the pregnancy, whether or not prenatal tests indicate a male child.

Your first order of business is to ascertain whether the *mohel* will be available around the due date. (*Mohalim* take vacations, too.) Ask about the fee. Most charge a flat rate for the ceremony and add travel expenses if any distance is involved. Don't be shy if the fee is beyond your means; many are willing to reduce the price if there is a problem.

During your conversation, try to get a sense of the *mohel's* style. Is he or she jovial? brusque? willing to answer your questions about the ceremony? Is this someone you look forward to meeting?

Be prepared to answer some questions, too. A traditional *mohel* might ask about your Jewish status. While you may not want to discuss the volatile issue of "Who is a Jew?" at this moment in your life, the *mohel* has obligations beyond providing you with a service and must remain faithful to his/her interpretation of Jewish law. Some Orthodox *mohalim* may decline to do a *bris* on a baby born of a mother who was converted by a non-Orthodox rabbi, for example. But even a *mohel* trained by one of the liberal movements may ask whether the mother is Jewish, so he or she knows whether to include the prayer for conversion at a *brit milah*.

Once your baby boy is born, your second or third phone call should be to the *mohel* to set up a date and time for the *bris*. You'll probably talk once again before the event, at which time the *mohel* should give you instructions about preparations you need to make at home. At that point you may be asked for your Hebrew names and the baby's Hebrew name. Do not leave the decision of a Hebrew name to the morning of the *bris*.

Questions for the *Mohel*

- Will you be available for the week before and after our due date?

- How long have you been performing circumcisions?

- Do you use a restraint?

- Do you use any anesthetic?

- How do you feel about parental participation?

- Can you help our guests understand the ritual? (You might want to inform the *mohel* if one of your families includes non-Jews.)

- Can we call you after the *bris* with questions?

- What will we need to have ready?

- What is your fee?

The *Mohel's* Responsibilities

The *mohel* generally leads the ceremony. He or she recites prayers, explains the procedure and its meaning, and informs the guests when the actual cutting is about to occur so they can choose to move away or gather near. Still, it is important to remember that the *mohel* is there to help *you* perform this mitzvah. According to Jewish law, the father is responsible for his son's *brit milah,* and technically the father performs the circumcision; the *mohel* acts only as his *shaliach,* or representative. This can be dramatized by having a parent hand the *izmail* (the circumcision knife) to the *mohel* immediately before the ritual.

On the day of your son's *brit milah,* the *mohel* will arrive early to examine the baby. If she or he has any questions about the baby's health, Jewish law obliges you to postpone the *bris.* Once the *mohel* is satisfied that your son is fine, he or she may discuss the ceremony with you and ask how you or other guests will participate. If the

---

Questions the *Mohel* May Ask You

- What is the baby's Hebrew name?

- What are your (the parents') Hebrew names?

- Who will act as *sandek* (holding the baby during the ceremony)?

- Is the mother Jewish?

- Will a rabbi be co-officiating?

- Will you or other guests be participating in the ceremony, and how?

- Are there special things you would like me to say—or not say?

---

mohel is to co-officiate with a rabbi, the two of them will need to confer. After the circumcision, the *mohel* may or may not stay for the meal and celebration, depending on his/her schedule. An envelope containing the fee should be ready in advance.

Prior to leaving, the *mohel* should examine the baby and give you complete instructions about taking care of the circumcision (see below). Some *mohalim* make a follow-up phone call or two in the days after a *bris*. But you should feel free to call with questions about your son's healing.

Guests and Participants

The only people who absolutely must be present at a *bris* are the baby, the *mohel,* and the *sandek,* who holds the baby. In general, you do not "invite" guests to a *bris,* and there certainly isn't time to mail formal invitations. However, it is a mitzvah to attend a *bris,* so it's a mitzvah to open the doors to as many people as possible. Most parents simply call or e-mail relatives and friends to tell them the date and time and leave the front door open.

There are a few special honors, or *kibbudim,* that can be assigned to relatives and close friends at a *bris.* Customarily, grandparents are given the most important roles, including that of *sandek.*

The word *sandek* is probably derived from the Greek *syndikos,* meaning patron.[18] The *sandek* assists the *mohel* by holding the baby, who is lying on a table or on a restraining board, during the circumcision. Traditionally, the *sandek* wears a *tallit,* or prayer shawl. He is the only one who sits during the ceremony; everyone else stands. In some Sephardic communities, fathers act as *sandek* for their own sons, though the custom in America has long been for grandfathers to fill this honored role.[19] (If you are fortunate enough to have both grandfathers present, the two can share the honors of *sandek,* with one holding the baby during the circumcision and the other one doing the honors during the naming.) The term *sandeket,* the feminine version, is used to honor a female guest or relative who participates in the ceremony.

Elijah

The prophet Elijah, who preached about the importance of *brit milah,* has been linked to the ritual since biblical times. His presence is invoked by the *kisei shel Eliyahu,* the chair of Elijah. By the Middle Ages, Elijah's chair was a well-established custom at *brisses.* In many European communities, the synagogue owned an elaborate throne used at all circumcisions. Today, any chair may be decorated or draped for the purpose, or a special pillow for the baby is used.[20]

Non-Jews at the Ceremony

In general, it is a considered a mitzvah to include as many people as possible, and it's a good way to affirm family unity. With the exception of the *sandek,* none of the roles or honors listed below need be limited to Jews. Non-Jewish grandparents, aunts, uncles, cousins, and friends can participate in many ways—depending on their comfort level, of course.

Among the honors you can give to guests at a *brit milah* are the roles of *kvatterin* (godmother) and *kvatter* (godfather), terms that come from eastern Europe. Unlike Christian godparents, the *kvatter* and *kvatterin* do not assume responsibility for the child's religious upbringing. Their roles are strictly ceremonial and limited to carrying the baby from the mother to the room where the *bris* takes place, and then to the ceremonial chair for Elijah, the legendary prophet who is a "guest" at every *bris.*

There are other ways to include guests in the proceedings, too. Invite four friends to hold a prayer shawl on poles over the *bris*— a touch that recalls the parents' wedding canopy. (See *"Hiddur Mitzvah*—Beautiful Touches.") Before the circumcision, pass the baby from the grandparents to the parents or, if you are so blessed, from great-grandparents to grandparents to parents, a powerful tribute to family continuity. If a sibling is mature enough to participate, he or she might carry the baby into the room, light a candle, or read a blessing or poem. In some communities, it is customary to assign a role to a couple trying to conceive, invoking the luck and blessings of the new parents on them.

It is also fine to keep things very simple and streamlined during the ritual. You can involve more people at the celebration afterward (see Part 4, *"Simcha*—Joy").

Women and *Brit Milah*

In the past, women had no active role in *brit milah,* and in some communities this is still the case. But women's participation in ritual life has expanded to include virtually all traditional honors—if they so choose. While some mothers participate fully, others find it too difficult to be in the room during the actual circumcision. Some wait in the next room, usually surrounded by supportive friends and family members, during the few minutes of the procedure. This is an entirely personal matter, and it is your choice.

A traditional prayer recited by new mothers at a *bris* is *Birkat Hagomel,* a blessing of thanks recited after recovering from an illness.

בָּרוּךְ אַתָּה יְיָ, אֱלֹהֵינוּ מֶלֶךְ הָעוֹלָם,
הַגּוֹמֵל לְחַיָּבִים טוֹבוֹת, שֶׁגְּמָלַנִי כָּל טוֹב.

*Ba-ruch a-ta Adonai, Eh-lo-hei-nu meh-lech
ha-o-lam, ha-go-mel l'cha-ya-vim to-vot,
sheh-g'ma-la-ni kol tov.*

Blessed are You, Adonai, Ruler of all, who does
good to the undeserving and who has dealt kindly
with me.

The community responds:

מִי שֶׁגְּמָלְךָ כָּל טוֹב, הוּא יִגְמָלְךָ כָּל טוֹב, סֶלָה.

*Mi sheh-g'ma-l'cha kol tov, hu yig-mol-cha kol
tov, seh-lah.*

May the One who has shown you kindness deal
kindly with you forever.

Liturgy and Ritual

As with most Jewish life-cycle rituals, the liturgy of *brit milah* is
very brief—no more than five or ten minutes long. It has three
basic parts: the circumcision; the *Kiddush*, which includes the
baby-naming; and the celebratory meal. Although no two ceremonies are identical, what follows is an outline of a typical *bris*. At
the end of this chapter, you will find two versions of *brit milah* that
elaborate on the basics.

Part I: *Milah*

The first part of the ceremony is as universal as anything in Jewish
religious life. As the baby is carried in, he is greeted with the
phrase *Baruch haba*, which means "Blessed is the one who
comes." "The One" refers to both the baby and the Holy One.

The baby may be taken to Elijah's chair for a moment and handed
to the *sandek*. The *mohel* prepares the baby for the circumcision and
usually says a few words of introduction. He then recites the blessing:

בָּרוּךְ אַתָּה יְיָ, אֱלֹהֵינוּ מֶלֶךְ הָעוֹלָם,
אֲשֶׁר קִדְּשָׁנוּ בְּמִצְוֹתָיו, וְצִוָּנוּ עַל הַמִּילָה.

*Ba-ruch a-ta Adonai, Eh-lo-hei-nu meh-lech
ha-o-lam, a-sher ki-d'sha-nu b'mitz-vo-tav,
v'tzi-va-nu al ha-mi-lah.*

Blessed are You, Adonai our God, Ruler of the universe, who sanctifies us with commandments and
commands us regarding circumcision.

The *mohel* removes the foreskin, making sure that at least one
drop of blood is visible. Then the father, mother, or both parents
recite this blessing, usually repeating it after the *mohel:*

בָּרוּךְ אַתָּה יְיָ, אֱלֹהֵינוּ מֶלֶךְ הָעוֹלָם,
אֲשֶׁר קִדְּשָׁנוּ בְּמִצְוֹתָיו, וְצִוָּנוּ
לְהַכְנִיסוֹ בִּבְרִיתוֹ שֶׁל אַבְרָהָם אָבִינוּ.

*Ba-ruch a-ta Adonai, Eh-lo-hei-nu meh-lech
ha-o-lam, a-sher ki-d'sha-nu b'mitz-vo-tav,
v'tzi-va-nu l'hach-ni-so biv-ri-to shel Av-ra-ham
a-vi-nu.*

Blessed are You, Adonai our God, Ruler of the universe, who sanctifies us with Your commandments
and commands us to bring our son into the
covenant of Abraham, our father.

Everyone says "Amen," and the guests repeat the traditional wish:

כְּשֵׁם שֶׁנִּכְנַס לַבְּרִית, כֵּן יִכָּנֵס לְתוֹרָה וּלְחֻפָּה
וּלְמַעֲשִׂים טוֹבִים.

*K'shem sheh-nich-nas la-b'rit, kein yi-ka-nes
l'to-rah ul-chu-pah ul-ma-a-sim to-vim.*

Just as he entered the covenant, so may he enter
into the study of Torah, the wedding canopy, and
the accomplishment of good deeds.

Part II: *Kiddush*

As soon as the baby is diapered, dressed, and swaddled, the second part of the ceremony begins with *Kiddush,* the blessing over wine. After the *mohel* says the blessing, he drinks some wine and gives some to the baby. This is followed by a longer chanted prayer that includes the baby-naming.

> Blessed are You, God, Source of Life, who sanctifies Your beloved from birth and who has impressed Your decree in his flesh, and marked this offspring with the sign of the holy covenant. Therefore, for the sake of this covenant, O living God, our portion, our rock, protect this child from all misfortune, for the sake of Your covenant that You have placed in our flesh. Blessed are You, Adonai, who establishes the covenant.
>
> Our God and God of our ancestors, sustain this child for his father and mother, and may he be called _____, son of _____.
>
> May his father rejoice in the issue of his loins, and may his mother exult in the fruit of her womb, as it is written, "Your father and mother will rejoice. She who bore you will exult."
>
> And it is said, "When I passed by you and saw you wallowing in your blood I said to you, 'Because of your blood you shall live!' and I said to you, 'Because of your blood you shall live!'"[21]
>
> And it is said, "God is ever mindful of God's covenant, the promise given for a thousand generations. That which God made with Abraham, swore to Isaac, and confirmed in a decree for Jacob, for Israel as an eternal covenant."
>
> And it is said, "When his son Isaac was eight days old, Abraham circumcised him, as God had commanded him."
>
> Praise God, for God is good. God's steadfast love is forever.

May this child, _____ grow into manhood. As he has entered the covenant, so may he enter the study of Torah, the wedding canopy, and the accomplishment of good deeds.

The ceremony may end here or continue with other prayers and blessings. The *mohel* may offer a traditional prayer that asks God to accept his work. The familiar words and melody of the *Sheheheyanu*, the prayer of thanksgiving for new blessings, is often included. In Israel, *Sheheheyanu* follows the father's blessing immediately after the circumcision.[22] Sephardic Jews follow the blessing over wine with the blessing for fragrant spices—Moroccan Jews use dried rose petals.

After the long *Kiddush*, it has become customary for one or both parents to talk about how the name was chosen. If the baby has been named for a relative who has died, this is invariably a moving moment. Typically, parents give voice to their hope that their son will grow up to be as learned, as quick to laugh, as devoted a friend and father as the man or men after whom he is named.

At this point, parents sometimes also add readings and prayers. Guests can offer impromptu blessings for the new baby, such as "May he grow up in a world free of want and fear," or "May he inherit his mother's good looks and his father's appetite."

If this idea appeals to you, ask a few guests to think about a blessing in advance. Wishes like these can also be written in a guest book.

Some parents now provide a printed guide to explain the history and meaning of *brit milah* or provide responsive readings for the ceremony. This pamphlet traditionally includes the prayers recited after meals, which include blessings for a meal after a *bris*. (See "*Hiddur Mitzvah*—Beautiful Touches.")

Part III: Celebration

Traditionally, the ceremony ends with the song, "Siman Tov Umazal Tov" (Good Fortune and Good Luck), a universal Jewish song of rejoicing, and a meal is served. This *s'udat mitzvah*, or meal of the commandment, usually begins with a *Motzi*, a blessing for bread, typically a specially made loaf of challah, a braided loaf of egg bread.

Variations

Although most ceremonies follow this general order, there are exceptions. Some parents separate the circumcision from the celebration, with only the immediate family present for the *milah* and

---

Sample Checklist of Things You Need for a *Bris*

Diapers

Kippah for the baby

Goblet for *Kiddush*

Kosher wine

Yarmulkes (*kippot,* or skullcaps) for guests

Sturdy table and chair

Prayer shawl for the *sandek*

Phone ringer turned off

Candles and matches

Elijah's chair

Shawl to cover Elijah's chair

Tape recorder, camera, booklets

Cotton balls*

Gauze pads*

Petroleum jelly*

Ointment*

Payment for the *mohel*

*The *mohel* will provide you with specifics.

---

then host guests for a *Kiddush* where the baby is given his name. Sometimes this is done because the mother is too ill to attend a *bris* eight days after the birth, but there are parents who simply prefer that the procedure not be connected to a party. There is even a biblical precedent for this choice, given that Abraham's celebration for Isaac's birth took place at his son's weaning, not at his circumcision.

Along the same lines, sometimes parents have the circumcision in a small room, away from most of the guests, and then move to a larger room where the company can witness the rest of the ceremony.

Parents who choose hospital circumcision sometimes request that a naming ceremony for their son be held later, in the synagogue. Responses to this request vary from rabbi to rabbi. The most traditional will insist on a *hatafat dam brit,* a ritual drawing of blood from the site of the circumcision, which fulfills the obligations of *brit milah,* before reciting the naming blessing; other rabbis routinely officiate at such namings. Still others apply the Talmudic category of *l'chat'chilah la, di-avad in,* which means, "If you ask me before you do it, I'll say, no; if you tell me after the fact, I'll say, all right." In such cases, a rabbi may insist on a private ceremony that will not encourage others to follow suit.

Adoption, Conversion, and Rituals for Already Circumcised Sons

Brit milah for an adopted infant is not very different from *brit milah* for a son who is born to you. An adopted son is circumcised as soon as possible. If the baby was not born to a Jewish mother, tradition calls for a *bet din,* a court of three Jews, to be present to witness that the *bris* was performed for the purpose of conversion. The only differences in the ritual are in the *mohel's* prayers. Before the circumcision, he says:

בָּרוּךְ אַתָּה יְיָ, אֱלֹהֵינוּ מֶלֶךְ הָעוֹלָם,
אֲשֶׁר קִדְּשָׁנוּ בְּמִצְוֹתָיו, וְצִוָּנוּ לָמוּל אֶת הַגֵּרִים.

*Ba-ruch a-ta Adonai, Eh-lo-hei-nu meh-lech
ha-o-lam, a-sher ki-d'sha-nu b'mitz-vo-tav,
v'tzi-va-nu la-mul et ha-ge-rim.*

Holy One of Blessing, Your Presence fills creation,
You make us holy with Your commandments, call-
ing us to circumcise the convert.

During the longer blessing after the circumcision, the *mohel* says:

בָּרוּךְ אַתָּה יְיָ, אֱלֹהֵינוּ מֶלֶךְ הָעוֹלָם, אֲשֶׁר קִדְּשָׁנוּ
בְּמִצְוֹתָיו, וְצִוָּנוּ לָמוּל אֶת הַגֵּרִים וּלְהַטִּיף מֵהֶם דַּם
בְּרִית, שֶׁאִלְמָלֵא דַם בְּרִית לֹא נִתְקַיְּמוּ שָׁמַיִם
וָאָרֶץ, שֶׁנֶּאֱמַר: אִם לֹא בְרִיתִי יוֹמָם וָלָיְלָה חֻקּוֹת
שָׁמַיִם וָאָרֶץ לֹא שַׂמְתִּי. בָּרוּךְ אַתָּה יְיָ, כּוֹרֵת
הַבְּרִית.

Holy One of Blessing, Your Presence fills creation,
You make us holy with Your commandments, call-
ing us to circumcise the convert and to draw the
blood of the convert. Were it not for the blood of
the covenant, heaven and earth would not have
been fulfilled, as it is said, without My covenant, I
would not set forth day and night and the laws of
heaven and earth. Holy One of Blessing, author of
the covenant.

There are many ways to acknowledge the particular dimension
of adoption at a *bris*. For example, parents might recite this
prayer, or ask others to read from it with them:

We are grateful to God
Who has made this miracle of creation
And given us this baby boy.
His coming into our home has blessed us.
He is part of our family and our lives.
This child has now become our son.

Out of our love of God and Torah and Israel,
We wish to raise him up as a Jew.
We come now before a Jewish court of three
To begin his entry into the Jewish people
Through the mitzvah of milah.

Let this be the beginning
Of his living a life of mitzvot.
May we be privileged to raise him up
As a true and loyal son of Abraham and Sarah.
This child comes into the covenant in our presence.
We welcome him with the words that God spoke to Abraham our
father:
Hit-halech l'fanai veh-yeh tamim
Walk before Me and be whole.[23]

If an adopted child was circumcised by a physician without
Jewish ritual, tradition also calls for a ritual called *hatafat dam
brit,* the covenant of the drop of blood. This involves drawing a
drop of blood from the site of the circumcision by a *mohel*. It is
performed as soon as possible, involves very little pain and virtually no wound, and is sometimes held at a *mikveh,* where the ritual of immersion follows. Technically, *hatafat dam brit* does not
require any blessings or a celebratory meal, but many adoptive
parents choose to celebrate as they would for a *brit milah,* with

Sheheheyanu, Kiddush, bestowal of a name, and other blessings and prayers.

According to *halachah,* the laws and rituals that apply to adopted sons also pertain to sons of Jewish fathers and non-Jewish mothers. At a *bris* for the son of a non-Jewish mother—even if she is committed to raising her child as a Jew—*mohalim* may use the blessings for conversion. According to Jewish law, the ritual conversion of a non-Jewish boy includes not only *brit milah* but also *mikveh,* immersion in a ritual bath. (See "Adoption" in Part 5 for a fuller discussion of laws, customs, and ceremonies.)

Caring for the Newly Circumcised Baby

The *mohel* should provide you with information about the care of the circumcision site. The advice is invariably simple: Most *mohalim* apply a gauze bandage saturated with petroleum jelly, which should be taken off in a day or two. During those first few days, you might see a drop of blood or even blood stains on the baby's diapers, but this is usually no cause for alarm. The penis will be bright red at first and perhaps even a bit swollen, but this should subside within two weeks, at most. A mucus-like lymphatic secretion may appear on the shaft of the penis; this is no cause for alarm. Just leave it alone, and it, too, will go away.

Your *mohel* may give you specific instructions about applying an antibacterial salve or ointment, but generally, the less you do, the better. By the time of your first visit to the pediatrician—within a month—the penis should be completely healed.

Complications are extremely rare, but do not hesitate to call the *mohel* and/or your pediatrician if the baby seems excessively fussy, has a fever, or develops an inflammation that surrounds the top of the penis. If you have any concerns or questions about how your son is healing, the *mohel* should be available and helpful.

Two Ceremonies for *Brit Milah*

In the past, most parents did not consider themselves active participants in a son's *brit milah.* The *mohel* would show up, do his job, and that would be that.

Given the power of the ancient ceremony and the anxiety associated with circumcision, many parents will simply follow the *mohel*'s and/or rabbi's directions. However, there are a few simple ways to customize and personalize the ritual. Just the addition of a poem, blessing, or special remarks about the baby's namesake turns the occasion into a powerful experience for everyone. Some parents are more ambitious and write ceremonies, complete with elaborate booklets that explain the ritual for their guests. Your rabbi or *mohel* should be able to offer some guidance.

The following pages include two ceremonies that may be copied and used. These are intended as guides for you in designing your own ceremony. More poems, readings, and prayers are found in the chapters *"Hiddur Mitzvah*—Beautiful Touches" and *"Brit Bat*—Welcoming Our Daughters," and in the "Adoption" section of Part 5.

Brit Milah Ceremony

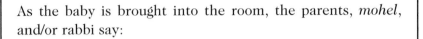

As the baby is brought into the room, the parents, *mohel*, and/or rabbi say:

בָּרוּךְ הַבָּא.

Ba-ruch ha-ba.

Blessed are you who bear the
Divine Presence.

Holding the baby, a parent says:

My son, my child, you have been as dear to me as my own breath. May I hold you gently now with the love to keep you close and with the strength to let you grow.

Parent says:

My son, my child, a piece of my life is you. You have grown to life apart from me, but now I hold you close to my heart and cradle you in my arms with my love.

One or both parents:

We have been blessed with the gift of new life. We have shared love and pain and joy in bringing our son into life.

By the way we live, we aspire to teach our son to become a caring and loving person. We hope that in seeking to fulfill himself, he will accept his responsibilities to others and to his heritage. We dedicate ourselves to the creation of a Jewish home and to a life of compassion for others, hoping he will learn from our example.

This material is from *The New Jewish Baby Book,* Second Edition, by Anita Diamant, © 2005, published by Jewish Lights Publishing, P.O. Box 237, Sunset Farm Offices, Woodstock, VT 05091. The publisher grants permission to you to copy this ceremony for distribution to your guests. All rights to other parts of this book are still covered by copyright and are reserved to the publisher.

Brit Milah Ceremony

God of our grandfathers, God of our grandmothers, we pray for covenant love, for life, for good. Keep us strong together.

בָּרוּךְ אַתָּה יְיָ, מְקוֹר הַחַיִּים מְשַׂמֵּחַ הַהוֹרִים עִם יַלְדֵיהֶם.

Ba-ruch a-ta Adonai, m'kor ha-cha-yim
m'sa-mei-ach ha-ho-rim im yal-dei-hem.

Blessed is the Holy Source of Life,
who causes parents to rejoice with their children.

Parents:

We are ready to fulfill the mitzvah of circumcision, as it is written in the Torah, "Throughout your generations every male among you shall be circumcised when he is eight days old."

When the baby is placed on Elijah's chair, the *mohel* or rabbi says:

In Jewish folklore, Elijah is regarded as the forerunner of messianic days, the one who announces the advent of the Messiah. As we recall Elijah now, we rekindle our faith that every human life may yet bring about *y'mot hamoshiah,* the era of harmony and peace for all people.

Mohel:

בָּרוּךְ אַתָּה יְיָ, אֱלֹהֵינוּ מֶלֶךְ הָעוֹלָם,
אֲשֶׁר קִדְּשָׁנוּ בְּמִצְוֹתָיו, וְצִוָּנוּ עַל הַמִּילָה.

Blessed by the Presence whose sanctity
fills our lives, we fulfill the mitzvah of
circumcision.

Circumcision is performed.

Brit Milah Ceremony

Parent/s, repeating after the *mohel*:

בָּרוּךְ אַתָּה יְיָ, אֱלֹהֵינוּ מֶלֶךְ הָעוֹלָם,
אֲשֶׁר קִדְּשָׁנוּ בְּמִצְוֹתָיו, וְצִוָּנוּ
לְהַכְנִיסוֹ בִּבְרִיתוֹ שֶׁל אַבְרָהָם אָבִינוּ.

*Ba-ruch a-ta Adonai, Eh-lo-hei-nu meh-lech
ha-o-lam, a-sher ki-d'sha-nu b'mitz-vo-tav,
v'tzi-va-nu l'hach-ni-so biv-ri-to shel
Av-ra-ham a-vi-nu.*

Blessed by the Presence whose sanctity fills
our lives, we bring our son into the covenant
of Abraham, our father.

Parent/s with *mohel*, rabbi, and/or guests:

זֶה הַקָּטֹן _____ גָּדוֹל יִהְיֶה.
כְּשֵׁם שֶׁנִּכְנַס לַבְּרִית,
כֵּן יִכָּנֵס לְתוֹרָה וּלְחֻפָּה וּלְמַעֲשִׂים טוֹבִים.

*Zeh ha-ka-ton _____ ga-dol yih-yeh.
K'shem sheh-nich-nas la-brit, kein yi-ka-nes
l'to-rah ul-chu-pah ul-ma-a-sim to-vim.*

As he has been brought into the covenant of
our people, so may he attain the blessings of
Torah, *huppah,* and a life of good deeds.

Raising the cup of wine, the *mohel* or rabbi says:

Brit Milah Ceremony

בָּרוּךְ אַתָּה יְיָ, אֱלֹהֵינוּ מֶלֶךְ הָעוֹלָם, בּוֹרֵא פְּרִי הַגָּפֶן.

בָּרוּךְ אַתָּה יְיָ, אֱלֹהֵינוּ מֶלֶךְ הָעוֹלָם, אֲשֶׁר קִדֵּשׁ יְדִיד מִבֶּטֶן, וְחֹק
בִּשְׁאֵרוֹ שָׂם, וְצֶאֱצָאָיו חָתַם בְּאוֹת בְּרִית קֹדֶשׁ. עַל כֵּן בִּשְׂכַר זֹאת,
אֵל חַי, חֶלְקֵנוּ צוּרֵנוּ, צַוֵּה לְהַצִּיל יְדִידוּת שְׁאֵרֵנוּ מִשַּׁחַת, לְמַעַן
בְּרִיתוֹ אֲשֶׁר שָׂם בִּבְשָׂרֵנוּ. בָּרוּךְ אַתָּה יְיָ, כּוֹרֵת הַבְּרִית.

אֱלֹהֵינוּ וֵאלֹהֵי אֲבוֹתֵינוּ וְאִמּוֹתֵינוּ, קַיֵּם אֶת הַיֶּלֶד הַזֶּה לְאָבִיו
וּלְאִמּוֹ, וְיִקָּרֵא שְׁמוֹ בְּיִשְׂרָאֵל _____ בֶּן _____. יִשְׂמַח
הָאָב בְּיוֹצֵא חֲלָצָיו, וְתָגֵל אִמּוֹ בִּפְרִי בִטְנָהּ, כַּכָּתוּב: יִשְׂמַח אָבִיךְ
וְאִמֶּךָ, וְתָגֵל יוֹלַדְתֶּךָ. וְנֶאֱמַר: וָאֶעֱבֹר עָלַיִךְ וָאֶרְאֵךְ מִתְבּוֹסֶסֶת
בְּדָמָיִךְ, וָאֹמַר לָךְ בְּדָמַיִךְ חֲיִי. וְנֶאֱמַר: זָכַר לְעוֹלָם בְּרִיתוֹ, דָּבָר
צִוָּה לְאֶלֶף דּוֹר. אֲשֶׁר כָּרַת אֶת אַבְרָהָם, וּשְׁבוּעָתוֹ לְיִצְחָק.
וַיַּעֲמִידֶהָ לְיַעֲקֹב לְחֹק, לְיִשְׂרָאֵל בְּרִית עוֹלָם. וְנֶאֱמַר: וַיָּמָל
אַבְרָהָם אֶת יִצְחָק בְּנוֹ, בֶּן שְׁמֹנַת יָמִים, כַּאֲשֶׁר צִוָּה אֹתוֹ אֱלֹהִים.
הוֹדוּ לַיְיָ כִּי טוֹב, כִּי לְעוֹלָם חַסְדּוֹ. הוֹדוּ לַיְיָ כִּי טוֹב, כִּי לְעוֹלָם
חַסְדּוֹ.

_____ בֶּן _____ זֶה הַקָּטֹן גָּדוֹל יִהְיֶה. כְּשֵׁם שֶׁנִּכְנַס
לַבְּרִית, כֵּן יִכָּנֵס לְתוֹרָה, וּלְחֻפָּה, וּלְמַעֲשִׂים טוֹבִים.

Blessed is the Presence whose sanctity fills our lives and ripens fruit on the vine.

You have sanctified your beloved from the womb, establishing your holy covenant throughout the generations. May devotion to the covenant continue to sustain us as a people. Blessed by the Presence whose sanctity fills our lives, we give thanks for the covenant.

God of all life, sustain this child and the let him be known in Israel as _____, son of _____ and _____.

Brit Milah Ceremony

May the father rejoice in his offspring and the mother be glad with her children. May you teach him through word and deed the meaning of the covenant forever, the word commanded to a thousand generations, the covenant made with Abraham, Isaac, Jacob, Sarah, Rebecca, Rachel, and Leah, an eternal covenant for Israel. As it is said, "And Abraham circumcised his son when he was eight days old, as God commanded." Give thanks to God for what is good, for covenant love that endures   forever.

May this little child, _____, son of _____ and _____, grow into manhood as a blessing to his family, the Jewish people, and humanity. As he has entered the covenant of our people, so may he grow into a life of Torah, *huppah,* and good deeds.

Parent/s drink the wine the baby has already tasted and explain the baby's name. Other readings may be included here.

Rabbi or *mohel*:

יְבָרֶכְךָ יְיָ וְיִשְׁמְרֶךָ,
יָאֵר יְיָ פָּנָיו אֵלֶיךָ וִיחֻנֶּךָּ,
יִשָּׂא יְיָ פָּנָיו אֵלֶיךָ וְיָשֵׂם לְךָ שָׁלוֹם.

May God bless you and keep you.
My God be with you and be gracious to you.
May God show you kindness and give
you peace.

Brit Milah Ceremony

Parent/s and guests:

בָּרוּךְ אַתָּה יְיָ, אֱלֹהֵינוּ מֶלֶךְ הָעוֹלָם,
שֶׁהֶחֱיָנוּ וְקִיְּמָנוּ וְהִגִּיעָנוּ לַזְּמַן הַזֶּה.

*Ba-ruch a-ta Adonai, Eh-lo-hei-nu meh-lech
ha-o-lam, sheh-heh-cheh-ya-nu v'ki-y'ma-nu
v'hi-gi-a-nu la-z'man ha-zeh.*

Blessed by the Presence whose sanctity fills
our lives, we give thanks for life, for health,
and for this sacred moment.[24]

Covenant Ceremony

As the baby is brought into the room, all say:

בָּרוּךְ הַבָּא בְּשֵׁם יְיָ.

Ba-ruch ha-ba b'shem Adonai.

Blessed are you who comes in the name of
the Eternal.

Parent/s:

הוֹדוּ לַייָ כִּי טוֹב, כִּי לְעוֹלָם חַסְדּוֹ.

Ho-du la-do-nai ki tov, ki l'o-lam chas-do.

Give thanks to the Eternal who is good,
whose goodness is everlasting.

Reader:

You are your parents' dream realized, their hopes fulfilled. You
are the latest and best chapter in the unfolding lives of your
family.

Reader:

You are a bridge over which we who welcome you can gaze
from this day into future days, from our generation into
yours. You are the newest link in the endless chain of our
people's history.

Covenant Ceremony

Grandparent/s:

Our God and God of all generations, we are grateful for new beginnings, for the bond of new life that links one generation to another. Thankful for the blessings of family, for the love and care that bring meaning and happiness to our lives, we rejoice with our children at the birth of our grandchild.

Reader:

If you hold a hand before your eyes, you can hide the tallest mountain. If we get caught up with what we do in our everyday lives, we can forget that miracles fill the world. You remind us of the many wonders that happen all around us.

All:

בָּרוּךְ אַתָּה יְיָ, אֱלֹהֵינוּ מֶלֶךְ הָעוֹלָם,
שֶׁהֶחֱיָנוּ וְקִיְּמָנוּ וְהִגִּיעָנוּ לַזְּמַן הַזֶּה.

*Ba-ruch a-ta Adonai, Eh-lo-hei-nu meh-lech
ha-o-lam, sheh-heh-cheh-ya-nu v'ki-y'ma-nu
v'hi-gi-a-nu la-z'man ha-zeh.*

Blessed are You, O God, who gives us life,
who sustains us, and who brings us here to
share in this occasion.

Reader:

A new son of Israel has come, and with him comes a great promise. In his soul is the potential to bring greatness into our world. He brings blessing to our lives, as he reminds us that the world is not yet complete. We each share in the task of perfecting this world.

Covenant Ceremony

Reader:

And so we set aside a chair for Elijah the prophet, may his memory be for a blessing. Recalling Elijah, we rekindle our faith that every human life has the potential to bring about an era of peace and harmony for all people.

Reader or *mohel*:

We welcome you to life with love. We rejoice in bringing this child into the *brit*, the covenant between God and the Jewish people.

Since the time of Abraham and Sarah, we Jews have been called to enter this covenant. As it says in Genesis, "I will establish My covenant between Me and you, to be God to you and to your offspring."

Parent/s:

We are ready to fulfill the mitzvah of circumcision as the Creator commanded us in the Torah. "Throughout your generations, every male among you shall be circumcised when he is eight days old."

Mohel:

בָּרוּךְ אַתָּה יְיָ, אֱלֹהֵינוּ מֶלֶךְ הָעוֹלָם,
אֲשֶׁר קִדְּשָׁנוּ בְּמִצְוֹתָיו, וְצִוָּנוּ עַל הַמִּילָה.

Ba-ruch a-ta Adonai, Eh-lo-hei-nu meh-lech ha-o-lam, a-sher ki-d'sha-nu b'mitz-vo-tav, v'tzi-va-nu al ha-mi-lah.

Blessed are You, Eternal Presence of the universe, who has sanctified us with Your commandments and commanded us concerning circumcision.

Circumcision is performed.

Covenant Ceremony

Parent/s:

בָּרוּךְ אַתָּה יְיָ, אֱלֹהֵינוּ מֶלֶךְ הָעוֹלָם,
אֲשֶׁר קִדְּשָׁנוּ בְּמִצְוֹתָיו, וְצִוָּנוּ
לְהַכְנִיסוֹ בִּבְרִיתוֹ שֶׁל אַבְרָהָם אָבִינוּ וְשָׂרָה אִמֵּנוּ.

*Ba-ruch a-ta Adonai, Eh-lo-hei-nu meh-lech
ha-o-lam, a-sher ki-d'sha-nu b'mitz-vo-tav,
v'tzi-va-nu l'hach-ni-so biv-ri-to shel
Av-ra-ham a-vi-nu v'Sa-rah i-mei-nu.*

Blessed are You, Eternal Presence of the
universe, who has sanctified us with Your
commandments and commanded us to bring
our son into the covenant of Abraham our
father and Sarah our mother.

All:

כְּשֵׁם שֶׁנִּכְנַס לַבְּרִית, כֵּן יִכָּנֵס לְתוֹרָה וּלְחֻפָּה
וּלְמַעֲשִׂים טוֹבִים.

*K'shem sheh-nich-nas la-b'rit, kein yi-ka-nes
l'to-rah ul-chu-pah ul-ma-a-sim to-vim.*

As he has entered the covenant, so may he
attain the blessings of Torah, marriage,
and a life of good deeds.

Covenant Ceremony

Reader:

May God who blessed our ancestors Abraham and Sarah, Isaac and Rebecca, Jacob, Rachel, and Leah, bless this child who is circumcised and bring him speedily to full healing. May his parents, _____ and _____, fulfill the privilege of raising him, educating him, and teaching him wisdom. May his hands and heart be faithful in serving God.

Reader, rabbi, or *mohel:*

בָּרוּךְ אַתָּה יְיָ, אֱלֹהֵינוּ מֶלֶךְ הָעוֹלָם,
בּוֹרֵא פְּרִי הַגָּפֶן.

Blessed is the Eternal Ruler of the universe,
Creator of the fruit of the vine.

Parent:

As we prepare to give you your name, we wrap you in this *tallit* [story of the *tallit*].

Parent tells stories about the baby's namesake(s).

Rabbi or *mohel*:

אֱלֹהֵינוּ וֵאלֹהֵי אֲבוֹתֵינוּ וְאִמּוֹתֵינוּ, קַיֵּם אֶת הַיֶּלֶד הַזֶּה לְאָבִיו
וּלְאִמּוֹ, וְיִקָּרֵא שְׁמוֹ בְּיִשְׂרָאֵל _____ בֶּן _____ . יִשְׂמַח
הָאָב בְּיוֹצֵא חֲלָצָיו, וְתָגֵל אִמּוֹ בִּפְרִי בִטְנָהּ. זֶה הַקָּטֹן גָּדוֹל יִהְיֶה.
כְּשֵׁם שֶׁנִּכְנַס לַבְּרִית, כֵּן יִכָּנֵס לַתּוֹרָה, וּלְחֻפָּה, וּלְמַעֲשִׂים טוֹבִים.

Our God, God of our mothers and fathers, sustain _____ through his parents' loving care. In the presence of loved ones, we give this child the name _____ to be known in the Jewish community as _____ ben _____ v' _____. May his name be a source of joy.

120

Covenant Ceremony

All:

May this family grow together in health and strength, in harmony, wisdom, and love, their home filled with words of Torah and acts of kindness. May we all share in the joy of seeing _____ grow into adulthood, a blessing to his family, his people, and all humanity.

Parent/s, to their son:

יְבָרֶכְךָ יְיָ וְיִשְׁמְרֶךָ,
יָאֵר יְיָ פָּנָיו אֵלֶיךָ וִיחֻנֶּךָּ,
יִשָּׂא יְיָ פָּנָיו אֵלֶיךָ וְיָשֵׂם לְךָ שָׁלוֹם.

Y'va-reh-ch'chah Adonai v'yish-m'reh-cha,
Ya-eir Adonai pa-nav ei-leh-kha
vi-chu-neh-ka, Yi-sah Adonai pa-nav ei-leh-kha
v'ya-seim l'chah sha-lom.

May God bless you and guard you.
May the light of God's Presence shine on you
and be gracious to you.
May the Presence of God lift you up and give
you a life of fulfillment, contentment,
wholeness, and peace.[25]

Brit Bat—Welcoming Our Daughters

The Jews are celebrating the birth of their daughters with cere-monies and celebrations. The ceremonies have been given many names: *simchat bat* (joy of the daughter), *brit hayyim* (covenant of life), *brit kedusha* (covenant of sanctification), *brit bat Zion* (covenant for the daughters of Zion), *brit b'not Yisrael* (covenant for the daughters of Israel), *brit e'dut* (covenant of wit-nessing), *brit ohel* (covenant of the tent), *brit hanerot* (covenant of candles), *brit Sarah* (covenant of Sarah), *brit rehitzah* (covenant of washing), *brit mikveh* (covenant of immersion), and simply, *brit bat,* covenant for a daughter.

The *brit bat* has given rise to enormous liturgical creativity inspired by several modern developments, including a renewed sense of Jewish identity after the 1967 war in Israel, and the fem-inist transformation of Jewish life. The disparity between the cel-ebration surrounding the birth of a boy and the lack of ceremony to mark the arrival of a baby girl inspired a generation of parents. Happily, the need to give public expression to the joy that attends the birth of a daughter coincided with the Jewish renewal move-ment, which stressed a hands-on, home-style, learn-as-you-do atti-tude toward tradition.

Using *brit milah*—the covenant of circumcision—as a model, and given the increasingly normative experience of bat mitzvah—the coming-of-age ceremony for daughters—parents began experimenting with covenant ceremonies for baby girls. What seemed experimental a generation ago is now entirely mainstream. Rabbis' manuals of all liberal movements now include naming or welcoming ceremonies for daughters, and Jewish rites of passage for baby girls are commonplace within Orthodox communities, too, as the absence of Jewish law on the subject frees traditionalists to improvise.

There is no typical liturgy for *brit bat*. Generations from now, *brit bat* may become as normative a ceremony as *brit milah*. However, it is probably more likely that our great-great-grandchildren will continue to enjoy many choices when they welcome their daughters into the covenant and community of Israel, following the tradition of the Passover Hagaddah (the book that contains the order of the Seder), which is constantly being reinterpreted, even as it retains a distinctive core of symbols, stories, and blessings.

This chapter contains the basic building blocks for creating a ceremony for your daughter. Here you will find a menu of possibilities: blessings, prayers, readings, and symbols culled from dozens of *brit bat* ceremonies, as well as an outline and several examples to help you plan your own distinctive celebration.

History

Brit bat may seem an entirely modern development, but it actually does have a long Jewish history. But because this is part of the counter-history of women's lives, much of it went unrecorded; what remains are tantalizing remnants and hints.

The Torah records that all new mothers owed the Temple ritual thanksgiving offerings of the same amount and kind, regardless of their baby's sex. The offering was due thirty-three days after birth for a boy, sixty-six days after for a girl, the difference representing the number of days she was prohibited from offering sacrifices following the birth of a male or female child.[27] What happened during those thirty-three or sixty-six days of separation from the community is the stuff of conjecture and midrash. There may well have been ceremonies for baby daughters during those days apart, rites not shared with the men and therefore not recorded.

Similarly, there may well have been folk customs for naming, welcoming, and blessing daughters throughout the undocumented history of Jewish women's lives. In Yiddish, the unfamiliar word *brisitzeh* (a feminine Yiddish form of *bris*) remains, suggesting an Ashkenazic covenant ceremony.[28] *Hollekreish,* another naming ceremony based on non-Jewish folk customs (later described in the chapter "Celebrations and Customs") may have had more significance for daughters than for sons.

The only formal acknowledgment of a daughter's birth in Ashkenazic tradition is the public naming in the synagogue. According to custom, the father is called to the Torah during the week after his daughter's birth on Shabbat or on any day there is a Torah service. There, he offers the *Mi Shebeirach* blessing, an all-purpose special-occasion blessing in which his daughter's name is announced for the first time:

> May the One who blessed our ancestors bless the
> mother _____ and her newborn
> daughter, whose name in Israel shall be
> _____. May they raise her for the
> marriage canopy and for a life of good deeds.[29]

After the regular service is concluded, the family then provides food and drink for those present. The mother and baby are generally not in attendance. If the mother is there, she may recite the *Birkat Hagomel,* the prayer of thanksgiving for having survived an ordeal (see pages 99–100).

Sephardic tradition, by comparison, has a variety of rituals and customs to herald a daughter's birth. For example, when Syrian Jews name daughters in the synagogue, the congregation sings songs in her honor and is then invited to attend a celebratory meal.[30] Moroccan Jews name their daughters at home in a ceremony led by a rabbi, who holds the child, quotes from the Bible, and pronounces a *Mi Shebeirach* that lists the names of the biblical matriarchs, Sarah, Rebecca, Rachel, and Leah. Songs are sung, and during the naming, the women raise their voices in ululation as an expression of joy.

The Jews of Spain perform a ceremony at home, after the mother has recovered. It is called *las fadas,* a word probably based on *hadas,* which means "fairies" and suggests that the celebration was borrowed from a local non-Jewish custom of seeking the blessing of good spirits.[31]

In *las fadas,* the baby is brought into the celebration on a pillow. She is dressed in a miniature bridal gown and is passed around the room, and each guest gives her a blessing. When the baby reaches the rabbi, he recites a blessing for her health and happiness. Verses from Song of Songs are recited, songs are sung, and a lavish feast follows.

The traditional Sephardic prayer book includes a ceremony that contains the following readings and prayer:

From Seder Zeved Bat— Celebration for the Gift of a Daughter

Oh my dove in the rocky clefts,
In the shelter of terrace high
Let me see your face
Let me hear your voice
For your voice is sweet
And your face is beautiful.

One alone is my dove, my perfect one,
The darling of her mother,
The delight of her who bore her.
Daughters saw her—they acclaimed her,
Queens and consorts—they sang her praises.

May the One who blessed our mothers, Sarah, Rebecca, Rachel and Leah, Miriam the prophetess, Abigail and Esther the queen, bless also this darling baby _____. May the One bless her to grow up in comfort, health, and happiness. May the One give to her parents the joy of seeing her happily married, a radiant mother of children, rich in honor and joy to a ripe old age. May this be the will of God, and let us say Amen.[32]

Planning a *Brit Bat*

Although there are precedents, there are no firm rules for *brit bat*. The rest of this chapter offers many choices, beginning with consideration of where and when to hold your celebration. The ceremonies that appear at the end of this chapter are yours to use, in their entirety or as models for your own creative efforts. There is no right or wrong here—only opportunities for creativity and holiness.

Where

Brit bat can take place at home or in a synagogue. Some people use a sanctuary or social hall because they need the space and also because they wish to create a community celebration. It may also be simpler to hire a caterer and keep the commotion out of the house. But others feel that home is the only place for a family occasion like *brit bat,* where it is easier to care for the baby, reassure older siblings, and host a celebration.

When

Generally, parents schedule a *brit bat* on a day that is convenient for family and friends and when the mother feels well enough to enjoy the event, but generally the selection involves some Jewish criteria as well.

- *Eight days.* Having the ceremony on the eighth day echoes the ancient rite of *brit milah.* The same traditional explanations apply, such as the sanctity associated with the number eight, and the spiritual strength the baby derives from her first contact with Shabbat. (See *"Brit Milah."*)

Holding the *brit bat* on the eighth day means that the miracle of birth is still very fresh in the parents' minds, and the ceremony will resound with the powerful emotions of labor and delivery. However, many women don't feel ready for a party so soon after giving birth and opt for a later date.

- *Fourteen days* has been advanced as another interval with traditional roots. In the Torah, after the birth of a daughter a mother's ritual impurity ends after fourteen days. Two weeks allows for the mother's recovery and, according to some pediatricians, is a reasonable amount of time to keep a newborn away from crowds.

- *Thirty days* is a popular choice, as it allows time to recover, plan, and invite. It too has a basis in tradition, as the rabbis of old believed that a child was viable only after thirty days.

- *Rosh Hodesh.* Some parents schedule the ceremony on the first day of the next new moon. A day for new beginnings, Rosh Hodesh is a semi-holiday that was traditionally a day of rest for women.

- *Shabbat.* Whether days or weeks after the baby is born, most *brit bat* ceremonies are scheduled for the Sabbath. Because Shabbat is itself a covenant between God and Israel, it seems an appropriate time for a covenantal ceremony.

A *brit bat* on Shabbat can take place at different times of day and in a number of contexts. In some congregations, the custom is to take the baby up to the *bimah* (the raised platform in the synagogue) during services on Friday night or Saturday morning. The rabbi generally conducts a brief ceremony that includes the announcement of the name. The rabbi may offer blessings, such as the traditional *Mi Shebeirach,* and others may speak or read as well. Afterward, refreshments might be sponsored by the new parents or in the family's honor.

Another option is to hold the *brit bat* immediately following the morning service, preceding *Kiddush.* The celebration can coincide with the Shabbat midday meal, either in the synagogue or at home.

Brit bat is sometimes included in *Havdalah,* the ceremony that marks the end of Shabbat and celebrates the distinctions between Shabbat and the rest of the week, the mundane from the holy. A *havdalah brit bat* marks the physical separation of mother and baby, and the child's entrance into the community of Israel.

Guests and Participants

Jewish tradition encourages the inclusion of as many people as possible at a *simcha* like this. Although some parents do mail invitations to their daughter's *brit bat* ceremony, most invite guests by telephone and/or e-mail.

Generally, when *brit bat* takes place at home, the baby's parents lead the ceremony. When it is held in a synagogue, the rabbi officiates, although sometimes with a great deal of parental participation. You do not need a rabbi to perform a *brit bat* ceremony. Parents or any honored guest can serve as the ceremonial leader.

Include as many people as you like in the *brit bat.* Grandparents are usually given the most important *kibbudim,* or honors, especially the roles and titles associated with *brit milah: kvatterin, kvatter* (godmother and godfather, respectively), and *sandek* (sponsor).The *sandek* or *sandeket* (the feminine version of *sandek*) holds the baby during the naming. The *kvatter* and *kvatterin* bring the baby into the room, hold her during some part of the ceremony, or perform other ceremonial tasks such as candle-lighting.

Many parents provide a printed guide to the proceedings (see "*Hiddur Mitzvah*—Beautiful Touches").

Non-Jews in the Ceremony

Non-Jewish grandparents, aunts, uncles, cousins, and friends can participate in many ways—depending on their comfort level. Unlike godparents in Christian ceremonies, the *kvatter* and *kvatterin* do not assume responsibility for the child's religious upbringing; their roles are strictly ceremonial. The same holds true for the *sandek,* a word that probably derives from the Greek for "patron."

Blessings, poems, readings, or prayers can be distributed to any and to as many guests as you choose. (See *"Hiddur Mitzvah—Beautiful Touches"* and Part 4, *"Simcha—Joy"* for more about ways to enhance the ceremony and involve guests.)

The legend that the prophet Elijah attends all *brit milah* ceremonies has been attached to *brit bat.* The *kisei shel Eliyahu* (Elijah's chair) invokes the presence of the prophet, angel, protector, peripatetic guest, and harbinger of *y'mot mashiach,* the days of the Messiah. (See page 98 for more about Elijah.)

Elements of a *Brit Bat* Ceremony

Brit bat can be short and simple, or long and elaborate: the ceremonies that appear at the end of this chapter provide an idea of the range. But for all the variations, there are a few nearly universal elements that fall into a four-part structure: introduction, covenant, naming and conclusion, and celebration.

- *Part I: Introductory blessings and prayers.* These include the greeting *brucha haba'a* (blessed is she who enters) and prayers or readings by the parents and/or rabbi. *Kiddush* (blessing over wine) is sometimes recited here as well.

- *Part II: Covenant prayers or ritual.* Using blessings and/or symbolic actions, a baby daughter is entered into the covenant of the people of Israel. Generally, this is followed by the threefold wish that she will also take on the blessings of Torah study, marriage, and a life of good deeds.

- *Part III: Naming and final blessings.* The name is announced and namesakes are lovingly recalled. Blessings, prayers, readings, and wishes from the guests may be read, and the ceremony ends with *Sheheheyanu* and/or the Priestly Benediction.

- *Part IV: Celebratory meal.* The *s'udat mitzvah*—meal of the commandment—is part of all major life-cycle events.

The following "menu" explains this four-part structure in greater detail. Remember that rituals tend to be as powerful as they are brief. If you include every item on this menu in your *brit bat,* your liturgical "meal" will be too rich, and the ceremony will go on too long.

Part I—Introduction

Brucha haba'a, "Blessed is she who enters": This greeting begins virtually all *brit bat* ceremonies. It not only recalls the beginning of *brit milah* (*Baruch haba*—Blessed is he who enters), it also acknowledges the divinity of the female or the female aspects of the Divine.

Candle-lighting can add to a beautiful beginning. Also a tradition associated with *brit milah,* lighting candles has an added dimension at a *brit bat* because the weekly honor of lighting Shabbat candles is traditionally given to women.

There are many ways to put candles to effective use. The mother can light a single braided *Havdalah* candle or a pair of white Shabbat candles. The female members of the family or all the women guests can be invited to bring their Shabbat candlesticks and light them together (traditional white or a rainbow of colored candles, as you wish). Seven candles, representing the days of creation, may be lit.

The baby's mother or both parents might use candlesticks that are a gift to the child. If a baby is named for a female relative who has died, using her candlesticks is a beautiful statement of continuity (see *"Hiddur Mitzvah*—Beautiful Touches"). Candles are sometimes also used as a covenantal *"brit* action."[33]

Introductory readings and prayers: These words set the tone, and often explain the "theology" of the ceremony. One of the more popular stories used in *brit bat* is the following, which comes from the Midrash:

> When Israel stood to receive the Torah, the Holy
> One, Blessed be the One, said to them, "I am giving
> you My Torah. Present to Me good guarantors that
> you will guard it, and I shall give it to you."
>
> They said, "Our ancestors are our guarantors."
>
> The Holy One, Blessed be the One, said, "Your
> ancestors are not sufficient guarantors. Yet bring Me

good guarantors, and I shall give you the Torah."

They said, "Master of the universe, our prophets are our guarantors."

The One said to them, "The prophets are not sufficient guarantors. Yet bring Me good guarantors, and I shall give you the Torah."

They said, "Our children are our guarantors."

And the Holy One, Blessed be the One, said, "They certainly are good guarantors. For their sake, I give the Torah to you."[34]

Kiddush: The blessing and drinking of wine is a part of virtually every Jewish celebration. After the blessing, the baby is given a drop to drink. The cup can then be passed to the parents, grandparents, and other guests. It's nice to use a special *Kiddush* cup—an heirloom, a gift to the baby from a grandparent, or the goblet used at the parents' wedding.

בָּרוּךְ אַתָּה יְיָ, אֱלֹהֵינוּ מֶלֶךְ הָעוֹלָם,
בּוֹרֵא פְּרִי הַגָּפֶן.

*Ba-ruch a-ta Adonai, Eh-lo-hei-nu meh-lech
ha-o-lam, bo-rei p'ri ha-ga-fen.*

Holy One of Blessing, Your Presence fills creation, forming the fruit of the vine.

Part II: Covenant

Daughters are most commonly entered into the covenant with a *bracha*, a blessing, such as this one:

בָּרוּךְ אַתָּה יְיָ, אֱלֹהֵינוּ מֶלֶךְ הָעוֹלָם, אֲשֶׁר קִדַּשׁ
יְדִיד מִבֶּטֶן. אֵל חַי חֶלְקֵנוּ צוּרֵנוּ, צַוֵּה לְהַצִּיל
יְדִידוּת שְׁאֵרֵנוּ מִשַּׁחַת, לְמַעַן בְּרִיתוֹ. בָּרוּךְ אַתָּה
יְיָ, כּוֹרֵת הַבְּרִית.

אֱלוֹהַּ כָּל הַבְּרִיאוֹת, קַיֵּם אֶת הַיַּלְדָּה הַזֹּאת
לְאָבִיהָ וּלְאִמָּא.

*Ba-ruch a-ta Adonai, Eh-lo-hei-nu meh-lech
ha-o-lam, a-sher ki-deish y'did mi-be-ten. El chai
chel-kei-nu tzu-rei-nu, tza-vei l'ha-tzil yi-dee-dut
sh'ei-rei-nu mi-sha-chat, l'ma'an b'ree-to. Ba-ruch
a-ta Adonai, ko-reit ha-b'reet.*

*E-lo-ha kol ha-b'ree-ot, ka-yeim et ha-yal-da
ha-zot l'a-vee-ha u'l'ee-ma.*

You have sanctified Your beloved from the womb,
establishing Your holy covenant throughout the
generations. May devotion to the covenant continue to sustain us as a people. Praised are You,
Eternal God, who has established the covenant.
Blessed by the Presence whose sanctity fills our
lives, we give thanks for the covenant.[35]

Some parents feel that *brit bat* requires a symbolic action as
well as words.[36] Many lovely gestures can serve this purpose,
including candle-lighting, touching the baby's hand to a Torah
scroll, wrapping or covering the baby with a prayer shawl, or some
form of washing or immersion.

Water is a traditional covenantal symbol. Although some people
are disconcerted by the similarity between washing and Christian
baptism, water rituals are very much a part of Jewish practice and,
indeed, the basis of Christian custom. Observant Jews wash their
hands and say a blessing before meals, and *mikveh* marks the
cycles of women's lives. Indeed, the Talmud suggests that as
Abram became Abraham through the covenant of circumcision,
Sarai became Sarah through the ritual of immersion in water.

The Torah is rich with water imagery associated with women.
Sarah and Abraham welcomed the three guests who brought them
news of their son by bringing them water for washing. Rebecca
makes her biblical appearance at a well, as does Rachel. Miriam is
associated with a well of water that sustained the Hebrews in the
wilderness.

The covenantal ritual act of *brit rehitzah* involves the parents
washing their daughter's feet.[37] As in *brit milah,* there is a bless-

ing before the act of covenant and another afterward. The familiar Hebrew (and Jewish summer camp) song "Mayyim" is a good accompaniment to any ceremony that involves water. Guests can hum the melody during the washing.

Before the washing, the rabbi or leader says:

בָּרוּךְ אַתָּה יְיָ, אֱלֹהֵינוּ מֶלֶךְ הָעוֹלָם,
זוֹכֵר הַבְּרִית.

*Ba-ruch a-ta Adonai, Eh-lo-hei-nu meh-lech
ha-o-lam, zo-cher ha'brit.*

Blessed are You, Adonai our God, Ruler of the universe, who is mindful of the covenant.

After the washing, the parents say:

בָּרוּךְ אַתָּה יְיָ, אֱלֹהֵינוּ מֶלֶךְ הָעוֹלָם,
זוֹכֵר הַבְּרִית בִּרְחִיצַת רַגְלָיִם.

*Ba-ruch a-ta Adonai, Eh-lo-hei-nu meh-lech
ha-o-lam, zo-cher ha'brit bir-chi-tzat rag-la-yim.*

Blessed are You, Adonai our God, Ruler of the universe, who is mindful of the covenant through the washing of the feet.

Here is part of one *brit* ritual that revolves around candlelighting. Parents, grandparents, and special guests each light one of six candles, corresponding to the six days of creation. Each person reads a prayer, poem, or one of the following six verses:

Your word is a lamp unto my feet, a light for my path.
(Ps. 119:105)

You are the One who kindles my lamp: the Lord my God lights up my darkness.
(Ps. 18:29)

Arise, shine, for your light has dawned, God's radiance shines upon you!

(Isa. 60:1)

May the Lord continue to shine upon you and God's brilliant presence surround you.

(Isa. 60:2)

Lift up your eyes all about you and behold: They have all gathered around you; your sons shall be brought from afar, your daughters like babes on your shoulders.

(Isa. 60:4)

May God be gracious to us and bless us. May God's face shine upon us.

(Ps. 67:2)

The parents lift the baby to the light. The parents or rabbi say:

Light was the first of God's creations; as light appeared, it brought with it the possibility of all the wondrous things to follow. We, too, kindle lights— of hope, of understanding, of celebration, of countless new possibilities. This little daughter with whom we (these parents) have been blessed has already brought light into our (their) lives. May God's radiance continue to shine upon us (them). May she grow to be a source of light to all those around her. May her radiance illuminate the world. May the light of Torah and mitzvot be reflected in her shining deeds. And may she help bring the light of redemption to the world. Amen.[38]

The Torah can be used as a central symbol for another covenantal gesture. During a synagogue service, the baby is taken up to the

Torah where her hands are placed on the scroll. These verses or others can be distributed among parents and honored guests:

> *Teach me, O Lord, the way of Your laws, and I shall treasure them always.*
>
> (Ps. 119:33)

> *Give me understanding and I shall treasure Your Torah; I shall keep it wholeheartedly.*
>
> (Ps. 119:34)

> *Your hands have made us and fashioned us. Give us understanding that we may learn Your commandments.*
>
> (Ps. 119:73)

> *I will lift up my hands and reach out to your commandments, which I love. Your laws will be on my lips.*
>
> (Ps. 119:48)

> As this little child has touched the Torah, so may the Torah touch her life, filling her mind with wisdom, and her heart with understanding. May we (these parents) who have brought her here today always strive to bring her close to the ways of God and of our people. May we (they) teach her Torah every day through our (their) words and our (their) deeds. May we (they) raise our (their) daughter to a joyful life of learning, and to deeds of loving kindness.[39]

The *threefold wish* for Torah, marriage, and good deeds, which is traditional at a *bris,* often follows the covenant ritual. It expresses the communal wish that this daughter will fulfill the three requirements of all Jews, now that she has become a member of the people of Israel.

כְּשֵׁם שֶׁנִּכְנְסָה לַבְּרִית,
כֵּן תִּכָּנֵס לְתוֹרָה וּלְחֻפָּה וּלְמַעֲשִׂים טוֹבִים.

*K'shem sheh-nich-n'sah la-brit, kein ti-ka-nes
l'to-rah ul-chu-pah ul-ma-a-sim to-vim.*

As she has entered the covenant, so may she enter
a life devoted to Torah, *huppah,* and the accomplishment of good deeds.

The following reading, which expounds on the threefold wish,
is popular in *brit* ceremonies of all kinds:

*We dedicate our child to Torah—to a never-ending fascination with
study and learning. With a book, she will never be alone.*

*We dedicate our child to huppah—to never-ending growth as a
human being, capable of giving and receiving love. With loving
family and friends, she will never be alone.*

*We dedicate our child to maasim tovim—to a never-ending con-
cern for family and community, justice and charity. While she
cares for others, she will never be alone.*[40]

Part III: The Name, Readings, and Conclusion

The baby's name is given in both Hebrew and (if different) in
English. Anything you say about how you chose your daughter's
name will be meaningful. Because so many Jews name children to
honor the memory of a family member who has died, the highlight
of the ceremony is often the stories told about that loved one. The
Hebrew meaning or biblical story associated with a name might
suggest a comment on how, for example, you hope your Esti will
grow up to be as loyal to her people as the Esther of the Purim
story.

There is an old custom of making an acrostic poem using the
first letters of the baby's name in Hebrew. Each Hebrew letter is
matched with a phrase or line from the Bible that also begins with
that letter. The most common source for this is Psalm 119, but you
can also try Song of Songs, Proverbs, other psalms, and the weekly

Torah portion closest to your baby's birth. Sometimes acrostics are calligraphed and made into beautiful wall hangings.

Among the other traditional blessings and readings for a *brit bat* are *Birkat Hagomel*, the blessing said after recovery from an illness; and *Ha-tov V'ha-mei-tiv*, another traditional prayer recited on the occasion of a great blessing (see page 11). The biblical poem *Shir HaShirim*, Song of Songs, is often quoted at *brit bat* ceremonies. Some couples use the theme of the seven wedding blessings, the *Sheva Brachot*, and recite seven blessings from the wedding liturgy and other sources. Similarly, you might reprise a song or reading from your wedding.

Contemporary and original blessings, prayers, poems, wishes, and readings are popular additions, and parents sometimes read a letter written to their baby daughter—something to be saved and read again, perhaps at her bat mitzvah.

Siblings old enough to participate can say or read something to their new sister. Participation by grandparents is always very meaningful. The following quotations from tradition are often used:

The crown of the aged are children's children. And the glory of children are their parents.

(Prov. 17:6)

and/or

In the Talmud there is the story of an old man who was seen planting a carob tree as the king rode by. "Old man," the king called, "how many years will it be before that tree bears fruit?" The old man replied, "Perhaps seventy years." The king asked, "Do you really expect to be alive to eat the fruit of that tree?" "No," answered the old man, "but just as I found the world fruitful when I was born, so I plant trees that later generations may eat thereof."

(Ta'anit 23a)

To add spontaneity and even a touch of humor to your *brit bat,* you can invite the company to offer spontaneous prayers and wishes for your new baby: "May her life be filled with laughter and people who love her," or "May she sleep through the night soon." If the group is small and the baby placid, you could even pass her from person to person as each one speaks. (And make sure the video camera is on!)

The end of the ceremony is signaled by the following three prayers, in any order or combination:

Sheheheyanu: This prayer of thanksgiving may be the most common element of all *brit bat* ceremonies.

בָּרוּךְ אַתָּה יְיָ, אֱלֹהֵינוּ מֶלֶךְ הָעוֹלָם,
שֶׁהֶחֱיָנוּ וְקִיְּמָנוּ וְהִגִּיעָנוּ לַזְּמַן הַזֶּה.

*Ba-ruch a-ta Adonai, Eh-lo-hei-nu meh-lech
ha-o-lam, sheh-heh-cheh-ya-nu v'ki-y'ma-nu
v'hi-gi-a-nu la-z'man ha-zeh.*

Holy One of Blessing, Your Presence fills creation,
You have kept us alive, You have sustained us, You
have brought us to this moment.

Traditional blessing for a daughter: On Friday night, after the Shabbat table blessings are made, many families add a blessing for their children. Reciting these words for the first time at *brit bat* can start that practice in your family. (Some families add the names of their grandmothers and great-grandmothers to this list of biblical matriarchs. And see the alternative blessing by Marcia Falk in Part 6, "The First Year.")

יְשִׂמֵךְ אֱלֹהִים כְּשָׂרָה רִבְקָה רָחֵל וְלֵאָה.

*Y'si-mech Eh-lo-him k'Sarah, Rivkah, Rachel,
v'Leah.*

May God make you as Sarah, Rebecca, Rachel,
and Leah.[41]

The Priestly Benediction concludes many Jewish rituals and services, and some parents include it in the Shabbat blessing of their children. If a rabbi is officiating, he or she most often recites this. If not, the parents or the entire company can say:

יְבָרֶכְךָ יְיָ וְיִשְׁמְרֶךָ,
יָאֵר יְיָ פָּנָיו אֵלֶיךָ וִיחֻנֶּךָּ,
יִשָּׂא יְיָ פָּנָיו אֵלֶיךָ וְיָשֵׂם לְךָ שָׁלוֹם.

Y'va-reh-ch'chah Adonai v'yish-m'reh-cha,
Ya-eir Adonai pa-nav ei-leh-kha vi-chu-neh-ka,
Yi-say Adonai pa-nav ei-leh-kha v'ya-seim l'chah
sha-lom.

May God bless you and protect you.
May God's presence shine for you and be favorable
to you.
May God's face turn to you and give you peace.

Part IV: *S'udat Mitzvah*

According to Jewish law, major life-cycle events are celebrated with a *s'udat mitzvah,* or meal of the commandment. Such meals traditionally begin with the blessing over challah *(Motzi)* and end with the prayers sung upon completion of a meal *(Birkat Hamazon).* (See part 4, "*Simcha*—Joy," for more on the meal and party.)

Sample List of Things You Need for a *Brit Bat*

- Kosher wine and goblet for *Kiddush*
- *Yarmulkes (kippot,* or skullcaps) for guests
- Candles and candlesticks
- Prayer shawl or scarf for swaddling the baby
- Elijah's chair
- Tape/video recorder, cameras
- Explanatory guides/pamphlets
- Phone ringer turned off

Naming Ceremony

All:

בְּרוּכָה הַבָּאָה בְּשֵׁם יְיָ.

Brucha ha-ba-a b'sheim Adonai.

May she who enters be blessed in the name
of the Lord.

Parent/s:

Through this covenant we affirm our daughter's part in the
covenant, the *brit,* made between God and Israel at Mount
Sinai.

According to our tradition, the entire Jewish people, women
and men, children and infants, born and unborn, were
included in the revelation of the Law and in its affirmation.
It has always been the central endeavor of each Jew in every
generation to understand this covenant and to live meaning-
fully by it. We give thanks for the opportunity to bring our
daughter into the covenant, and we say:

בָּרוּךְ אַתָּה יְיָ, אֱלֹהֵינוּ מֶלֶךְ הָעוֹלָם,
אֲשֶׁר קִדְּשָׁנוּ בְּמִצְוֹתָיו, וְצִוָּנוּ
לְהַכְנִיסָהּ בִּבְרִיתוֹ שֶׁל עַם יִשְׂרָאֵל.

כְּשֵׁם שֶׁנִּכְנְסָה לַבְּרִית,
כֵּן תִּכָּנֵס לְתוֹרָה וּלְחֻפָּה וּלְמַעֲשִׂים טוֹבִים.

Naming Ceremony

*Ba-ruch a-ta Adonai, Eh-lo-hei-nu meh-lech
ha-o-lam, a-sher ki-d'sha-nu b'mitz-vo-tav,
v'tzi-va-nu l'hach-ni-sah biv-ri-to shel
am Yisrael.*

*K'shem sheh-nich-n'sah la-brit, kein
ti-ka-nes l'to-rah ul-chu-pah ul-ma-a-sim
to-vim.*

Blessed are You, Lord our God, Ruler of the
universe, who has made us holy through Your
commandments and commanded us to bring
our daughter into the covenant of Israel.
As our daughter enters the covenant, so may
she attain love of learning through the study
of Torah, happiness in partnership with
another human being, and the capacity to act
toward others in honest, respectful, and
ethical ways.

At our marriage, seven blessings were recited. Today in celebration of our joy at the birth of our daughter, we ask loved
ones to recite seven blessings over this *Kiddush* cup filled
with wine, the symbol of joy.

Rabbi or guest:

בָּרוּךְ אַתָּה יְיָ, אֱלֹהֵינוּ מֶלֶךְ הָעוֹלָם,
בּוֹרֵא פְּרִי הַגָּפֶן.

*Ba-ruch a-ta Adonai, Eh-lo-hei-nu meh-lech
ha-o-lam, bo-rei p'ri ha-ga-fen.*

Praised are You, Lord our God, Source of the
universe, Creator of the fruit of the vine.

Naming Ceremony

Guest:

בָּרוּךְ אַתָּה יְיָ, אֱלֹהֵינוּ מֶלֶךְ הָעוֹלָם, יוֹצֵר הָאָדָם.

*Ba-ruch a-ta Adonai, Eh-lo-hei-nu meh-lech
ha-o-lam, yo-tzer ha-a-dam.*

Praised are You, Lord our God, Source of the
universe, Creator of humanity.

Guest:

בָּרוּךְ אַתָּה יְיָ, אֱלֹהֵינוּ מֶלֶךְ הָעוֹלָם,
אֲשֶׁר יָצַר אֶת הָאָדָם בְּצַלְמוֹ, בְּצֶלֶם דְּמוּת תַּבְנִיתוֹ,
וְהִתְקִין לוֹ מִמֶּנּוּ בִּנְיַן עֲדֵי עַד.
בָּרוּךְ אַתָּה יְיָ, יוֹצֵר הָאָדָם.

*Ba-ruch a-ta Adonai, Eh-lo-hei-nu meh-lech
ha-o-lam, a-sher ya-tzar et ha-a-dam
b'tzal-mo, b'tzeh-lem d'mut tav-ni-to, v'hit-kin
lo mi-meh-nu bin-yan a-dei ad. Ba-ruch
a-ta Adonai, yo-tzer ha-a-dam.*

Praised are You, Lord our God, Source of the
universe, who created human beings in Your
image and Your likeness. And out of their
very selves You prepared for them a
perpetual spiritual being. Praised are You,
our Lord, Creator of humanity.

Naming Ceremony

Guest:

בָּרוּךְ אַתָּה יְיָ, אֱלֹהֵינוּ מֶלֶךְ הָעוֹלָם,
אֲשֶׁר קִדְּשָׁנוּ בְּמִצְוֹתָיו,
וְצִוָּנוּ עַל קִדּוּשׁ הַחַיִּים.

*Ba-ruch a-ta Adonai, Eh-lo-hei-nu meh-lech
ha-o-lam, a-sher ki-d'sha-nu b'mitz-vo-tav,
v'tzi-va-nu al ki-dush ha-cha-yim.*

Praised are You, Lord our God, Source of the
universe, who commands us to sanctify life.

Guest:

בָּרוּךְ אַתָּה יְיָ, אֱלֹהֵינוּ מֶלֶךְ הָעוֹלָם,
זוֹכֵר הַבְּרִית וְנֶאֱמָן בִּבְרִיתוֹ וְקַיָּם בְּמַאֲמָרוֹ.

*Ba-ruch a-ta Adonai, Eh-lo-hei-nu meh-lech
ha-o-lam, zo-cheir ha-brit v'neh-eh-man
biv-ri-to v'ka-yam b'ma-a-ma-ro.*

Praised are You, Lord our God, Source of the
universe, who remembers the covenant and
who is steadfastly faithful in Your covenant,
keeping Your promise.

Naming Ceremony

Guest:

בָּרוּךְ אַתָּה יְיָ, מְשַׂמֵּחַ הוֹרִים עִם יַלְדֵיהֶם.

*Ba-ruch a-ta Adonai, m'sa-mei-ach ho-rim
im yal-dei-hem.*

Praised are You, Lord our God, Source of the
universe, who causes parents to rejoice with
their children.

Guest:

בָּרוּךְ אַתָּה יְיָ, אֱלֹהֵינוּ מֶלֶךְ הָעוֹלָם,
שֶׁהֶחֱיָנוּ וְקִיְּמָנוּ וְהִגִּיעָנוּ לַזְּמַן הַזֶּה.

*Ba-ruch a-ta Adonai, Eh-lo-hei-nu meh-lech
ha-o-lam, sheh-heh-cheh-ya-nu v'ki-y'ma-nu
v'hi-gi-a-nu la-z'man ha-zeh.*

Praised are You, Lord our God, Source of the
universe, for giving us life, for sustaining us,
for enabling us to reach this day.

Parent or rabbi:

This baby is named in loving remembrance of _____.
She lives in her. Let her life make _____
known to all who see her.

May the one who blessed our mothers, Sarah, Rebecca, Leah,
and Rachel, and our fathers, Abraham, Isaac, and Jacob,
bless these parents and their newborn daughter. Her name
shall be _____. May her parents rear their
daughter with love of Torah and the performance of good
deeds, and may they be privileged to bring her to the marriage canopy. Let us say Amen.

Naming Ceremony

Rabbi or parent/s:

יְבָרֶכְךָ יְיָ וְיִשְׁמְרֶךָ,
יָאֵר יְיָ פָּנָיו אֵלֶיךָ וִיחֻנֶּךָּ,
יִשָּׂא יְיָ פָּנָיו אֵלֶיךָ וְיָשֵׂם לְךָ שָׁלוֹם.

Y'va-reh-ch'chah Adonai v'yish-m'reh-cha,
Ya-eir Adonai pa-nav ei-leh-kha
vi-chu-neh-ka,
Yi-sah Adonai pa-nav ei-leh-kha v'ya-seim
l'chah sha-lom.

May God bless you and protect you.
May God's presence shine for you and be
favorable to you.
May God's face turn to you and give
you peace.

Parent/s:

Bread is the symbol of sustenance and honey the sign of sweetness. We dip the bread in honey in hope that our daily strivings will be sweetened by our love for each other.

בָּרוּךְ אַתָּה יְיָ, אֱלֹהֵינוּ מֶלֶךְ הָעוֹלָם,
הַמּוֹצִיא לֶחֶם מִן הָאָרֶץ.

Ba-ruch a-ta Adonai, Eh-lo-hei-nu meh-lech
ha-o-lam, ha-mo-tzi leh-chem min ha-a-retz.

Praised are You, Lord our God, Source of the
universe, who provides us with the staff
of life.[42]

Brit Ohel Shel Sarah Imeinu

Covenant of the Tent of Sarah Our Mother

Song: "Ma to-vu"

(How wonderful are your tents, Jacob, your dwelling places, Israel)

The baby is brought in and everyone says:

בְּרוּכָה הַבָּאָה.

B'ru-cha ha-ba-a.

We welcome you into our midst. We greet
you as you enter into the covenant of Israel.

Rabbi:

As Abraham was father to the Jewish people, so Sarah was its
mother. Our sages say, Abraham dealt with the men, and
Sarah dealt with the women.

Abraham would bring men into relationship with God and his
people through *milah* and the covenant of religious circumcision. Sarah would bring the women into relationship with
God and her people through their coming into her tent and
taking formal residence there.

In Sarah's name, we now perform this ceremony of *brit ohel*
and bring this daughter of the Jewish people into her tent and
into the covenant of Sarah our mother.

Brit Ohel Shel Sarah Imeinu

We thank You, Adonai, our God and universal Sovereign, who has made us holy by means of the mitzvot, commanding us regarding the covenant of the tent.

The *sandeket* is seated in the center of the room. Four friends raise a scarf over her head. The parents hand the baby to the *sandeket* and say:

בָּרוּךְ אַתָּה יְיָ, אֱלֹהֵינוּ מֶלֶךְ הָעוֹלָם,
אֲשֶׁר קִדְּשָׁנוּ בְּמִצְוֹתָיו, וְצִוָּנוּ
לְהַכְנִיסָה לִבְרִיתָה שֶׁל שָׂרָה אִמֵּנוּ.

*Ba-ruch a-ta Adonai, Eh-lo-hei-nu meh-lech
ha-o-lam, a-sher ki-d'sha-nu b'mitz-vo-tav,
v'tzi-va-nu l'hach-ni-sah liv-ri-tah shel
Sa-rah i-mei-nu.*

We are grateful to You, Adonai, for You are
our God and Ruler of the universe. You have
made us holy by means of the mitzvot,
commanding us to bring our daughter into
the covenant of Sarah our mother.

All:

כְּשֵׁם שֶׁנִּכְנְסָה לַבְּרִית,
כֵּן תִּכָּנֵס לְתוֹרָה וּלְחֻפָּה וּלְמַעֲשִׂים טוֹבִים.

*K'shem sheh-nich-n'sah la-brit, kein ti-ka-nes
l'to-rah ul-chu-pah ul-ma-a-sim to-vim.*

As she has entered into the covenant, so may
she enter into Torah, *huppah,* and a life of
good deeds.

Brit Ohel Shel Sarah Imeinu

The *sandeket* wraps the scarf around the baby and hands her to her mother:

Rabbi or parent/s:

בָּרוּךְ אַתָּה יְיָ, אֱלֹהֵינוּ מֶלֶךְ הָעוֹלָם,
בּוֹרֵא פְּרִי הַגָּפֶן.

*Ba-ruch a-ta Adonai, Eh-lo-hei-nu meh-lech
ha-o-lam, bo-rei p'ri ha-ga-fen.*

We praise You, Adonai, our God and
universal Ruler, who creates the fruit of the vine.

בָּרוּךְ אַתָּה יְיָ, אֱלֹהֵינוּ מֶלֶךְ הָעוֹלָם,
אֲשֶׁר קִדֵּשׁ אֶת הָאֹהֶל וְכָל הַנִּכְנָסִים בּוֹ,
תַּפְרִיחַ אֹהֶל צַדִּיקִים שֶׁנֵּדַע כִּי שָׁלוֹם הוּא.
בָּרוּךְ אַתָּה יְיָ, מוֹשִׁיבֵנוּ בְּאֹהָלִים.

*Ba-ruch a-ta Adonai, Eh-lo-hei-nu meh-lech
ha-o-lam, a-sher ki-deish et ha-o-hel v'chol ha-
nich-na-sim bo, taf-ri-ach o-hel
tza-di-kim sheh-nei-da ki sha-lom hu. Ba-ruch
a-ta Adonai, mo-shi-vei-nu b'o-ha-lim.*

We praise You, Adonai, our God and Ruler,
who has sanctified the tent and all who enter it.
Cause the tent of the righteous to flourish,
that we may know that it is all peace.
We are grateful to You Adonai, for making
us dwell in tents.

Brit Ohel Shel Sarah Imeinu

Eloheinu, our God and our ancestor's God,
sustain this child, who is to be known in
Israel as _____ and referred to
in the world as _____.

Parent/s:

Help us nurture her and encourage her to fulfill the blessing
in her name.

All:

May her mother and father rejoice and find delight in their
daughter. Let her coming into the covenant of the tent be at
a favorable time for God and for Israel.

Parent/s:

May we find joy in this moment and pleasure in all that she
becomes. May our tiny daughter grow to be great.

Rabbi or guest:

יְבָרֶכְךָ יְיָ וְיִשְׁמְרֶךָ,
יָאֵר יְיָ פָּנָיו אֵלֶיךָ וִיחֻנֶּךָּ,
יִשָּׂא יְיָ פָּנָיו אֵלֶיךָ וְיָשֵׂם לְךָ שָׁלוֹם.

Y'va-reh-ch'chah Adonai v'yish-m'reh-cha,
Ya-eir Adonai pa-nav ei-leh-kha
vi-chu-neh-ka,
Yi-sah Adonai pa-nav ei-leh-kha v'ya-seim
l'chah sha-lom.

May Adonai turn to each of you
and to all of us
and make for us a life
of wholeness and hopefulness and peace.
Amen.[43]

Brit E'dut

Covenant of Witnessing

Parent/s:

We come together today to welcome our new daughter into our family and into the covenant of the Jewish people. More than 3,000 years ago, our ancestors stood at Mount Sinai and entered into a covenant with God. Men, women, children, officers, elders, hewers of wood, and drawers of water all stood before the Lord and proclaimed:

כֹּל אֲשֶׁר דִּבֶּר יְיָ נַעֲשֶׂה וְנִשְׁמָע.

Kol a-sher di-ber Adonai na-a-she v'nishma.

All the words the Lord has spoken we will do.

The covenant that was established at Sinai was made not only with our ancestors but with those who would follow. This covenant has been reaffirmed throughout the millennia. Today we, too, are gathered: men, women, and children, our heads and our elders and a drawer of water. For Sarah, as she came into the world, drew out of her mother the waters that had sustained her before her birth.

We too, through our words today, with this drawer of water in our midst, reaffirm the pledge of our ancestors:

Brit E'dut

כֹּל אֲשֶׁר דִּבֶּר יְיָ נַעֲשֶׂה וְנִשְׁמָע.

Kol a-sher di-ber Adonai na-a-seh v'nishma.

All that the Lord has spoken we will do
and obey.

All:

בְּרוּכָה הַבָּאָה.

B'ru-cha ha-ba-a.

May she who comes before us today
be blessed.

Parent/s:

When Abraham and Sarah dwelt at Mamre, three men
appeared at the door of their tent. As a sign of hospitality,
they offered these travelers water to drink and to wash their
feet. In the same way that Abraham and Sarah welcomed the
travelers, so do we welcome our daughter into this world,
with food and drink and the washing of her feet.

All:

בָּרוּךְ אַתָּה יְיָ, אֱלֹהֵינוּ מֶלֶךְ הָעוֹלָם,
שֶׁהֶחֱיָנוּ וְקִיְּמָנוּ וְהִגִּיעָנוּ לַזְּמַן הַזֶּה.

*Ba-ruch a-ta Adonai, Eh-lo-hei-nu meh-lech
ha-o-lam, sheh-heh-cheh-ya-nu v'ki-y'ma-nu
v'hi-gi-a-nu la-z'man ha-zeh.*

Holy One of Blessing, Your Presence fills
creation, You have kept us alive,
You have sustained us, You have brought us
to this moment.

Brit E'dut

Parent:

As you begin your journey through life, we pray that you will find sustenance in *mayyim hayyim,* the living waters that Judaism offers to all who draw from the well of our tradition.

Baby's feet are washed.

Parent:

As your father and I stood under the shelter of this *tallit* to be joined together as husband and wife, so now do we encircle you within it as you enter the circle of our family. As we wrap you in this *tallit,* so may your life be wrapped in justice and righteousness. As we embrace you today, so may you embrace your tradition and your people.

Guest:

As your eyes are filled with wonder when you gaze at the world, so, too, may you be filled with wonder at the everyday miracles of life.

Guest:

As you startle to the world around you, so may you remain ever open both to the happiness and to the pain of those you encounter in the world.

Guest:

As you cry for food and comfort now, so may you one day cry out to correct the injustices of the world, to help clothe the naked and feed the hungry.

Guest:

As your hand tightly grasps your mother's finger, so may you grasp hold of learning and grow in knowledge and in wisdom.

Brit E'dut

Rabbi or parent/s:

אֱלֹהֵינוּ וֵאלֹהֵי אִמּוֹתֵינוּ, קַיֵּם אֶת הַיַּלְדָה הַזֹּאת לְאָבִיהָ וּלְאִמָּהּ, וְיִקָּרֵא שְׁמָהּ בְּיִשְׂרָאֵל _____ בַּת _____. יִשְׂמַח הָאָב בְּיוֹצֵאת חֲלָצָיו, וְתָגֵל אִמּוֹ בִּפְרִי בִטְנָהּ. זֹאת הַקְּטַנָּה גְדוֹלָה תִהְיֶה. כְּשֵׁם שֶׁנִּכְנְסָה לַבְּרִית, כֵּן תִּכָּנֵס לְתוֹרָה, וּלְחֻפָּה, וּלְמַעֲשִׂים טוֹבִים.

Eh-lo-hei-nu vei-lo-hei i-mo-tei-nu, ka-yeim et ha-yal-dah ha-zoht l'a-vi-ha ul-i-mah, v'yi-ka-rei sh'mah b'yis-ra-el _____ bat _____. Yis-mach ha-av b'yo-tzeit cha-la-tzav, v'ta-geil i-mo bif-ri vit-nah. Zoht ha-k'ta-nah tih-yeh g'dolah. K'shem sheh-nich-n'sah la-brit, kein ti-ka-nes l'to-rah ul-chu-pah ul-ma-a-sim to-vim.

Oh God, God of all generations, sustain this child and let her be known in the house of Israel as _____. May she bring us joy and happiness in the months and years to come. As we have brought her into the covenant of Torah today, so may she enter into the study of Torah, the blessings of marriage, and the performance of good deeds.

Baby's namesakes are remembered.

Grandparent/s:

Our God and God of all generations, we are grateful for new beginnings, for the bond of new life that links one generation to another. Thankful for the blessings of family, for the love and care that bring meaning and happiness to our lives, we rejoice with our children at the birth of their child, our grandchild.

Brit E'dut

May they grow together as a family in health and in strength, in harmony, wisdom, and love, their home filled with words of Torah and acts of kindness.

May we be enabled to share in the joy of seeing this child grow into adulthood, a blessing to her family, her people, and all humanity.

All:

יְבָרֶכְךָ יְיָ וְיִשְׁמְרֶךָ,

יָאֵר יְיָ פָּנָיו אֵלֶיךָ וִיחֻנֶּךָּ,

יִשָּׂא יְיָ פָּנָיו אֵלֶיךָ וְיָשֵׂם לְךָ שָׁלוֹם.

Y'va-reh-ch'chah Adonai v'yish-m'reh-cha,
Ya-eir Adonai pa-nav ei-leh-kha vi-chu-neh-ka,
Yi-sah Adonai pa-nav ei-leh-kha v'ya-seim
l'chah sha-lom.

May God bless you and protect you.
May God's presence shine for you and be
favorable to you.
May God's face turn to you and give
you peace.[44]

Brit Shomrot Hamachzorim

Covenant of the Guardians
of the Sacred Cycles

Rabbi or guest, as baby is taken to the chair of Elijah:

In Jewish tradition, Elijah the prophet represents the coming of the messianic time. Elijah is present at the covenant whose sign is circumcision, at the Pesach Seder, and at the weekly *Havdalah* ceremony, and he is known as the guardian of young children. The presence of Elijah at this covenant ceremony bids us to look through the life of one child to the fulfillment of all life.

Guest:

"When the men saw that Moses was so long in coming down from the mountain, they went to Aaron and asked him to make them a god. He said to them, 'Take off the gold rings that are on the ears of your wives, your sons, and your daughters, and bring them to me.'

"And the men took off the gold rings that were in their ears, too impatient to notice that the women refused their gold." (Exod. 32:1–3)

Guest:

And so, the Holy Ancient One made the special relationship of women to Rosh Hodesh. Celebrating the new moon, women became guardians of the cycles of sacred time. They watched the light grow bright and diminish and, with the light, welcomed holy days and Shabbat days in their order.

Brit Shomrot Hamachzorim

And the ebb and flow of the cycles within their bodies made them watchful, mindful of the gifts of heaven and earth.

Today, we publicly announce the birth of our new daughter and sister, welcoming her into this covenant our mothers have guarded in secret for so long.

Guest:

Ever since Avraham and Sarah began helping people discover God, this has been our vision: a world of men and women acting together, sharing the tasks needed to nurture and teach, to sustain and develop, that we reach the sacred time for which we wait.

בָּרוּךְ אַתָּה יְיָ, אֱלֹהֵינוּ מֶלֶךְ הָעוֹלָם,
שֶׁהֶחֱיָנוּ וְקִיְּמָנוּ וְהִגִּיעָנוּ לַזְּמַן הַזֶּה.

*Ba-ruch a-ta Adonai, Eh-lo-hei-nu meh-lech
ha-o-lam, sheh-heh-cheh-ya-nu v'ki-y'ma-nu
v'hi-gi-a-nu la-z'man ha-zeh.*

Let us bless the Source of all, who has
breathed life into us, sustained us, and
brought us to this precious moment.

Awakening of the Five Senses

Parent lights two Shabbat candles and says:

Jewish women have been guardians of the light, kindling the spiritual flame for home and community since ancient times. With every Shabbat and holy day we remember the spark of spirit within and manifest its beauty and wonder through lighting the fire of enlightenment, love, and peace.

Brit Shomrot Hamachzorim

בָּרוּךְ אַתָּה יְיָ, אֱלֹהֵינוּ מֶלֶךְ הָעוֹלָם, בּוֹרֵא מְאוֹרֵי הָאֵשׁ.

*Ba-ruch a-ta Adonai, Eh-lo-hei-nu meh-lech
ha-o-lam, bo-rei m'o-rei ha-eish.*

Let us bless the Source of all, who creates
the illuminations of the flame.

The baby is given a taste of wine as parent or guest says:

Why do we make a blessing over wine rather than water?
Water, after all, symbolizes purity and was created directly by
God. But wine involves a partnership between people and
God. God provides the fruit that we transform into wine,
which in turn alters our awareness and lifts our spirit.[45]

May _____ take what God provides and
make it holy.

בָּרוּךְ אָתָּה יְיָ, אֱלֹהֵינוּ מֶלֶךְ הָעוֹלָם,
בּוֹרֵא פְּרִי הַגָּפֶן.

*Ba-ruch a-ta Adonai, Eh-lo-hei-nu meh-lech
ha-o-lam, bo-rei p'ri ha-ga-fen.*

Let us bless the Source of all, who creates
the fruit of the vine, symbol of our rejoicing.

Parent, guest, or leaders lead a *niggun,* a wordless melody.

May the sound of blessing caress her ears and fill her heart.

Brit Shomrot Hamachzorim

בָּרוּךְ אַתָּה יְיָ, אֱלֹהֵינוּ מֶלֶךְ הָעוֹלָם, שׁוֹמֵעַ תְּפִלָּה.

*Ba-ruch a-ta Adonai, Eh-lo-hei-nu meh-lech
ha-o-lam, sho-mei-ah t'fi-lah.*

Let us bless the Source of all, who listens to
prayer from the heart.

Flowers are held beneath the baby's nose as parent or guest
says:

The sense of smell unites us with our breath and reminds us
of the soul. May the fragrance of beauty and peace surround
_____ as she remembers the wisdom of her soul.

בָּרוּךְ אַתָּה יְיָ, אֱלֹהֵינוּ מֶלֶךְ הָעוֹלָם, בּוֹרֵא עִשְׂבֵי בְשָׂמִים.

*Ba-ruch a-ta Adonai, Eh-lo-hei-nu meh-lech
ha-o-lam, bo-rei is-vei v'sa-mim.*

Let us bless the Source of all, who creates
the sweet-smelling grasses.

The baby's hands are washed with water that was collected
from rain, lake, river, or sea water.

Parent, guest, or leader:

Brit is the covenant of our separate male and female realities,
united and transformed by an awareness of Spirit.

With the purifying water from the Garden of Eden do we
wash, wake, and welcome you into the covenant of women,
guarding the sacred cycles of time. From the Source of
Oneness are we all born. Remember and return often to the
pure spring of life. Immerse yourself in truth, joy, and hope.

158

Brit Shomrot Hamachzorim

בָּרוּךְ אַתָּה יְיָ, אֱלֹהֵינוּ מֶלֶךְ הָעוֹלָם,
אֲשֶׁר קִדְּשָׁנוּ בְּמִצְוֹתָיו, וְצִוָּנוּ עַל נְטִילַת יָדָיִם.

*Ba-ruch a-ta Adonai, Eh-lo-hei-nu meh-lech
ha-o-lam, a-sher ki-d'sha-nu b'mitz-vo-tav,
v'tzi-va-nu al n'ti-lat ya-da-yim.*

Let us bless the Source of all, who guides us
on the path of holiness and directs us to lift
up our hands through washing with water.

Naming

Parent, rabbi, or leader:

מִי שֶׁבֵּרַךְ אִמּוֹתֵינוּ שָׂרָה, רִבְקָה, רָחֵל, וְלֵאָה
וּמִרְיָם הַנְּבִיאָה וַאֲבִגַיִל, וְאֶסְתֵּר הַמַּלְכָּה בַּת אֲבִיחַיִל
הוּא יְבָרֵךְ אֶת הַנַּעֲרָה הַנְּעִימָה הַזֹּאת

וְיִקָּרֵא שְׁמָהּ בְּיִשְׂרָאֵל ‎_____‎ בַּת ‎_____‎
בְּמַזָּל טוֹב וּבִשְׁעַת בְּרָכָה.
וְיִגְדְּלָהּ בִּבְרִיאוּת, שָׁלוֹם וּמְנוּחָה
לְתוֹרָה וּלְחֻפָּה וּלְמַעֲשִׂים טוֹבִים.
וְיִזְכֶּה אֶת אָבִיהָ וְאֶת אִמָּהּ לִרְאוֹת בְּשִׂמְחָתָהּ
בְּבָנִים וּבָנוֹת עֹשֶׁר וְכָבוֹד
דְּשֵׁנִים וְרַעֲנַנִּים יְנוּבוּן בְּשֵׂיבָה
וְכֵן יְהִי רָצוֹן וְנֹאמַר אָמֵן.

*Mi sheh-bei-rach i-mo-tei-nu Sa-rah, Riv-kah, Ra-chel,
v'Lei-ah u'Mir-yam ha-n'vi-ah, va'A-vi-ga-yil, v'Es-ter bat
A-vi-cha-yil hu y'va-reich et ha-na-a-rah ha-n'i-mah ha-zoht*

Brit Shomrot Hamachzorim

v'yi-ka-rei sh'mah b'Yisrael

_____ *bat* _____ *v'*_____

b'ma-zal tohv u-vish-at b'racha.
Vi-gad'lah biv-ri-ut, she-lohm um-nu-chah
l'torah ul-chu-pah ul-ma-a-sim tovim.
Vi-za-keh et a-vi-ha v'et i-mah lir-oht b'sim-cha-tah
b'va-nim u-va-noht, oh-sher v'cha-vohd
d'shei-nim v'ra-a-na-nim y'nu-vun b'sei-vah
v'chein y'hi ra-tzohn v'no-mar a-mein.

May God who blessed our mothers,
Sarah, Rebecca, Rachel, and Leah,
Miriam the prophet and Avigayil,
bless this beautiful little girl
and let her name be called in Israel _____,
daughter of _____
at this favorable moment of blessing.
May she be raised in health, peace, and tranquility
to study Torah,
to stand under the *huppah* (if that is her choice)
to do good deeds.
May her parents merit to see her happy,
blessed with children, wealth, and honor,
peaceful and content in their old age.
May this be God's will.
Amen.

Parent explains the meaning of the baby's name.

Let us bless the Source of all, who has brought us to a life of service and given us the opportunity to introduce our daughter to the covenant of the sacred cycles.[46, 47]

Brit Banot

As the baby is brought into the room all rise and say:

Who is she who shines though like the dawn,
Beautiful as the sun, radiant as the moon?
(Song of Songs 6:10)

The following lines may be read by the rabbi or leader, by selected guests, responsively, or by the entire company:

Look to Abraham your father and to Sarah who bore you. (Isa. 51:2)

God appeared to Abram and said to him: I am *El Shaddai*; walk wholeheartedly before Me.... Then I will establish a covenant between Me and you and your descendants who will come after you: A covenant in which I will be your God and your children's God, forever and ever. (Gen. 17:1, 17:7)

The baby is held at the center of a large *tallit*. Each of the four corners is held by parents and honored guests and is folded around the baby.

How precious is Your constant love, O God; you shelter us under Your wings. (Ps. 36:8)

Brit Banot

Let all my being praise the Lord, who is clothed in splendor and majesty; wrapped in light like a garment, unfolding the heavens like a curtain.... You send forth Your spirit and there is creation. You renew the face of the earth. (Ps. 104:1–2, 104:30)

O you who dwell in the shelter of the Most High and abide in the protection of *Shaddai*. My God, in whom I trust, will cover you; you will find shelter under God's wings.

Rabbi or parent/s:

Our God and God of our ancestors, we thank you for the gift of this child (our daughter) whom we welcomed into God's covenant today. May she grow to maturity embraced by God's love and the love of all who know her. May the *Shekhinah*, God's sheltering presence, be with her always. May the words of Torah surround her. Clothed in majesty and honor, may she always look to the future with joy.

Parent/s:

בָּרוּךְ אַתָּה יְיָ, אֱלֹהֵינוּ מֶלֶךְ הָעוֹלָם,
אֲשֶׁר קִדְּשָׁנוּ בְּמִצְוֹתָיו, וְצִוָּנוּ
לְהַכְנִיסוֹ בִּבְרִיתוֹ שֶׁל אַבְרָהָם אָבִינוּ וְשָׂרָה אִמֵּנוּ.

*Ba-ruch a-ta Adonai, Eh-lo-hei-nu meh-lech
ha-o-lam, a-sher ki-d'sha-nu b'mitz-vo-tav,
v'tzi-va-nu l'hach-ni-so biv-ri-to shel
Av-ra-ham a-vi-nu v'Sa-rah i-mei-nu.*

Brit Banot

O Lord our God, Ruler of the universe,
who sanctifies us with Your mitzvot and
commanded us to bring our daughter into the
covenant of Abraham our father and
Sarah our mother.

All:

כְּשֵׁם שֶׁנִּכְנְסָה לַבְּרִית,
כֵּן תִּכָּנֵס לְתוֹרָה וּלְחֻפָּה וּלְמַעֲשִׂים טוֹבִים.

*K'shem sheh-nich-n'sah la-brit, kein ti-ka-nes
l'to-rah ul-chu-pah ul-ma-a-sim to-vim.*

As she has entered the covenant, so may she
attain the blessings of Torah, marriage under
the *huppah,* and a life of good deeds.

Guest or rabbi:

בָּרוּךְ אַתָּה יְיָ, אֱלֹהֵינוּ מֶלֶךְ הָעוֹלָם,
בּוֹרֵא פְּרִי הַגָּפֶן.

*Ba-ruch a-ta Adonai, Eh-lo-hei-nu meh-lech
ha-o-lam, bo-rei p'ri ha-ga-fen.*

Praised are You, Lord our God, Ruler of the
universe, who creates the fruit of the vine.

Our God and God of our ancestors, sustain this child. We
declare that her name shall be _____, daughter
of _____ and _____.

May the father rejoice in his offspring; may her mother
delight in the fruit of her womb. As it is written: Gladness and
joy shall abide with her; thanksgiving and happy song.
(Isa. 51:3)

Brit Banot

God makes a covenant with her, a covenant of life and peace. (Malachi 2:5)

As it is written: This is the child for whom I prayed; God has granted my desire. (I Samuel 1:27)

O Praise our God, whose goodness endures forever.

May this little one _____ become great.

As she has entered the covenant, so may she attain the blessings of Torah, marriage under the *huppah,* and a life of good deeds.

Let us say Amen.[48]

Hiddur Mitzvah— Beautiful Touches

The urge to decorate and beautify our surroundings seems like a basic human impulse. Jewish law codified this joyful instinct with a rabbinic principle: according to *hiddur mitzvah* (*hiddur* means "beautiful"), when a physical object is needed to fulfill a mitzvah or commandment, the object should be as lovely as possible. So although it is perfectly kosher to bless wine in a paper cup, it is considered praiseworthy to put the wine into a beautiful goblet that was made expressly for *Kiddush*, or sanctification. In the past, communal ritual objects were used by individual families—for example, synagogues had elaborate chairs used for the prophet Elijah's ceremonial seat, and even the clamps and scalpels used for *brit milah* were decorated. The objects you use for your baby's *brit* ceremony can become family heirlooms that will recall powerful memories for you and hold a strong fascination for your child as he or she grows. Likewise, the songs and words you use and remember will always have a kind of magic.

Ideas and Readings for Your Celebration

Guides

Some families provide a printed guide or booklet to accompany a *brit* or any of the other ceremonies mentioned in this book. The explanations, translations, responsive readings, poems, or prayers you provide can help guests feel more comfortable and involved.

Copies will become family treasures, so be sure to store or even frame one.

Guides can be simple or elaborate, a single photocopied sheet or a pamphlet of many pages. Sometimes the cover is a copy of the birth announcement and the contents include the entire ceremony. A booklet might also contain the *Birkat Hamazon,* the blessings that are sung after eating. Alternately, a guide can simply provide basic information about the ritual and customs, including an announcement of *tzedakah* (righteous giving or charity) donated in honor of the birth.

Candles

Although few Americans are familiar with the custom, lighting candles at a *brit milah* is a common practice in Jewish communities around the world. The practice may date back to times when circumcision was performed in defiance of anti-Semitic edicts, and candles burning in the window of a Jewish home signaled friends and neighbors to come celebrate a clandestine *bris*.[49] Because lighting Shabbat candles is traditionally a woman's mitzvah, candles seem appropriate at ceremonies for daughters as well.

Light, a universal symbol of both the Divine Presence and of the human soul, is used in many ways at ceremonies for new babies. Sometimes a single candle is lit for the baby—two for twins. But in some parts of the world, thirteen candles are lit, because there are thirteen references to *brit milah* in the Book of Genesis.[50]

Parents might each kindle a candle and then, using their lit tapers, light a third (or fourth, or fifth), signifying the new light in their family. For some parents, this ceremony marks the addition of a new candle to their weekly Friday night Shabbat ritual.

Candles may be placed anywhere in the room. A circle of light surrounding parents and baby makes a powerful visual statement, and the honor of lighting candles can be given to various family members or friends. Use white Shabbat candles, braided *Havdalah* candles, or a rainbow of colored candles—whatever you like.

Candles can be lit in silence or with a reading, like this one for parents:

There is a new light in our hearts and in our home.
These candles celebrate the birth of our child.
Out of the creative darkness of the womb s/he has come.
These candles celebrate her/his emergence into light.
Blessed is the woman who bears a child, for she knows how love
covers pain.
Blessed is the man who fathers a child, for he makes a bridge
between earth and heaven.
Child of light, you know not yet the love and joy overflowing from
our hearts.[51]

Elijah's Chair

Decorating the *kisei shel Eliyahu*—the chair of Elijah—is a *brit milah* custom practiced by Jews worldwide. The prophet Elijah, who is associated with the coming of the Messiah, is similarly welcomed at *brit bat* celebrations today.

Spanish Jews drape the prophet's chair with fabrics of purple and gold and leave a prayer book or *Chumash* (the book version of the Torah) on it. In other nations, Jews place a beautiful pillow or brightly colored scarves on the chair. Another option is to cover Elijah's chair with a piece of cloth that will later be made into a *tallit* or *wimpel* (Torah binder). Similarly, the baby can be brought into the room wrapped in the *wimpel* fabric (see below). Other coverings for the chair might include your *huppah* cover—the top from your wedding canopy—or a shawl that belonged to a great-grandmother or beloved aunt who is not present or did not live to see the birth of your baby.

Baby Clothes

Some communities favor white clothing for the baby, while others dress the baby in colorful attire—the choice is yours. It is customary for baby boys to wear a tiny *kippah* (skullcap), which might be a special gift from a relative or friend who crochets. Because women in many liberal congregations now wear *kippot* as well, the custom is sometimes used in ceremonies for baby girls. If you wish your guests to wear *kippot,* as is customary, have several on hand.

Huppah

Sometimes parents will raise their own marriage canopy to welcome the newest member of the family. Family members and special friends can be honored by holding the poles during the *brit*. The presence of older siblings under the canopy can provide a much-needed moment of recognition for older brothers and sisters, who might feel lost in all the commotion surrounding the new baby.

Kiddush Cup

The principle of *hiddur mitzvah* applies to any object used in the ceremony. Because wine is blessed at virtually all *brit milah* and *brit bat* ceremonies, a cup will be necessary—the more beautiful the better. A distinctive goblet, a gift for the baby, might be unveiled at the ceremony, or the *Kiddush* cup you used at your wedding might be filled as the following words are recited:

> This cup is the vessel of our hopes. We first drank from it under our wedding *huppah*. Today, it is filled with the new wine of a life just begun, and from it we taste the sweetness of the great joy that *(baby's name)* has brought us.

Wimpels

In Eastern Europe, the cloth used to wrap an infant at his *brit milah* was later cut and sewn into a long strip for use as a Torah binder—in Yiddish, *wimpel,* pronounced *"vimpel."* (The Hebrew is *mappah.*)

The *wimpel* was presented as a family's gift to the synagogue, usually in time for use on the Shabbat closest to the child's first birthday. The Torah binder then belonged to the synagogue and would be used when the child reached bar mitzvah. In Germany and Italy, *wimpels* were painted or embroidered with the child's name, his parents' names, the date of birth, and a Hebrew inscription and were lavishly decorated with all sorts of images, including (in some communities) the baby's zodiac sign. The *wimpel* is enjoying a modest revival for daughters as well as for sons.[52]

Borrowing from the idea of the *wimpel*, a piece of fabric or cloth-ing used during the *brit* ceremony can later be incorporated into an *atarah*, the neckpiece on a *tallit*, or a prayer shawl. That *tallit* can be given to the child at the time of his or her bar or bat mitzvah.

Music

Music, song, and dance are traditional at Jewish celebrations. Although the Ashkenazic repertoire is not nearly as rich as the Sephardic, there are particular melodies American Jews associate with baby rituals.

"Siman Tov Umazal Tov" (Good Fortune and Good Luck) is the all-purpose song of rejoicing, proclaiming the event as a source of joy for those gathered and for all Israel. Because of the prophet Elijah's association with *brit milah*, "Eliyahu Hanavi" is often sung during a *bris*. Now that Elijah's chair is a common feature at *brit bat*, it seems appropriate to sing the prophet's song there as well. A second verse honoring the prophetess Miriam may be added or substituted at a *brit bat*.

"Hiney Ma Tov Umanayim" (How Good and Pleasant It Is) is another favorite at baby celebrations, because it extols the pleasure of community. "Yevarechecha Adonai Mitzion" (May the Lord Bless You from Zion) is popular because it includes the line "May you see your children's children." Cantors are probably your best resource when researching music for a ceremony. Even if you do not belong to a synagogue, many cantors are glad to share their expertise.[53]

Words

It is customary in some circles to offer a *d'var Torah*, a word of Jewish learning, on an occasion as important as a birth. Sometimes this is part of the ceremony, and sometimes it is pre-sented later, during the celebratory meal. Traditionally, such a *d'rash* (teaching) is based on the baby's name; the weekly Torah portion; or a section from Proverbs, Song of Songs, or the Book of Psalms. According to one tale, a psalm is given to each Jew for every year of life. Thus, if you are thirty years old, Psalm 31 is yours to study and enjoy. Psalm 1 is given to newborns.

For the *brit* ceremony itself, however, nothing is more mean-ingful or more powerful than your own thoughts and feelings about the birth of your child and the person or people for whom your baby is named. To recount these stories, you don't have to be a poet or a Jewish scholar. If you say what's in your heart, there won't be a dry eye in the house.

For readings and inspiration, this book contains dozens of prayers, poems, and creative translations of traditional texts. Several of these appear in the chapters *"Brit Milah"* and *"Brit Bat"* and in the "Adoption" section of Part 5. So even if you are planning a *brit milah*, glance through these other sections as well as the original poems, readings, and prayers that follow.

A Blessing

May your eyes sparkle with the light of Torah,
and your ears hear the music of its words.
May the space between each letter of the scrolls
bring warmth and comfort to your soul.
May the syllables draw holiness from your heart,
and may this holiness be gentle and soothing
to you and all God's creatures.
May your study be passionate,
and meanings bear more meanings
until Life itself arrays itself to you
as a dazzling wedding feast.
And may your conversation,
even of the commonplace,
be a blessing to all who listen to your words
and see the Torah glowing on your face.

Danny Siegel
Berachot 17a and *Eruvin* 54a[54]

Blessing the Children

Parent/s place hands on their children's heads and recite:

For the boys—

May you be as Ephraim and Menashe
of whom we know nothing
but their names
and that they were Jews.
And may you be as all Jews
whose names are lost
as witnesses to God's care,
love, and presence.
Remember them in your words,
and live Menschlich *lives*
as they lived Menschlich *lives.*

For the girls—

May you be as Sarah, Rivka, Rachel, and Leah,
whose names and deeds
are our inheritance;
who bore us, raised us,
guided and taught us
that a touch
is a touch of Holiness,
and a laugh is prophecy;
that all that is ours,
is theirs;
that neither Man nor Woman alone
lights the sparks of Life,
but only both together,
generating light and warmth
and singular humanity.
Danny Siegel[55]

Blessing the Children

May you be as Henrietta Szold,
raising and building,
that your People
need not suffer
the loneliness of pain.

May you be as Herzl and Ben Yehuda,
stung and raving with visions
for the sake of Israel
and the Jews.

And may our family be together
as Sholom Aleichem and his children,
passing on our stories to each other
with a radiance of joy
and a laugh of love.

Danny Siegel[56]

Above All, Teach This Newborn Child

Above all, teach this newborn child to touch,
to never stop,
to feel how fur is other than the leaf or cheek
to know through these hands diamond from glass,
Mezuzah from anything else in the world
The same with Challah and a book.

As the baby grows,
teach this child to embrace the shoulders of another
before sadness brings them inhumanly low,
to stroke the hair softly of one younger who is weeping,
one older who cries.

Let these hands be a gentle Yes
When Yes is the Truth,
and gently, a No when No is right.
Whatever these fingers touch—
may they be for new holiness and blessing,
for light, life, and love.

Amen.

Danny Siegel[57]

On the Birth of a Brother or Sister

Welcome to the world!
You are so small and you cry so much.
People make such a fuss.
I don't know why.

I think I will take care of you
And play with you sometimes,
Because I am big.
I hope you like me.
I hope you learn to say my name.

Sometimes you will pull my hair
But I will not mind,
Unless you pull it very hard.
Sometimes I will fight with you
Because you want my toys.
I hope you will not mind.

Sometimes I will be angry at Mom and Dad
Because they spend too much time with you.
I hope you will forgive me.

Thank you, God, for little fingers and tiny toes
Just like mine.
Thank you God, for arms that are large enough to hold one more.

Thank you, God, for a love that is big enough
To include my brother/sister and ME!

Sandy Eisenberg Sasso[58]

So you have been born

So you have been born, ben Sarah*
your first great birth:

from water to air
from water to land
from the mikvah/womb to the midwife's hands.

The Great-Moon-Mother-of-Miracles
brought you to birth

(from the dark, where the secret light is sown)
to sunlight!
moonlight!
candlelight!!!!!!!!

By this light, with God's aid be born
again and again
Shanah shanah [year after year]
hodesh hodesh [month after month]
hag hag [holiday after holiday]
shabbat shabbat [Sabbath after Sabbath]
nes nes [miracle after miracle]

Great-Moon-Mother-of-Miracles, multiply miracles
bless with your light the yoledet,† her child
With wave upon wave of your light, renew, replenish your daughter,
your daughter's child.

Miryam bat Bayla/Stephanie Loo[59]

---

* For a daughter, "bat Sarah"
† A *yoledet* is a woman who has recently given birth.

Child at the Gate of Covenant

So recently an expert
on the universe,
the furrow from his nose
down to his lips
drawn by an angel
at the gate of birth,
the child, ancient
as the earth, endowed
with words his mouth
can't yet pronounce,
watched by Elijah,
dabbed with wine,
a party to the covenant,
his parents' stories soon
to be like ancient history:
he is gently disengaged
from pleasures of eternity,
and entered in the rolls
of life, the surge
of worldly business
like a sea swell
rolling under him,
to bear him up,
the teaching life
will soon enough
extract from him
tucked almost inaccessibly
away, behind the furrow,
deep inside.

Joel Rosenberg[60]

For the Naming of a Girl-Child

Between a boy-child and a girl-child,
    only the latter has the soul's shape.
    For he will grow up,
    huffing and thrusting,
    with a plate of armor
    'round his life-breath,
    and, if fortunate, will watch
    this outer veil grow limber
    and translucent, to reveal
    his true shape with advancing age.
    If not for circumcision,
    he would suffocate.

    But she
    was husked in heaven from the start.
    Her natural radiance will be
    tempered by the world.
    And she, more conscious of her exile,
    will accept the ring someday
    beneath the canopy, as if
    in willful diminution of her light
    (as once, of old, the moon),
    and she will take the future
    in her womb, as if in trust.
    And she, the nurse and blueprint
    of the universe, is Israel
    and the Presence quite enough,
    and so the contour of the soul,
    right from the first day of her life.

No sign of covenant is made in her:
she is a sign herself already,
for, waxing and waning with the moon,
she is the imprint of a world
that breathes—her own small breath
a tiny metronome by which
the world is tuned.

Joel Rosenberg[61]

Brucha Haba'a—Blessed She Comes

Welcome Woman-Child
  Newborn guardian
  of the sacred gift
  of cycles and seasons.
Within and all around you
Be witness to the rhythms of
  surrender and renewal
  faith and love
Awaken intuition and knowledge
to the indwelling presence—Shechinah

We welcome you
  into the world
  into your family
  into your people

May you know from your early days
  how we travel through the dance
  of dark and light
  slavery and freedom
  wandering and revelation
  planting and harvest
  new moon and full moon
from the illumined place of now
  the sanctuary in time—Shabbat
  Hanna Tiferet Siegel[62]

Poem of Thanksgiving

With all my heart, with all my soul, with all my might
I thank You, God, for the gift of this wonderful child.
I thank You for a healthy pregnancy, a safe
*   delivery and a speedy recovery.*

With all my heart, with all my soul, with all my might
I pray for the continued health of this child.
I pray for her to be strong in mind and body,
To grow steadily and sturdily in a home filled with joy.
I pray for her to become a person who greets the world
With passion, courage, humility, humor and patience.

With all my heart, with all my soul, with all my might
I pray for God to watch over me and my family.
I pray for the ability to love and nurture this child
To provide for her and to educate her,
To understand her and to allow her the freedom to grow.

Adapted by Rabbi Maggie Wenig
from the poem by Rabbi Judith Shanks[63]

Parents' Blessing

May you live to see your world fulfilled,
May your destiny be for worlds still to come,
And may you trust in generations past and yet to be.

May your heart be filled with intuition
and your words be filled with insight.
May songs of praise ever be upon your tongue
and your vision be on a straight path before you.
May your eyes shine with the light of holy words
and your face reflect the brightness of the heavens.
May your lips speak wisdom
and your fulfillment be in righteousness
even as you ever yearn to hear the words
of the Holy Ancient One of Old.

Berachot 17a[64]

Blessings

In every birth, blessed is the wonder.
In every creation, blessed is the new beginning.
In every child, blessed is life.
In every hope, blessed is the potential.
In every transition, blessed is the beginning.
In every existence, blessed are the possibilities.
In every love, blessed are the tears.
In every life, blessed is the love.[65]

Parents' Prayer

We dedicate our child to Torah,
To a never-ending fascination with study and learning
With a book, s/he will never be alone.

We dedicate our child to huppah,
To never-ending growth as a human being capable of giving and
*   receiving love.*
With a loving mate, s/he will never be alone.

We dedicate our child to maasim tovim,
To a never-ending concern for family and community, justice and
*   charity.*
If s/he cares for others, s/he will never be alone.

We pray for wisdom to help our child achieve these things,
To fulfill the needs of his/her mind and body,
To be strong when s/he needs us to be strong,
To be gentle when s/he needs us to be gentle,
But always there when s/he needs us.
The birth of a child is a miracle of renewal.
We stand together this day, contemplating a miracle.[66]

Every person born into this world represents something new, something that never existed before, something original and unique. It is the duty of every person in Israel to know and consider that he is unique in the world in his particular character, and that there has never been someone like him before. For if there had been someone like him before, there would be no need for him to be in the world. Every single person is a new thing in the world and is called upon to fulfill his particularity in the world.

Adapted from a passage by Martin Buber

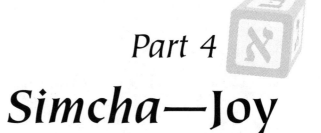

Part 4

Simcha—Joy

Simcha Means "Party"

The word *simcha* means "joy," and it also means "party." The birth of a Jewish baby is always occasion for both. A ceremony to welcome your new son or daughter to the Jewish people actually requires that you have a *simcha,* complete with food and drink.

Partying is not just part of Jewish culture; it is embedded in traditional Jewish law, which mandates that all major life-cycle events include a *s'udat mitzvah*—a commanded meal.

The meal to honor the birth of a new baby can be a lavish sit-down affair at a catering hall, but informal repasts are far more common. A *s'udat mitzvah* can be a bagel-and-lox breakfast after a morning *bris,* dessert and coffee at the *Oneg Shabbat* after a Friday night synagogue ceremony, or a buffet lunch after a Shabbat morning *brit bat.* Because of most new parents' states of mind and energy levels, the celebration tends to be simple, with guests called or e-mailed regarding the time and location of the ceremony.

It is customary to start a *s'udat mitzvah* with a blessing over a large, braided loaf of challah, and there is at least one ceremonial glass of wine for a blessing.

Traditional foods are all suggestive of fertility: chickpeas, eggs, and olives—round foods that are, in some sense, seeds for the next generation. The olive, which was also a source of heat and light in the ancient world, embodies the warmth and joy a baby brings; parsley, or any green vegetable, signifies a wish for the earth's continued bounty; pastries, cakes, and cookies symbolize the sweetness of the occasion. Persian Jews offer a plate of apples, a symbol of easy labor and delivery, to young couples in attendance at the meal.[1]

Some people bake and freeze the goodies for their baby's *simcha* well in advance. For parents- and grandparents-to-be who enjoy baking, this can provide a useful outlet for the nervous energy that comes with waiting. Likewise, if you plan to have a catered meal, you might want to contact a caterer and make menu selections in advance. (If you find yourself with time to spare before the baby comes, it's a good idea to compile a guest list, complete with e-mail addresses and/or phone numbers.)

In the best of all possible worlds, new parents are not the ones to organize and host their own *s'udat mitzvah.* In Sephardic communities, paying for the food and drink at a *brit* is considered an honor assumed by the *sandek,* the person who holds the baby during the circumcision. Similarly, the *s'udat* is often a gift from grandparents.

Close friends and relatives may offer to bring food to the *s'udat mitzvah,* but if you really prefer to do it yourself or let a caterer take care of everything, ask people who offer to help for a rain check in the form of a covered-dish meal, to be delivered during your first weeks at home with the new baby. In any event, remember that your guests are coming to share your joy and see the baby—and do not expect a feast.

However, it is important to remember that some of your guests might be offended by the presence of shrimp on the buffet table. Even for people who don't observe kashrut (the laws that govern what Jews eat), following its basic rules at the *simcha* is a thoughtful gesture and an act of hospitality for those who do. Remember that the *mohel,* cantor, or rabbi who officiates at your ceremony may not be able to share in the meal if you do not honor the dietary laws. Generally, if your party takes place in a synagogue, you will be required to serve a kosher meal.

Kashrut is not an ancient health code. It is a way of sanctifying the basic human need for food. The laws of kashrut are based on specific proscriptions in the Bible against eating birds of prey and fish lacking fins or gills. The separation of milk and meat is an elaboration on the Torah's command not to "boil a kid in its mother's milk."

Briefly, kashrut permits the following foods: all vegetables and fruits, fish with fins and scales (no shellfish or bottom-feeding fish), domestic fowl, and animals that chew a cud and have split hooves. For meat to be kosher, the animal must also be killed according to specific ritual laws by a trained butcher who recites a blessing. The meat is then soaked and salted to remove all traces of blood. Finally, meat and milk products are not eaten at the same meal and must be kept separate. Thus, *milchig* (dairy) and *flayshig* (meat) foods are not cooked in the same pots or served on the same dishes. The waiting period between consumption of meat and milk varies according to community custom.

A simple way to prepare or organize a kosher meal is to keep it vegetarian, or *milchig*. To find a kosher caterer, ask for recommendations from friends, family, or your rabbi. Failing that, consult the "Yellow Pages" under "Catering." In larger cities and towns, there is usually a special listing of kosher services. "Kosher style" means the restaurant or caterer specializes in Jewish-identified foods, such as knishes and lox, but it is usually a signal that the food is not designated as kosher, so be sure to make your wishes clear.

Blessings and Toasts

Before beginning the meal, you can honor a special guest by asking him or her to say the *Motzi,* the blessing over bread, traditionally made over a large braided loaf of challah, or the *Kiddush,* the blessing over wine.

If your *brit* ceremony did not include an opportunity for guests to offer their blessings and wishes for the baby and family, the meal is a good time to do this. As always, it's a good idea to ask one or two guests to think about what they might like to say in advance. If there was no appropriate time for an older sibling to participate during the *brit* ceremony, the baby's brother(s) or sister(s) can be given a chance to shine here. If siblings are old enough, they might even compose a few words of welcome for the new baby or simply present a gift.

You can even appoint a "master of ceremonies" (perhaps an uncle or sister who has a snappy comeback for every occasion) to make merry, start songs, call on people to speak, make toasts, and read telegrams or other messages from afar.

In some families, while everyone is finishing dessert and coffee, a friend or relative rises to deliver a *d'var Torah,* words of Torah or learning that are related to the baby's name, the weekly Torah portion, or some other aspect of the *simcha.*

The traditional ending for a *s'udat mitzvah* is the singing of *Birkat Hamazon,* the blessings after eating. There is a special *Birkat Hamazon* for the meal following a *bris* that includes blessings for the baby, parents, *mohel,* and *sandek.* It is an honor to be asked to lead these prayers, which are printed in booklets called *benchers.*[2]

Photography

Some rabbis, *mohels,* and parents object to the presence of cameras during *brit* ceremonies, especially during the ritual circumcision itself. Others welcome all forms of photography—video or still. A tape recorder is still probably the most unobtrusive form of recording technology.

Whatever your feelings about pictures at the ceremony, the *s'udat mitzvah* is a fine time for documenting the events of the day. In general, people don't hire professional photographers for such intimate celebrations, but it may be a good idea to ask a particular relative or friend who is good with a camera to do the honors. Although candid pictures are wonderful, posed shots of proud grandparents holding the baby and other family groupings will become treasured keepsakes.

Gifts

Jewish baby gifts range from the silly (bibs with Yiddish phrases such as *Bubbe's fresser*—Grandma's big eater) to the sublime (Grandpa's engraved *Kiddush* cup). But there is also a middle path, filled with Jewish children's books, CDs, and art for the baby's room. There are cloth, plastic, and cardboard books that feature the Hebrew alphabet and baby blankets with the words *layla tov* (good night) woven into the design. Works of Jewish art for the nursery include bright posters of the *aleph-bet,* special *tzedakah* (charity) boxes, and winsome mezuzot for the doorpost to the baby's room. Calligraphers and artists have created special birth "certificates" and limited-edition prints especially for Jewish children. In some families, a handcrafted silver, ceramic, or brass Hanukkah *draydl* (spinning top) has replaced the proverbial silver loving cup as the heirloom gift. Judaica shops and art museum gift stores are great resources for these kinds of presents, as are Judaica websites.

Some gifts become heirlooms the moment they are given. A prayer shawl given by grandparents to a grandson becomes a tangible link between the generations. Handmade gifts are always welcome. A hand-crocheted *kippah* for the baby to wear during the *brit* is a gift beyond price. Other ideas for craftspeople include needlepoint hangings based on a baby's name, a cross-stitched Hebrew alphabet, wooden blocks with a baby's name painted in Hebrew and English on the sides, or personalized appliqué on a baby quilt or soft fabric blocks.

Although they are not exactly gifts, charitable contributions in honor of a baby's birth is a time-honored Jewish custom and a way of acting upon the wish that this child will live in a more peaceful and just world. (See "Celebrations and Customs" for more about *tzedakah.*)

Finally, thoughtful guests often bring a small gift for the baby's sibling(s), who invariably feel left out. It need not be a big present—just a token to help older kids know that they haven't been forgotten.

Announcements

A birth announcement may be the most welcome piece of mail anyone can receive, and the most joyful to send. In terms of Jewish history, the printed birth announcement is a relatively recent custom.

In general, birth announcements tend to be simpler than wedding announcements, mostly because you want to get the news out as quickly as possible. They are usually sent out within a month of the baby's arrival. Not everyone is able to meet that short a deadline, however, and it really makes no difference when your cards go out, as people are delighted to get the "official" news whenever it arrives.

There are no rules about what you should or should not say. Etiquette and tradition suggest nothing but the baby's name, the parents' names, date of birth, and the baby's size. Because few people stray from these basics, any personal message is sure to make an impact.

The presence of Jewish or Hebrew elements is an announcement of Jewish identity and pride. The addition of the baby's Hebrew name—in transliteration and/or with Hebrew letters—is the most common way to accomplish this. Similarly, you can give the birth date in both Gregorian and lunar Jewish dates; 5 April 2005—25 Adar II 5765. You might also want to tell people whether yours was a Shabbat baby or whether she was born during a holiday:

> *Yael enunciated her arrival*
> *on the third day of Hanukkah.*
> *26 Kislev 5765—December 9, 2004*
> *Susan, Jordan & Ela Kohn*

Many announcements now mention the person or people in whose honor the baby was named. For example:

> *Karen Appel and Mark Fine*
> *joyfully announce the birth of their son*
> *Avi Appel Fine*
> *May 25, 2005—16 Iyar 5765*
> *Named after Mark's grandfather, Abraham Fine*

> *We have a daughter!*
> *Dory Rebecca is named after*
> *Marty's grandmother Rivka*
> *and Esther's grandfather Dov*

While it is customary to include the baby's weight and length at birth on the announcement, some parents omit this mundane information in favor of more personal and evocative details: "Leora was born with a full head of soft, dark hair." Or, "When Michael was born, he did not cry, but opened his eyes and looked around the room until he seemed to find our faces." Or, "Ben has the long fingers and toes of his father's family and shares the gift of healthy lungs with his big brother Adam." Or, "Mimi is a good eater and, thank God, a good sleeper!"

Parents sometimes add a phrase from the Bible, in English or both English and Hebrew. If your baby has a biblical name, you might search out a line that mentions it. For example, "He was called Solomon, and the Lord loved him," or "Awake Devorah and sing." To find such a quotation, check a biblical concordance or ask your rabbi or cantor.

The Book of Psalms and the Song of Songs are full of graceful phrases, as are the poems and prayers you'll find in *"Brit Milah," "Brit Bat," "Hiddur Mitzvah*—Beautiful Touches," and "Adoption." A few favorites from various sources include the following:

For this child we have prayed.
I Samuel 1:27

Light shine upon us
Our people have increased
And our joy is made great
For we have borne a child
May there be no end of peace.
Isaiah: 9:1–2

With each child, the world begins anew.
Midrash

By the breath of children God sustains the world.
Shabbat 119b

Today is the birthday of the world.
Rosh Hashanah liturgy

This little child, may he (she) grow big.
The daily prayer book

A good name is better than great riches.
Proverbs 22:1

How shall we bless her?
With what will this child be blessed?
With a smile like light,
With eyes, large and wide, to see every flower,
*   animal, and bird,*
And a heart to feel all she sees.

Adoption announcements bring the same good news as birth announcements: a new member of the family has arrived, and there is a new member of the Jewish people in the world. The suggestions and quotations above all apply to the announcement of an adoption, including the custom of noting the baby's familial namesake(s).

Some adoption announcements do not make any mention of adoption at all, while others make a point of it. You can, for example, note two dates: the child's birthday and the date of his or her arrival home. If yours is an international adoption, place of birth might be included. And some parents incorporate names that were given to their children before adoption. A few examples follow.

195

Alexander Micah
Born: December 12, 2004, in Bogota, Columbia
Arrived home: February 18, 2005

Our daughter is home!
Rachel Susan Feldman-Bright
born
Seong Ae Han
(Beauty and Sincerity)
She is a gift and a wonder. (Psalms)

Not by our planting
But by heaven, our harvest
Nina Maya Gruber.
For this child we have prayed. (I Samuel 1:27)

Alice and Philip Stein
joyfully announce the arrival of their son
Joshua Moshe
born June 15, 2004
adopted July 7, 2004

The creative possibilities for design and decoration are endless. Your wonderful news can be printed inside pink or blue cards from a stationery shop; or you can write personal notes inside museum art cards, compose an announcement on the computer, or have a professional printer set it in type.

Some calligraphers do baby announcements, and those who create designs in English and Hebrew are most easily found on the Internet or in a local Jewish newspaper. If your wedding invitation was the work of a calligrapher, you might get in touch for this assignment. If you don't know where to begin looking for a calligrapher, your rabbi may be able to recommend someone.

If you opt for a calligrapher, it's a good idea to be in touch in advance of the baby's birth. Some couples who know their child's sex and have selected the child's name commission the whole announcement in advance and simply call the calligrapher with relevant details once the baby is born. Others select a design, give the artist a boy's name and a girl's name, and phone with the final outcome. (See the appendix for a directory of the artists whose work appears on these pages.)

Artist: Peggy Davis

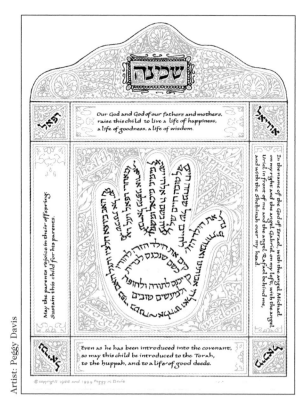

Artist: Peggy Davis

With God's blessing,
יברכך ה'
be kept safe always
וישמרך
With God's grace, see the
יאר ה' פניו
light of the Creator
אליך ויחנך
around you
ישא ה' פניו אליך
With God's favor, find peace
וישם לך שלום
and wholeness in this world

NUMBERS VI

In celebration of the birth of
Rachel Batya Stein
daughter of Susan and Alfred Stein
רחל בתיה בת עזרא ושדה לאה
April 5, 2004 · 13 Nisan 5765

Artist: Jonathan Kremer

WITH GOD'S GRACE, SEE THE LIGHT OF THE CREATOR AROUND YOU

WITH GOD'S FAVOR, FIND PEACE AND WHOLENESS IN THIS WORLD

WITH GOD'S BLESSING, BE KEPT SAFE ALWAYS

WELCOME! ברוך הבא!

In celebration of the birth of
Daniel Alexander Wolf
son of Laura Sterner and Mark Wolf
born on October 22, 2004
דניאל אברהם בן מאיר הלוי ואליעבע
י"ב חשון תשס"ה

Artist: Jonathan Kremer

199

Artist: Mickie Caspi

Artist: Elaine Adler

With each child the world begins anew
Midrash

Matthew and Miriam
joyfully welcome

Eve Madeline Askin
חיה מיכל

March 5, 2004 ~ 12 Adar 5764
7:03 a.m.
6 pounds, 5 ounces
18½ inches

200

Kensuke Solomon
Carlo DeLisi

賢輔

שלמה עזריאל בן דניאל וקוקו

born April 5, 2003 ~ Nisan 3, 5763

Daniel
and Koko

God gave Solomon immense wisdom and understanding

ויתן אל הים חכמה לשל מה ותבונה הרבה מאד ורהב לב כחל אשר על שפת הים

and a heart as vast as the sand on the seashore

מלכים א ה:ט ~ Kings I 5:9

כי ברך אברכך והרבה ארבה את זרעך ככוכבי השמים וכחול אשר על שפת הים

Israel·Rachel·Erez·Shelly·Elital·Lior·Hadas·Noam·Alon·Talia·Jennifer·Allison·David·Stephanie·Larry

Jennifer, Alon and Talia Markowitz
joyfully announce the birth of

גבריאל דוד·Gabriel David

ל·שבט שהוא ראש חדש אדר תשס"ב·February 12, 2002
8 lb. 11 oz.

I WILL BLESS YOU, AND YOUR DESCENDANTS WILL BE AS NUMEROUS
AS THE STARS OF THE SKY AND THE SAND UPON THE SEA SHORE.

GENESIS 22:17

201

Celebrations and Customs

Spreading happiness is a basic human impulse and a Jewish mandate. All joyful Jewish life-cycle events do this in a variety of ways.

Tzedakah

Perhaps the most important and beautiful of these customs is the tradition of marking happy occasions like births with charitable donations, or *tzedakah*—a word based on the Hebrew *tzedek,* which means "justice." Judaism does not view charity as an act of personal goodness but as a mitzvah, a holy obligation, and a privilege for the giver. *Tzekadah* is a way of sharing one family's joy while acknowledging that personal happiness is incomplete in a world so badly in need of repair. A donation made to honor the birth of a child is a kind of investment in the happier, more just society we wish for our children. The act of giving in a child's name also expresses a hope that the child will grow up to be a person who gives *tzedakah.*

Among Sephardic Jews, a large tray—the *seneet Eliyahu hanabi* (tray of Elijah the prophet)—decorated with flowers and candles, is passed at a *brit milah.* Guests are expected to fill it with gifts of money, and after the meal, the tray is auctioned off to the highest bigger, who distributes his bid, along with the money collected on the tray, to charity.[3] The reason many Jews make contributions of eighteen dollars or some multiple of eighteen dollars is that the numerical value of eighteen is spelled out with the same Hebrew letters that mean "life"—*chai.*

One way to make *tzedakah* an integral part of your *simcha* is to join with families and congregations that assess a gift of 3 percent of the food costs associated with Jewish celebrations. The money is sent to Mazon, an organization that helps soup kitchens, food pantries, and other feeding programs in the United States and around the world (Mazon: A Jewish Response to Hunger, 1990 S. Bundy Dr., Suite 260, Los Angeles, CA 90025-5232; 310-442-0020; www.mazon.org).

Although it is customary to give money to Jewish organizations, donations can also be made to efforts and institutions that have meaning to your family—from the American Cancer Society to a rabbinical seminary, from AIDS research to Israel bonds.

Many people have trees planted in Israel in honor of a birth. This gesture has a centuries-old precedent: In ancient times, a cypress sapling was planted for the birth of a girl, a cedar for a boy. Later, branches would be cut from those trees for the child's wedding canopy. The Jewish National Fund (www.jnf.org or 888-JNF-0099) will take your order and send an acknowledgement to the baby's family.

Although tradition teaches that *tzedakah* is best given anonymously, a simple announcement of charitable gifts given in the baby's name—as part of the *brit* ceremony, included in a printed explanation of the ceremony, or in a birth announcement—may encourage others to make a contribution on this or a similar occasion. And that would be an extra mitzvah.

Pidyon Haben

Every baby is cherished, but the birth of a first child is an unparalleled experience that marks one of life's great passages into parenthood. *Pidyon haben,* the redemption of the firstborn son, is one of the oldest of all Jewish rituals and celebrates this occasion.

In many ancient cultures, the firstborn child, especially sons, enjoyed special status, a fact that made the tenth plague visited upon the Egyptians in the story of Exodus—the killing of all first-born sons—a truly unspeakable punishment. The exemption of Jewish firstborns on that terrible night placed an obligation on all firstborn Jewish sons thereafter to serve God as members of the Temple priesthood.

Even when priestly service became limited to Levites and their descendants, all firstborn sons were still seen as obligated and thus in need of a ritual release from their duty. This "redemption" was accomplished by asking a *kohane,* a priest or descendant of priests, to accept five shekels in exchange for the son's obligation.

According to Jewish law, *pidyon haben* must take place on the thirty-first day after birth and is required only when a Jewish woman's first pregnancy results in a baby boy.[4] If the mother has previously given birth to a girl, if she has miscarried, or even if the delivery was by cesarean section, the ceremony is not performed.[5]

Like all Jewish ceremonies, *pidyon haben* is very brief, consisting of a few exchanges between the father and a *kohane* or a rabbi. The father presents the baby and offers money, traditionally five silver dollars, as a substitute for giving up his son. The rabbi accepts the offer, announces the substitution ("This is instead of that; this is in exchange for that"), pronounces the Priestly Benediction, and the company proceeds to eat, drink, and be merry.

Until recently, liberal Jews abandoned this custom or observed it perfunctorily. For one thing, the ceremony, in which parents buy their firstborn sons back from a representative of the priesthood, is based on a system of priests and sacrifices that no longer exists. It also treats daughters as nonpersons. However, some parents have revived the custom by focusing on the elements of *pidyon haben* that speak to the powerful feelings of gratitude and awe evoked by a first child.

Pidyon haben has inspired new ceremonies given various names, including *pidyon habat* (redemption of the firstborn daughter), *kiddush petter rechem* (sanctification of the one who opens the womb),[6] and *seder kedushat chaye hamishpachah* (ceremony of consecration to family life).[7] All emphasize the unique experience of becoming parents for the first time and are inclusive of all firstborn children, girls as well as boys, children born by cesarean section or after a miscarriage. The focus is not on redeeming a child from obligations, but on sanctifying and dedicating the child for a life of service. (See the example at the end of this chapter.)

Certain ritual elements of traditional *pidyon haben* are usually maintained, including the presentation of the child to a rabbi or ceremonial leader. The Passover story is also recalled, connecting the beginning of parenthood and the birth of the Jewish people, and there is usually a dialogue between the rabbi and parents that includes an exchange of coins to be donated to a Jewish charity and representing the child's first contribution to the community. And, of course, there is a meal of celebration. Because few people are familiar with the ritual, parents often distribute copies of the ceremony or information explaining its significance.

Pidyon Ceremony

Parent/s:

This is our son/daughter, our firstborn, who opened the womb of his/her mother. As it is written: Consecrate to Me all the firstborn; whatever is the first to open the womb among the people of Israel. (Exod. 13:2)

Having been privileged to realize the fulfillment of the potential for life within us, may our sense of reverence for the sanctity of all life be awakened.

The consecration of the firstborn also serves as a reminder of the Exodus from Egypt. It is written: And when in time to come your child asks you, "What does this mean?" you shall say, "By strength of hand the Eternal brought us out of Egypt, from the house of bondage." (Exod. 13:14)

The experience of the Exodus from Egyptian bondage sensitized our people to the values of human freedom and dignity. May we exemplify these values as we grow together as a family, creating a home where love of Torah, awareness of that which is godly, and compassion for humanity always abide; where the hearts of the parents and the hearts of the children shall always be turned to one another.

Rabbi or leader:

Blessed with the sacred trust of new life, will you dedicate yourselves to the redeeming of life?

Parent/s:

I/we desire that the birth of my/our son/daughter inspire us all to work for the redemption of all life. We express our partnership with that which is godly in the process of *tikkun olam*, world redemption, as we, in honor of the birth of our

Pidyon Ceremony

child _____, *bat/ben* _____ ע׳
_____, present a gift of *tzedakah*. May it be a
symbol of my/our and his/her commitment to Torah, to involve-
ment in the life of our people, and to the upholding of those values that make for human dignity, fellowship, and peace.

Blessed by the presence whose sanctity fills our lives, we
redeem every firstborn and engage in *tikkun olam*.

Parent/s present a gift of *tzedakah* and say:

For a son:

זֶה תַּחַת זֶה, זֶה חָלוּף זֶה, זֶה מָחוּל עַל זֶה.

> *Zeh ta-chat zeh, zeh cha-luf zeh,*
> *zeh ma-chul al zeh.*

For a daughter:

זֶה תַּחַת זֹאת, זֶה חָלוּף זֹאת, זֶה מָחוּל עַל זֹאת.

> *Zeh ta-chat zot, zeh cha-luf zot,*
> *zeh ma-chul al zot.*

> This *tzedakah* instead of greed,
> This gift in place of selfishness,
> This commitment because of the blessing of
> new life.

May my/our son/daughter enter into life, Torah, and a commitment to all that is godly. As he/she has entered into the
covenant, may he/she grow into a life of Torah, *huppah,* and
good deeds.

Parents and guests recite the *Sheheheyanu*, the prayer for
new blessings. After *Kiddush*, the blessing over wine, and
Motzi, the blessing over bread, which is dipped in honey for
a sweet life, the *s'udat mitzvah* is served.[8]

First Days

In the tight-knit communities of the past, the first days of a child's life, especially of a son, were marked by ritual visits to the family's home by relatives, friends, and neighbors. *Shalom Zachar* (peace of the male or son) was celebrated on the first Friday night after the birth of a son. If the baby was born on a Friday evening after Shabbat candles had been lit, people would arrive, unannounced but expected, that very night. Guests assembled in the new baby's home to recite psalms, sing songs, and discuss Torah. Little children were invited to recite the *Shema* (the prayer that declares God's unity) near the cradle. Adult visitors offered prayers on behalf of the new arrival and his mother, tuning the baby's ears to the sound of Hebrew from his first days on earth.

Legend has it that, while in the womb, babies learn the entire Torah, but just before birth an angel causes the infant to forget all he or she knows. *Shalom Zachar* was considered an opportunity to console the baby for this loss.[9]

In addition to gifts of food, friends would bring charms and amulets to banish the evil spirits attracted to newborns, who were thought to be especially vulnerable before *brit milah.*

Today, the first Shabbat of a baby's life may be spent in the hospital, and even if the baby is home, the family may prefer privacy to a house full of guests. However, for those who feel ready for a communal expression of welcome, a *Shalom Zachar* or a *Shalom Nekavah* (peace of the daughter) can be organized by relatives or friends as a brief coffee-and-dessert visit. A blessing over wine, a *Sheheheyanu,* a chorus of "Siman Tov Umazal Tov," and *voilà!* It's a *simcha.*

Shalom Zachar/Nekavah can also provide a model for welcoming an adopted child or a baby brought home after a hospital stay necessitated by medical complications. The first Shabbat evening at home might be an appropriate time for a simple gathering. A shared meal, song, candlelight, and loving support can make an auspicious beginning and a cherished memory.

Another celebration held the night before a *bris* was called *Vach Nacht,* watch night, or *Lel Shemurim,* the night of the vigil. Newborn sons and their mothers would not be left alone for an instant on this night, when they were perceived to be in mortal danger from Lilith and other demons. To protect the little one, a mixture of magic and piety was employed; a minyan (a prayer quorum of ten men) surrounded mother and child, and a chalk circle was drawn on the floor to keep out the demons.

Sephardic Jews celebrate a similar custom called *Zocher HaBris,* "remembering the *bris,*" but without the preoccupation with demons and darkness. In some communities, the night before a *bris* is celebrated with a festive meal in the grandfather's home, complete with dancing and singing. Elsewhere, the celebration is held at the home of the *sandek* and then moves in a torch-lit, singing procession to the home of the new baby.[10] Parents who view the mitzvah of *brit milah* with trepidation report that the presence of sympathetic friends the night before the *bris* can be a comfort.

Another eastern European custom, *Hollekreish,* was borrowed from Christian neighbors and based on ancient pagan custom. The original meaning of the name is obscure. *Kreisch* comes from the German for "scream" or "shriek." And although some rabbis trace *Holle* to the Hebrew *chol* ("profane" or "secular"), it more likely refers to an ancient Teutonic goddess Holle or Holda, who played the part of Lilith in the pantheon of German mythology. *Hollekreish* was probably meant to scare the demon Holle away from a baby and mother until baptism would protect them.[11] In some communities, *Hollekreish* was celebrated only for boys; elsewhere the practice included girls.[12]

The children of the community were invited to the new baby's home on the fourth Shabbat of his or her life, where they assembled around the baby's cradle. The father, cantor, or the children themselves would read selected biblical verses. Then the cradle would be lifted into the air three times, and three times the question would be asked:

> *Hollekreish, Hollekreish; wie soll das*
> *kindchen heissen.*
> What should the little child be called?

The children would shout the baby's name each time and then be rewarded with sweets.

Fear of the evil eye and other dark and malicious spirits prompted many of these customs. In some communities, packets of nuts and sweets were attached to the cradle to keep the spirits occupied. Elsewhere, red ribbons were tied on the crib or even around the baby's wrist. Biblical verses were sometimes posted around the baby's room.[13] The pervasive dread of the *ayn horeh,* evil eye, also made for strange baby etiquette. For example, one would never extol the beauty of a baby, at least not without mentioning some "flaw," spitting three times, or saying, *"Kayn ayn-horeh"* ("Let there be no evil eye"), lest you attract the jealousy of the demon world.

The unspoken awe and fear that surround the mystery of birth are still with us. Many Jews will not buy a layette, have a crib in the house, or allow a baby shower before the birth. When asked why, we claim that our reticence is based on concern that something might, God forbid, happen to the baby and then it would be too painful to have all that paraphernalia around. But then, even thinking such a thought requires that you spit three times to dispel the evil eye. Old superstitions die hard.

First Shabbat

Wherever you find yourself on your first Shabbat with the baby, take a moment to savor the double blessing of the new life and the day of rest. Whether you are still in the hospital or at home, light the candles—perhaps adding a new one for your new son or daughter—hold the baby up to the warm glow, and read:

For All Newborn Children on Their First Shabbat

When the sun sets
And the stars pull an evening blanket
　　across the sky
　　coaxing the world to rest and sleep
　　and us—to dream
We kindle lights
　　Eternal light
　　Remembrance light
　　Shabbat light
The light in children's eyes
Hands cupped over candle's flame
Drawing setting sun inside our souls
We build a memory and a home for light
We bless this moment
　　and give thanks.

Paused between day and night
We breathe a new soul into the world
We take a breath and sing.[14]

　　Rabbi Sandy Eisenberg Sasso

Part 5

The Changing Jewish Family

The Changing Jewish Family

The Jewish community has never been more diverse or more open, which explains why it's difficult to make meaningful generalizations about the nature or shape of "the Jewish family." Adoption and conversion give new visibility to the historical fact that Jews of color have always been part of the people of Israel. Single parents and gay and lesbian parents find ever warmer reception in organized Jewish life. The most far-reaching change, however, is the presence of non-Jewish relatives in the majority of extended Jewish families. Intermarriage, conversion, and open adoption all make it more than likely that at least some of the family guests at the celebrations for your new Jewish baby will not be Jewish.

This is a new level of openness for the Jewish world, which historically was far more homogeneous and insular. And while there is a growing welcome for families that fall outside traditional expectations (married, white, heterosexual couples where both parents were born Jewish), change is always challenging. It is entirely possible that your baby celebration will not meet with a single objection regardless of your family constellation; but sometimes—if the adopted baby is Asian, if the mother chose to conceive and bear a child without a father's participation, if Hannah is going to have two mommies (or two daddies), if Mama is Episcopalian—convening your community to celebrate may raise some eyebrows and temperatures.

Grandparents and other family members—both Jewish and non-Jewish—may be confronting preconceptions, if not prejudices, in a very personal way and in a very public setting. If you suspect that your ceremony and celebration may present such challenges, be sure to give family and friends as much time as possible to get used to the idea. Send a letter or e-mail as soon as you're comfortable announcing your plans, and be as open and positive as possible.

Think of your ceremony as a new beginning for everyone. The arrival of any baby signals a profound shift in any family. As children become parents and parents become grandparents, the family structure realigns. The arrival of a new life, a new generation, a beautiful new baby can provide an opening to an honest, respectful dialogue about differences and decisions of all kinds.

Interfaith Families

Many interfaith families—including intermarried couples and those where one partner has converted to Judaism—enjoy the full support of both extended families in their decision to raise children as Jews. But in some cases, the Jewish ceremony announcing this commitment raises difficult issues, even after a conversion and/or a Jewish wedding preceded the baby's birth.

Whatever the specific circumstances, a public *brit* ritual can stir strong feelings. The prospect of attending a *brit milah,* the covenant of circumcision, may be downright disturbing to non-Jews who have never attended a *bris* and may harbor fears and misconceptions about what's going to happen. Your Jewish ceremony may also remind non-Jewish family members of religious and/or family traditions they will not be sharing with this new child. Some family members may even see your Jewish decisions as signaling a rejection of them and all they stand for, and some Christians genuinely fear for the fate of an unbaptized baby's soul.

It is important to be sensitive and show respect for such concerns. Invite questions, and explain the mechanics and the meaning of any planned ritual. Provide information and offer reassurance. People are often afraid that they will say or do something wrong at a religious ceremony that is new to them, so the more you let them know about what to expect, the better. Giving this book to non-Jewish relatives to read before the ceremony—even before the birth of your baby—might be a good way to prepare them for what's going to happen and why. Consult "Resources for New Parents," and look over the appendixes provided for non-Jewish guests at *brit milah* and *brit bat*.

If a family member says something that seems anti-Semitic, confront the issue directly, giving him or her the benefit of the doubt. Perhaps there has been some misunderstanding. Maybe there are unspoken fears that need to be discussed. This is not to say that you should tolerate bigotry. Try a firm but positive statement: "I'm really surprised to hear you talk that way about Judaism. You raised me to be tolerant of other religious traditions."

Remember to be clear about what you are doing and why, and take the time to reassure your non-Jewish family that your actions are not intended to hurt them in any way and that your choices are not a repudiation of them. Grandparents may need to hear you say the obvious: that you want them to play an important part in your baby's life. Let them know that you want them to share your joy.

You can demonstrate your wish to be inclusive and loving by inviting non-Jewish family members to participate in ceremonies and celebrations in appropriate and comfortable ways. Grandparents and other guests may offer personal prayers or read from nonreligious sources, offer toasts, sing songs, hold or carry the baby into the room, and give treasured gifts. Every ceremony in this book includes readings and prayers that can be read by any honored guest.

Most ceremonies for new babies are held at home, giving parents a great deal of discretion in terms of who participates and how. If a ceremony is going to be held in a synagogue, however, the customs of the congregation should be honored. Thus, if non-Jews are never called up to the *bimah* (the raised platform or altar) on other occasions, they probably will not be called up for a baby-naming.

There are some other roles that are generally limited to Jewish participation. The leader of any Jewish ritual should be Jewish him- or herself. At a *bris*, the role of the *sandek*, the one who holds the baby during the circumcision, traditionally goes to a Jewish man who himself underwent the procedure while being held by another Jewish man. Hebrew prayers and blessings that invoke the idea of being commanded (*asher kid'shanu b'mitzvotav,* "who has commanded us") are recited by Jews, who are "commanded" to perform ritual deeds, or mitzvot. If a rabbi or *mohel* will be participating in the ceremony, you might want to discuss the honors you plan to bestow on non-Jews with him or her.

One important difference between Jewish and Christian birth rituals concerns godparents. In many Christian churches, godparents speak on behalf of the child at a baptism or christening and sometimes agree to act as the child's spiritual guides in the future, especially if the parents are unable to. In the Jewish tradition, however, godparents play a strictly honorary role at the ceremony. There is no real religious significance attached to them.

The party that accompanies your ritual is a wonderful setting to celebrate your family's diversity. While the religious observance should be unambiguously Jewish, the *simcha* can serve to highlight and honor all the aspects of your baby's birthright. By featuring distinctive elements from the non-Jewish family—food, music and dance, songs, ceremonial clothing and gifts, family toasts—you show respect and demonstrate your intention to maintain and teach a sense of pride in your extended family's varied heritage.

For the Non-Jewish Parent of a Jewish Child

Although you and your spouse may have discussed the choice and agreed to raise your child as a Jew, the ceremony that makes this decision public may leave you feeling awkward or confused. You might worry about saying or doing something inappropriate during the ritual, or be concerned about your family's reaction, or wonder how you can affirm a religious tradition that is not entirely familiar to you.

It is important to talk to your spouse about these feelings and to know that you are not alone. Many non-Jews have struggled with the same emotions. To become comfortable with the ceremony itself, learn as much as possible about its history, and then find ways to make it as personally meaningful as you can.

Participate in a fashion that is comfortable for you: read a poem or nonsectarian prayer or even part of a children's book that you love, either during the ritual or at the celebration afterward. Play a favorite piece of music. Make sure the food being served satisfies your tastes and celebrates your ethnic and cultural tradition. Lox and bagels are not mandatory.

Your decision to raise your child as a Jew doesn't imply mastery or expertise. You don't have to "know it all" to provide your child with a Jewish childhood. You and your child have a lifetime in which to explore the tradition, the art, the history, the lore, and the customs—together. Many Reform and Reconstructionist congregations run support groups for interfaith families that provide a safe and helpful forum for non-Jews in the community.

Most important, choosing to give your child an unambiguous sense of identity, history, and community is the act of a loving parent, which is what Jewish children, like all children, need more than anything.

Finally, in cases where a non-Jewish mother has made the decision to raise her child as a Jew, the question of conversion may or may not arise. (This is not an issue for children born of Jewish mothers and non-Jewish fathers, because legally, Jewish status is handed down through the mother.) The Reform and Reconstructionist movements recognize the Jewishness of children in families with a Jewish father when parents are committed to providing a Jewish education and home observance. However, even with this affirmation of patrilineal descent, some parents choose to convert their children formally—with the attendant rituals and celebrants of *brit* and *mikveh*. This is a matter to discuss with input from your rabbi. (Read the section on "Adoption" for more about formal conversion, and consult the "Resources for New Parents" at the back of this book.)

Adoption

We did not plant you, true.
 But when the season is done,
 When the alternate prayers
 For sun and for rain are counted,
 When the pain of weeding
 And the pride of watching are through,
 I will hold you high,
 A shining sheaf
 Above the thousand seeds grown wild.
 Not by our planting,
 But by heaven,
 Our harvest.
 Our own child.

Author unknown

If you turned to this chapter first, you probably already know the statistics: as many as one in six American couples may have difficulty conceiving, which explains why more and more Jews are turning to adoption. But even if you did start reading on this page, remember that nearly all of this book can be helpful for you, too. While this section focuses on some of the issues specific to adoption, the chapters on names, covenant ceremonies, celebrations, and announcements apply to all new parents, whether you meet your bundle of joy in a delivery room, in an orphanage, at an airport, or in an attorney's office.

For many people, adoption is a difficult choice, a last resort. The decision may represent a great loss that some compare to the pain of losing a loved one. Adopting may mean acknowledging that you do not ever expect to have a child of your own flesh. Thoughtful adoption professionals believe that people need to mourn that loss before looking ahead to adoption; fortunately, there are excellent resources available to help. "Resources for New Parents," at the back of this book, includes books for parents facing the challenges of genetic testing, infertility, and pregnancy loss.

People who decide to fulfill the mitzvah of "be fruitful and multiply" through the mitzvah of adoption face a complex process that begins with a series of important questions: International or domestic? Through an agency or privately? Infant or older child? Then comes the paperwork, the home study, and the waiting. Fortunately, you do not have to go through any of this alone. There are welcoming networks of people who have been there before you and can guide and comfort you through the process.

Adoption is no longer a rarity in the Jewish world, nor is it a secret kept from the child and the community. Indeed, adoption is a source of public joy, celebration and ceremony, and *nachas*—a word that conveys the intense and unique pleasure parents take in their children's existence.

Judaism and Adoption

Neither biblical nor rabbinic Judaism provides much guidance for modern couples considering adoption. Jewish law on adoption includes few specific rules or guidance. *Halachah* does address the care of needy children, and the rabbis certainly looked kindly upon the actions of Pharaoh's daughter, who adopted Moses. It has always been considered a mitzvah—a good and holy act—to take orphaned children into one's home, and foster or adoptive parents were expected to assume all the burdens and the rewards of parenthood. The Talmud says, "Those who raise a child are called its parents, and not the ones who conceived it."

What little Jewish law exists on the subject of adoption relates to Jewish orphans, who required assistance from the Jewish community. Today, however, the release of Jewish children for adoption is relatively rare, and most adoptions involve non-Jewish children.

Adopting a non-Jewish child generally raises the question of conversion. Some parents feel that a commitment to raising a child as a Jew is sufficient and that formal conversion rituals are irrelevant, especially for infants. Others feel it is important to follow the spirit and letter of Jewish law, declaring the adopted child as fully theirs and a full member of the Jewish community.

According to Jewish law, conversion to Judaism requires *mikveh* (ritual immersion) for both girls and boys, and *brit milah* for boys; both are traditionally done in the presence of a *bet din,* a rabbinical court of three. The children of a woman who has converted to Judaism are Jewish and are welcomed with the same *brit* celebrations and ceremonies as any other Jewish child.

An uncircumcised adopted male newborn is given a *brit milah* on the eighth day after birth or as soon as possible, in the presence of a *bet din,* one of whom is generally the *mohel,* the person who performs the circumcision. The chapter on *brit milah* contains a full discussion of the practice, laws, and customs pertaining to circumcision, including a special section on *bris* for conversion and adoption. For a baby adopted later than three months of age, the procedure is generally done in a hospital by a physician and under general anesthesia. If a baby was circumcised without religious ceremony, the Jewish ritual is reenacted in a ceremony called *hatafat dam brit,* in which the *mohel* draws a drop of blood from the site of the circumcision and recites the prayers of *brit milah.* This ceremony may be done in the home or synagogue, regardless of the child's age.

Mikveh is required of all converts to Judaism, male and female, adults and children of all ages. Immersion in a *mikveh* is an act of renewal and rebirth and also symbolizes a change of legal status—in the case of conversion, from not Jewish to Jewish. The water of the ritual bath symbolizes the mystical source of all water and thus all life—the river whose source is Eden.[1] The *mayyim hayyim,* or living water, of *mikveh* also represents the physical source of human life, the waters of the womb.

If you live in a temperate climate or if the adoption of your child occurs during the summer, it is perfectly kosher to perform the *mikveh* in any body of fresh, running water. Ponds, lakes, rivers, and oceans are natural *mikvaot.* For many people, the outdoors provides a more spiritually satisfying experience; however, weather, family custom, or rabbinical preference may discourage this option.

Your rabbi can convene a *bet din,* a court of three Jews, generally rabbis, to witness the immersion. Immersion must be total, as it was in the womb. The naked child is held loosely and lowered into the water by one or both of the child's adoptive parents. When the child is raised from the water, the following blessing is recited by one or both parents:

בָּרוּךְ אַתָּה יְיָ, אֱלֹהֵינוּ מֶלֶךְ הָעוֹלָם,
אֲשֶׁר קִדְּשָׁנוּ בְּמִצְוֹתָיו, וְצִוָּנוּ עַל הַטְּבִילָה.

*Ba-ruch a-ta Adonai, Eh-lo-hei-nu meh-lech
ha-o-lam, a-sher ki-d'sha-nu b'mitz-vo-tav,
v'tzi-va-nu al ha-t'vi-lah.*

Praised are You, Adonai, God of all creation, who sanctifies us with Your commandments and commands us concerning immersion.

The *Sheheheyanu* is then recited.

For boys, a *mikveh* appointment is scheduled sometime after the circumcision has healed. *Brit milah* and *mikveh* are delayed if there is the least suspicion of a health risk.

For girls, *mikveh* is the only ritual requirement. Traditionally, girls are named after *mikveh,* either immediately following immersion or sometime later in a ceremony at a synagogue or at home. The chapter on *brit bat* contains many suggestions for celebrating the arrival of a daughter into your lives and into the covenant of the Jewish people.

The overwhelming majority of Jews have their sons circumcised as infants, a practice that is widely followed with adopted infant sons. However, if a child is adopted after infancy, circumcision is a far more difficult decision to make and explain. The fear and pain associated with having the procedure done on a school-age boy cannot be wished away, and some parents refuse to subject a new son to such a bewildering operation. But for others, a decision not to circumcise seems just as wrong. One adoptive parent wrote eloquently of her decision to have two sons, ages seven and eleven, circumcised: "We considered letting the boys grow up and make the decision for themselves. It would have been an easier way out for us as parents," she wrote. However, she and her husband decided to go ahead with the procedure, despite her fears that "it might make them hate Judaism, not to mention make them hate us. I could only say to them that if I did not have them circumcised, I would not be treating them like my true sons ... the same as if they had been born to me as babies."[2]

Although circumcision is performed at the earliest possible date, there is some difference of opinion regarding *mikveh*. It is not uncommon to take newborns to the *mikveh*. If you blow directly into a baby's face, the child will hold his or her breath for the few seconds of immersion. However, some parents prefer to wait until the child is old enough to hold his or her breath. Some have also suggested postponing *mikveh* until a child is preparing for his or her bar or bat mitzvah, so the immersion becomes an intentional rite of passage for a young person preparing to receive and accept the responsibilities of the Torah.

This approach dovetails with Talmudic law regarding converted children. When a child not born to a Jewish mother reaches adulthood (traditionally, thirteen years old for boys, twelve for girls), he or she has the right to affirm or renounce his or her Jewish identity. Legally, the right to renounce expires when a child reaches adulthood.[3]

There are serious objections to the idea of waiting so long, on both halachic and psychological grounds. Without *mikveh,* an adopted child is not legally Jewish. And formally reminding a child who is twelve or thirteen that she or he is not "really" Jewish can create distress during early adolescence, when identity issues can become confusing and even painful. According to *halachah,* a simple declaration of one's Jewish identity at bar or bat mitzvah is sufficient acknowledgment of the Talmudic right to renounce.

Whatever you decide to do about *mikveh,* there is widespread support among adoption professionals, Jewish and non-Jewish, for full disclosure about your child's origins. In the case of international or interracial adoption, there is often no question of concealment; but the same principles apply even if the child resembles his or her adoptive parents. The story of how Mommy and Daddy waited and hoped for little Sarah's arrival, complete with pictures of their airport meeting, can easily become part of a child's sense of who she is and how she belongs.

Names for an Adopted Child

There is virtually no difference in the ways adoptive parents and birth parents select names, which means that when American Jews adopt, they tend to name their children in memory of family members who have died. Typically, a child's full Hebrew name includes his or her parents' names as well, as in *David ben Moshe v'Rivka,* David, the son of Moses and Ruth; or *Gila bat Raphael v'Leah,* or Gila, the daughter of Raffi and Lee. It is much rarer to follow the custom for adult converts, in other words, *David ben Avraham avinu v'Sara imenu,* David the son of Abraham our father and Sarah our mother. This "generic" convert's name was more common in the past, when adopted children were likely to be Jews by birth.[4] (For more about naming customs, see Part 2, "A Jewish Name.")

Who Is a Jew?

For Jews, religious affiliation and commitment are not only a matter of soul and heart, but a legal status as well. According to Jewish law, any person born to a Jewish mother is a Jew. But *halachah* also spells out the ways that any person born to a non-Jewish mother may become Jewish, through study, religious practice, and finally, the rituals of conversion. Even in the most perilous times, Judaism has always opened the door for sincere converts.[5]

Because personal status is a halachic matter, there are profound differences of opinion about how one legally becomes Jewish. Adoptive Jewish parents affiliated with liberal movements (Conservative, Reconstructionist, Reform, Renewal) sometimes worry that their child will not be recognized as a Jew by Orthodox Jews or in the State of Israel.

It is a misconception that Jews-by-choice whose conversions are supervised by non-Orthodox rabbis will be prevented from immigrating to Israel and rejected outright by Orthodox Jews. According to the Israeli Law of Return, citizenship is automatically granted to all Jews who seek it—without regard to affiliation. Any Jew-by-choice who converted under liberal Jewish auspices and "makes *aliyah*" (moves to Israel) will be issued an identity card that declares him or her a Jew. A problem arises only when that person wishes to marry, because in Israel, converts wishing to

עד ימלא שחוק פיד ושפתיד תרועה

איוב ח: כא

©2000 Peggy H. Davis

He fills our mouth with laughter and our lips with rejoicing

Job 8:21

Ron and Risa joyfully announce
the arrival of
Daniel Maxim Stern
שמחה יאיר
named for his maternal great-grandmother
Sarah Schwartz ז"ל
Born in Murmansk, Russia
April 9, 1999
Arrived home December 4, 1999

Artist: Peggy Davis

have a Jewish wedding must prove their Jewishness according to Orthodox standards: the Orthodox rabbinate exercises legal control over issues of personal status for Jewish citizens. (In fact, the same problem exists for all Jewish immigrants who wish to marry in Israel; they are asked to provide proof that their mothers were born Jewish.)[6]

Jews-by-choice find varying degrees of welcome in the Orthodox communities of the Diaspora, but generally, there is no issue until a convert wishes to marry an Orthodox Jew. At that point, an Orthodox conversion may be required.

In order to avoid any challenge to authenticity, some parents seek out Orthodox rabbis in hopes of arranging a conversion that will satisfy the requirements of the entire Jewish world. While there are exceptions, Orthodox rabbis tend to discourage conversion and are, in fact, bound to turn away parents unwilling to commit to traditional practices for themselves and their children.

Whatever your concerns, issues of personal status and identity are complex and personal and are best discussed with your rabbi.

Challenges and Services

Although overt xenophobia and racism is, by and large, socially unacceptable in the Jewish community, there are still some who fear and reject people—even children—who look "different" from what they think Jews "should" look like. This fear finds expression in everything from the garden-variety cruelty that kids display on the playground, to a grandfather who worries that his grandson might one day grow up to marry the Chinese-born Rosenbloom girl.

Such prejudices are withering quickly. Just as the Jewish population in Israel includes black-skinned Ethiopians and blue-eyed redheads from the former Soviet Union, the global Jewish community of the twenty-first century is both taller and blonder, and more petite and darker-skinned than ever before. This is not a departure from the Jewish past, but an expression of the fact that conversion and adoption are ancient, normative elements of our history. The Jewish people has never been a "race"; we are a community that chooses—person by person, generation by generation—to enter into a special, covenantal relationship with God and with other Jews.

While all Jewish parents worry about their children's commitment to Judaism as they grow up (Will they identify as Jews? Will they intermarry?), adoptive families do face particular issues and needs. Most Jewish family agencies provide assistance and offer a spectrum of support services, from culturally sensitive family counseling to Hanukkah parties.

Additionally, all members of adoptive families benefit from contact with other parents and children who share similar histories, questions, and challenges. Just being part of a group of families who look like yours is an important form of validation. The following organizations may be of help:

- *Stars of David International: A Jewish Adoption Information & Support Network* is a non-profit organization providing a compassionate network of support, adoption information, and education to prospective parents, adoptive families, adult adoptees, birth families, and the Jewish community. www.starsofdavid.org 1-800-STAR-349.

- *The Jewish Multiracial Network* brings Jewish multiracial families and individuals together to learn about and celebrate their Judaism, with opportunities for learning, nurturing, and support for a large and growing part of the Jewish community. infoJMN@isabellafreedman.org.

Ceremonies

The adoption of a child is an occasion as momentous as a birth and merits the same attention and care that Jews lavish on all joyous life-cycle events. For parents who wish to have a Jewish ceremony that sanctifies the act of adoption itself, an example is provided at the end of this chapter.

Any and all ceremonies related to an adoptive child's homecoming, including *brit milah, brit bat,* and *mikveh,* may be tailored to honor the special circumstances of his or her arrival. Many parents do this by telling the unique story of how this child came to them, and by reading poems and prayers that address the particulars of the miracle. The poem at the beginning of this chapter, and the prayer that follows, are favorites.

An Adoption Blessing

We have been blessed with the precious gift of this child. After so much waiting and wishing, we are filled with wonder and with gratitude as we call you our son/daughter. Our son/daughter, our child, you have grown to life apart from us, but now we hold you close to our hearts and cradle you in our arms with love. We welcome you into the circle of our family and embrace you with the beauty of a rich tradition.

We pledge ourselves to the creation of a Jewish home and to a life of compassion for others, hoping that you will grow to cherish and emulate these ideals.

God of new beginnings, teach us to be mother and father, worthy of this sacred trust of life. May our son/daughter grow in health, strong in mind and kind in heart, a lover of Torah, a seeker of peace. Bless all of us together within Your shelter of Shalom.

Rabbi Sandy Eisenberg Sasso[7]

Brit Immuts

Covenant of Adoption

The baby is escorted into the room by one or more grand-parents and then is handed to other relatives or friends. The parent/s explain the ceremony and tell the story of the baby's name.

The baby is given to the parent/s, who say/s:

נִשְׁבָּעִים אֲנַחְנוּ בְּשֵׁם מִי שֶׁשְּׁמוֹ רַחוּם וְחַנּוּן שֶׁנְּקַיֵּם אֶת הַיֶּלֶד הַזֶּה
כְּאִלּוּ הָיָה מִזַּרְעֵנוּ יוֹצֵא חֲלָצֵינוּ. וּנְגַדְּלוֹ וְנַחֲזִיקוֹ וְנַדְרִיכוֹ בְּדַרְכֵי
תוֹרָתֵנוּ, כְּכֹל מִצְוֹות הַבֵּן עַל הָאָב וְהָאֵם. יְהִי יְיָ אֱלֹהֵינוּ עִמּוֹ בְּכֹל
מַעֲשֵׂי יָדָיו. אָמֵן, כֵּן יְהִי רָצוֹן.

*Nish-ba-im a-nach-nu b'sheim mi sheh-sh'mo
ra-chum v'cha-nun sheh-n'ka-yeim et
ha-yeh-led ha-zeh k'i-lu ha-yah mi-zar-ei-nu
yo-tzei cha-la-tzei-nu. Un-ga-d'lo v'na-cha-zi-ko
v'nad-ri-cho b'dar-chei to-ra-tei-nu,
k'chol mitz-vot ha-bein al ha-av v'ha-eim.
Y'hi Adonai Eh-lo-hei-nu i-mo b'chol ma-a-sei
ya-dav. A-mein, kein y'hi ra-tzon.*

I/we solemnly swear, by the One who is called loving and mer-ciful, that I/we will raise this child as my/our own. I/we will nurture him/her, sustain him/her, and guide him/her in the paths of Torah, in accordance with the duties incumbent upon Jewish parents. May God ever be with him/her. I/we pray for the wisdom and strength to help this child, _____, become a man/woman of integrity and kindness.

Brit Immuts

For a boy:

הַמַּלְאָךְ הַגֹּאֵל אֹתִי מִכָּל רָע יְבָרֵךְ אֶת הַנְּעָרִים, וְיִקָּרֵא בָהֶם שְׁמִי
וְשֵׁם אֲבֹתַי אַבְרָהָם וְיִצְחָק, וְיִדְגּוּ לָרֹב בְּקֶרֶב הָאָרֶץ.

Ha-mal-ach ha-go-eil o-ti mi-kol rah
y'va-reich et ha-n'a-rim, v'yi-ka-rei va-hem
sh'mi v'sheim a-vo-tai Av-ra-ham v'Yitz-chak,
v-yid-gu la-rov b'keh-rev ha-a-retz.

May the One who saved me from all evil,
bless this boy, and let him be called by our
name and the names of our ancestors, and may
he multiply throughout the land. (Gen. 48:16)

For a girl:

בְּרוּכָה אַתְּ לַיָי בִּתִּי, וְעַתָּה בִּתִּי אַל תִּירָאִי, כֹּל אֲשֶׁר תֹּאמְרִי
אֶעֱשֶׂה לָךְ כִּי אֵשֶׁת חַיִל תִּהְיִי.

B'ru-chah at la-do-nai bi-ti, v'a-ta bi-ti al
ti-ra-i, kol a-sher to-m'ri eh-eh-she lach ki
ei-shet cha-yil tih-yi.

Be blessed of the Lord, daughter! And now,
daughter, have no fear. I will do in your
behalf whatever you ask, for you will be a
fine woman. (Ruth 3:10–11)

Brit Immuts

Parent/s:

יְבָרֶכְךָ יְיָ וְיִשְׁמְרֶךָ,
יָאֵר יְיָ פָּנָיו אֵלֶיךָ וִיחֻנֶּךָּ,
יִשָּׂא יְיָ פָּנָיו אֵלֶיךָ וְיָשֵׂם לְךָ שָׁלוֹם.

Y'va-reh-ch'chah Adonai v'yish-m'reh-cha,
Ya-eir Adonai pa-nav ei-leh-kha vi-chu-neh-ka,
Yi-sah Adonai pa-nav ei-leh-kha v'ya-seim
l'chah sha-lom.

May God bless you and protect you.
May God's presence shine for you and be
favorable to you.
May God's face turn to you and give
you peace.

All:

בָּרוּךְ אַתָּה יְיָ, אֱלֹהֵינוּ מֶלֶךְ הָעוֹלָם,
שֶׁהֶחֱיָנוּ וְקִיְּמָנוּ וְהִגִּיעָנוּ לַזְּמַן הַזֶּה.

Ba-ruch a-ta Adonai, Eh-lo-hei-nu meh-lech
ha-o-lam, sheh-heh-cheh-ya-nu v'ki-y'ma-nu
v'hi-gi-a-nu la-z'man ha-zeh.

Holy One of Blessing, Your Presence fills creation,
You have kept us alive,
You have sustained us, You have brought us to
this moment.

Guests offer personal blessings and prayers. Kiddush is
recited, and the meal is served.[8]

Part 6

The First Year

The First Year

For all parents, the first year of a child's life is a series of milestones. The first smile, the first step, the first word are all breathlessly reported to doting grandparents and half-interested friends alike.

The first year of a Jewish baby's life is also a series of *Sheheheyanus*—the prayer of thanksgiving that greets all sorts of milestones. You can say *Sheheheyanu* after the first full night's sleep as well as before your child's first Passover Seder. As the seasons change during your child's first year, Jewish holidays are experienced and remembered differently: giving Jonathan his first applesauce on Rosh Hashanah; trying to get Dan to look at all the candles on the eighth night of Hanukkah; hauling Shira's diaper bag and playpen to a Purim party.[1]

The Sabbath provides ways to celebrate your newly reconstituted family with sweet and simple rituals that will stay with your children as long as they live. Many families have rediscovered the custom of adding a candle for each child on Friday night. And reciting the traditional Shabbat blessing for children reminds everyone—no matter how cranky or exasperated—of the love that makes you a family.

The traditional Shabbat blessing of children takes place after candle-lighting. Either or both parents say:

For girls:

יְשִׂמֵךְ אֱלֹהִים כְּשָׂרָה רִבְקָה רָחֵל וְלֵאָה.

Y'si-mech Eh-lo-him k'Sarah, Rivkah, Rachel, v'Leah.

May God make you as Sarah, Rebecca, Rachel, and Leah.*

For boys:

יְשִׂמְךָ אֱלֹהִים כְּאֶפְרַיִם וְכִמְנַשֶּׁה.

Y'sim-chah Eh-lo-him k'Ef-ra-yim v'chi-m-na-sheh.

May God make you as Ephraim and Menasheh.†

Some parents add the Priestly Benediction:

יְבָרֶכְךָ יְיָ וְיִשְׁמְרֶךָ,
יָאֵר יְיָ פָּנָיו אֵלֶיךָ וִיחֻנֶּךָּ,
יִשָּׂא יְיָ פָּנָיו אֵלֶיךָ וְיָשֵׂם לְךָ שָׁלוֹם.

Y'va-reh-ch'chah Adonai v'yish-m'reh-cha,
Ya-eir Adonai pa-nav ei-leh-kha vi-chu-neh-ka,
Yi-sah Adonai pa-nav ei-leh-kha v'ya-seim
l'chah sha-lom.

May Adonai bless you and protect you. May Adonai shine the countenance upon you and be gracious to you. May Adonai favor you and grant you peace.

---

* The matriarchs of Judaism.
† The sons of Joseph and Osenath.

Poet Marcia Falk has written a beautiful alternative blessing of the children for use at the Shabbat table:

Blessing of the Children

To a girl: _____ • _____ :לבת
child's name   (שם הילדה)

הֲיִי אֲשֶׁר תִּהְיִי–
וַהֲיִי בְּרוּכָה
בַּאֲשֶׁר תִּהְיִי.

Ha-yi a-sher ti-h'yi
va-ha-yi b'ru-chah
ba'a-sher ti-h'yi.

Be who you are—
and may you be blessed
in all that you are.

To a boy: _____ • _____ :לבן
child's name   (שם הילד)

הֱיֵה אֲשֶׁר תִּהְיֶה–
וֶהֱיֵה בָּרוּךְ
בַּאֲשֶׁר תִּהְיֶה.

He-yei a-sher ti-yeh
ve-he-yei ba-ruch
ba'a-sher ti-yeh.

Be who you are—
and may you be blessed
in all that you are.

—from *The Book of Blessings*

Some parents celebrate their child's first birthday by planting a tree or by making a donation of *tzedakah*—righteous giving, or charity. If you created a *wimpel,* or Torah binder, to honor your child's *brit,* it is customary to take the completed band to your synagogue on or near the child's first birthday as a gift to the congregation.

Weaning

Nursing is a powerful and primal connection between a mother and child. Rabbinic literature used the image of a nursing mother as a metaphor for the bond between God and the people of Israel.[2]

The end of nursing is an important milestone for both child and mother. Weaning can provide an occasion for a celebration that hearkens back to Judaism's first baby and embodies contemporary Jewish women's spirituality.

In the past, when infant mortality was a terribly common fact of life, weaning may have been celebrated with more ceremony than birth or circumcision. There is no mention of a celebration in honor of Isaac's *brit*; the Torah says, "And the child grew and was weaned, and Abraham made a feast on the day Isaac was weaned" (Gen. 21:8). In the Bible, Hannah's prayer of thanksgiving was offered after Samuel's weaning.

Contemporary weaning celebrations tend to be brief, consisting of a series of prayers, personal reflections and commentary, and a meal. Because weaning often takes place over the course of weeks or months, a celebration like this can be scheduled sometime during or after the process, whenever you feel it is time to observe this very personal rite of passage.

Weaning celebrations are held at home, either as part of a Shabbat lunch or incorporated into the ceremony that ends the Sabbath, *Havdalah. Havdalah,* which means "separation," is clearly an appropriate theme. Just as the weekly *Havdalah* sanctifies and celebrates the difference between sacred and secular time, weaning marks a new separation of mother and child.

It is customary to begin the meal at a weaning celebration by having someone other than the mother feed the child his or her first solid food. (A symbolic "first" is fine, too. If your baby is already eating rice cereal, offer a first taste of barley cereal.) The honor of feeding the baby might be given to the father, a sibling, or a grandparent. Another custom associated with this rediscovered rite of passage is the giving of *tzedakah* in the amount of the baby's weight. The gift might be designated for a charity having to do with hunger or children.

Some parents make a point of using white wine for *Kiddush,* symbolizing mother's milk. If the baby has not already been given a *Kiddush* cup, this can be a nice occasion to buy one and offer the baby a first sip from it.

Weaning celebrations can be as simple as the addition of a *Sheheheyanu* on the first Shabbat meal after a full week without nursing. Or you can create a more public milestone, complete with a printed program of readings, songs, and blessings. You might reprise lines or readings from your child's *brit* ceremony, reflecting on the distance between that day and this. The sample ceremony that follows has a big, fun finish.

The familiar lines from Ecclesiastes 3 seem particularly appropriate at weaning:

A season is set for everything, a time for every experience under
  heaven:
A time for being born and a time for dying,
A time for planting and a time for uprooting the planted;
A time for slaying and a time for healing,
A time for tearing down and a time for building up;
A time for weeping and a time for laughing,
A time for wailing and a time for dancing;
A time for throwing stones and a time for gathering stones,
A time for embracing and a time for shunning embraces;
A time for seeking and a time for losing,
A time for keeping and a time for discarding;
A time for ripping and a time for sewing,
A time for silence and a time for speaking;
A time for loving and a time for hating;
A time for war and a time for peace.
A time for nursing, and a time for weaning.

Weaning Celebration

Parent/s:

Just as Abraham and Sarah rejoiced at the weaning of their son Isaac, our hearts, too, are glad that our child has grown into full childhood, sustained in good health by God's gift of milk.

Mother:

בָּרוּךְ אַתָּה יְיָ, אֱלֹהֵינוּ מֶלֶךְ הָעוֹלָם,
אֲשֶׁר פָּתַח אֶת שָׁדַי וְהֵנַקְתִּי אֶת פְּרִי רַחְמִי.

*Ba-ruch a-ta Adonai, Eh-lo-hei-nu meh-lech
ha-o-lam, a-sher pa-tach et sha-dai
v'hei-nak-ti et p'ri rach-mi.*

Blessed are You, God, Ruler of the universe,
who opened my breasts to nurse the fruit of
my womb.

Father/parent/guest:

בָּרוּךְ אַתָּה יְיָ, אֱלֹהֵינוּ מֶלֶךְ הָעוֹלָם,
מְשַׂמֵּחַ הוֹרִים עִם יַלְדֵיהֶם.

*Ba-ruch a-ta Adonai, Eh-lo-hei-nu meh-lech
ha-o-lam, m'sa-mei-ach ho-rim im
yal-dei-hem.*

Blessed are You, God, Ruler of the universe,
who enables parents to rejoice in their
children.

Weaning Celebration

Parent/s:

In love, I/we will continue to give sustenance to my/our child and provide for her/his physical needs. May I/we also provide her/him with spiritual sustenance through examples of loving kindness and through the teaching of Torah and the traditions of our people.

A donation of $_____, two times _____'s weight, has been made to _____ (name of a charity).

Today, we present our child, _____, with a *Kiddush* cup, symbolizing her/his independence from the breast and the hope that she/he will grow to participate in the mitzvah of *Kiddush*.

The blessings over wine and bread are recited, and the baby is given a piece of challah.

Parents break a baby bottle.

Everyone shouts: *Mazal tov!*[3]

Appendix 1:
What Non-Jews Should Know about *Brit Milah*—The Covenant of Circumcision

This appendix restates some of the material found in earlier chapters and provides a general explanation of the ritual and its meaning.

Jews and Christians look at many things differently. We have different theologies, different liturgies, different holiday cycles, and different ways of celebrating the life cycle. Nevertheless, Jews and Christians share many things, and what we share is no less profound than our differences.

We share a belief in a God who can be approached through prayer and worship, a God who loves and is revealed in the Bible and in history. We share a book, the Hebrew Bible, which most Christians call the Old Testament. And both Jews and Christians celebrate religious rituals at the beginning of life.

In virtually all cultures, rituals for babies are moments of sacred initiation, and many share certain elements—especially joy and gratitude for the gift of a new person in the world. Most Jewish and Christian birth rituals also bestow a name upon a new baby. By doing this within a religious framework, both traditions give a spiritual dimension to the child's identity.

But there are important differences between the rites of the two faiths. The Christian ritual of baptism, for example, uses water as a sign of identification with the death and resurrection of Jesus and as a sign of welcome into the Christian community. Jewish baby ceremonies, including those that use water, all signify a child's entry into the Jewish covenant with God. The Hebrew word for covenant is *brit.*

Brit refers to the relationship between the Jewish people and God. A covenant is a contract—an agreement between responsible parties, a two-way street. Circumcision is one of the terms of that agreement, which was set forth in the Bible. Since the beginning of the Jewish people, starting with Abraham and Sarah, Jewish parents have been called to welcome their eight-day-old sons into this covenant with a ceremony that is also called *brit.* Girls are welcomed into the covenant with a ceremony called *brit bat,* which features some of the same prayers, songs, and traditions found in *brit milah.*

The covenant of circumcision *(brit milah, brit,* or *bris)* is the oldest continuous Jewish rite, a ritual that unites Jews throughout ages and across cultures and signifies the connection between individual human life and the Holy. With this ancient ceremony, parents announce their commitment to taking on the responsibilities and joys of raising a Jewish son.

The procedure itself may be unsettling to some people, and at most *brisses,* guests who do not wish to watch the removal of the foreskin from the baby's penis may simply avert their eyes or keep their distance during the procedure. However, the circumcision itself is not the core element of the service. It is the blessings and intention to bring the child into what is also known as "the covenant of Abraham" that give the ritual its religious significance. A Jewish male who has not been circumcised is still Jewish—he is considered simply a Jew in need of a *bris.* Likewise, a Jewish male who was circumcised without Jewish rites is considered in need of a symbolic, ceremonial *bris.*

Circumcision itself has been deemed safe by the American Academy of Pediatrics. Circumcision in the home, rather than in the hospital, is also very safe and probably easier on the baby. Although he does feel some pain, the baby's discomfort will be brief (the procedure takes only a few seconds), and he is easily soothed afterward.

The person who performs circumcisions for the purpose of bringing a child into the Jewish covenant is called a *mohel* (pronounced mo-*hail* or *moil*). The *mohel* is not ordained but is trained in the procedures and blessings of *brit milah,* and some are also physicians.

As at a christening, a Jewish boy receives his name at a *bris.* A Hebrew name, which may or may not be different from his English name, will be announced. The Hebrew name is used on religious documents and to summon readers to the Torah, the first five books of the Hebrew Bible. Names are most often given in memory of a loved one who has died, as a tribute.

One interesting difference between Jewish and Christian birth rituals concerns godparents. Christian godparents often have an important religious function, speaking on behalf of the child at a baptism or christening, and sometimes agreeing to act as the child's spiritual guides in the future. In the Jewish tradition, however, godparents *(kvatter* and *kvatterin)* play a strictly honorary role at the ceremony, which often entails little more than bringing the baby into the room or holding him or her during some part of the ritual.

The Hebrew word for joy, *simcha,* is also the Hebrew word for party. A *bris* is a *simcha* that signifies the triumph of life, the promise of a new generation. According to Jewish law and tradition, all life-cycle events include a meal of celebration and expressions of happiness. A joyful heart is the most important gift you can bring to a *bris.*

Appendix 2:
What Non-Jews Should Know about *Brit Bat*—The Covenant for a Daughter

This appendix restates some of the material found in earlier chapters and provides a general explanation of celebrations that welcome baby girls into the Jewish people.

Jews and Christians look at many things differently. We have different theologies, different liturgies, different holiday cycles, and different ways of celebrating the life cycle. Nevertheless, Jews and Christians share many things, and what we share is no less profound than our differences.

We share a belief in a God who can be approached through prayer and worship, a God who loves and is revealed in the Bible and in history. We share a book, the Hebrew Bible, which most Christians call the Old Testament. Both Jews and Christians celebrate religious rituals at the beginning of life.

In virtually all cultures, rituals for babies are moments of sacred initiation, and many share certain elements—especially joy and gratitude for the gift of a new person in the world. Most Jewish and Christian birth rituals also bestow a name upon a new baby. By doing this within a religious framework, both traditions give a spiritual dimension to the child's identity.

However, there are important differences between the rituals of the two faiths. The Christian ritual of baptism, for example, uses water as a sign of identification with the death and resurrection of Jesus and as a sign of welcome into the Christian community. Jewish baby ceremonies, including those that use water, all signify a child's entry into the Jewish covenant with God. The Hebrew word for covenant is *brit.*

Brit refers to the relationship between the Jewish people and God. A covenant is a contract—an agreement between responsible parties, a two-way street. Boys become part of the covenant through the ancient ritual of *brit milah,* the covenant of circumcision. *Brit bat*—which means "covenant for a daughter"—is how parents welcome their infant daughters to this historic holy relationship. The ceremony is also a way of announcing a family's commitment to taking on the responsibilities and joys of raising a Jewish daughter.

Brit bat ceremonies have a long history among Mediterranean and Middle Eastern Jews. In recent years, this ancient tradition has inspired a burst of liturgical creativity, and while there is no single or standard ceremony, certain elements are nearly universal: blessings and prayers, songs and wishes, and a convenant prayer or gesture that enacts the baby's entry into the Jewish people.

One of the most important moments at the ceremony is the announcement of the baby's name. As at a christening, a Jewish girl receives her name at a *brit bat.* Indeed, many ceremonies are called "namings." A Hebrew name, which may or may not be different from her English name, will be announced.

The Hebrew name is used on religious documents and is the name by which Jews are summoned to read from the Torah scroll, which contains the first five books of the Hebrew Bible. Names are most often given in memory of a loved one who has died, as a tribute.

One difference between Jewish and Christian birth rituals concerns godparents. Christian godparents often have an important religious function, speaking on behalf of the child at a baptism or christening, and sometimes agreeing to act as the child's spiritual guides. In the Jewish tradition, however, godparents *(kvatter* and *kvatterin)* play a strictly honorary role at the ceremony, which often entails little more than bringing the baby into the room or holding her during some part of the ritual.

The Hebrew word for joy, *simcha,* is also the Hebrew word for party. A *brit bat* is a *simcha* that signifies the triumph of life, the promise of a new generation. According to Jewish law and tradition, all life-cycle events include a meal of celebration and expressions of happiness. A joyful heart is the most important gift you can bring to a *brit bat.*

Resources for New Parents

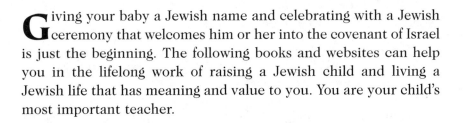

G iving your baby a Jewish name and celebrating with a Jewish ceremony that welcomes him or her into the covenant of Israel is just the beginning. The following books and websites can help you in the lifelong work of raising a Jewish child and living a Jewish life that has meaning and value to you. You are your child's most important teacher.

Pregnancy

Cardin, Nina Beth. *Out of the Depths I Call to You: A Book of Prayers for the Married Jewish Woman.* Northvale, N.J.: Jason Aronson, 1995.

Falk, Sandy, M.D., and Rabbi Daniel Judson. *The Jewish Pregnancy Book: A Resource for the Soul, Body and Mind during Pregnancy, Birth and the First Three Months.* Woodstock, Vt.: Jewish Lights Publishing, 2004.

Frymer-Kensky, Tikva. *Motherprayer: The Pregnant Woman's Spiritual Companion.* New York: Riverhead Books, 1995.

Klirs, Tracy Guren, ed. *The Merit of Our Mothers: A Bilingual Anthology of Jewish Women's Prayers.* Cincinnati, Ohio: Hebrew Union College Press, 1992.

Infertility, Genetic Testing, Pregnancy Loss

The "Jewish" genetic disorders are a group of conditions that are more common among individuals of Jewish descent. Although these disorders can occur in the general population, they do so at a significantly lower rate than in the Jewish population. These devastating genetic conditions include Tay-Sachs disease, Gaucher disease, Canavan disease, familial dysautonomia, Niemann-Pick Type A and B diseases, and cystic fibrosis. For up-to-date information about genetic testing, see www.nfjgd.org and www.jewishgenetics.org.

Cardin, Rabbi Nina Beth. *Tears of Sorrow, Seeds of Hope: A Jewish Companion for Infertility and Pregnancy Loss.* Woodstock, Vt.: Jewish Lights Publishing, 1999.

Dorff, Elliot. *Matters of Life and Death: A Jewish Approach to Modern Medical Ethics.* Philadelphia: Jewish Publication Society, 2004.

Feldman, Emanuel, and Joel Wolowelsky, eds. *Jewish Law and the New Reproductive Technologies.* Hoboken, N.J.: KTAV, 1998.

Gold, Rabbi Michael. *And Hannah Wept: Infertility, Adoption and the Jewish Couple.* Philadelphia: Jewish Publication Society, 1993.

Kohn, Ingrid, Perry-Lynn Moffitt, Isabelle A. Wilkins, and Michael Berman. *A Silent Sorrow: Pregnancy Loss—Guidance and Support for You and Your Family.* New York: Routledge, 2000.

See also *The Jewish Pregnancy Book* (complete details on previous page).

Brit Rituals

Breger, Jennifer, and Lisa Schlaff. *The Orthodox Jewish Woman and Ritual: Options and Opportunities.* New York: Jewish Orthodox Feminist Alliance, 2000.

Cohen, Debra Nussbaum. *Celebrating Your New Jewish Daughter: Creating Jewish Ways to Welcome Baby Girls into the Covenant—New and Traditional Ceremonies*. Woodstock, Vt.: Jewish Lights Publishing, 2001.

Janner-Klausner, Laura, ed. *Neshama Hadasha/A New Life: An Anthology of New Birth Celebrations from Kehilat Kol Haneshamah*. Jerusalem: Kehilat Kol Haneshama, 1999.

Klein, Michele. *A Time to Be Born: Customs and Folklore of Jewish Birth*. Philadelphia: Jewish Publication Society, 1998.

Kunin, Samuel A., M.D. *Circumcision: Its Place in Judaism, Past and Present*. Los Angeles: Isaac Nathan Publishing, 1998.

Mark, Elizabeth Wyner. *The Covenant of Circumcision: New Perspectives on an Ancient Jewish Rite*. Hanover, N.H.: University Press of New England, 2003.

Orenstein, Rabbi Debra, ed. *Lifecycles, Vol. 1: Jewish Women on Life Passages & Personal Milestones*. Woodstock, Vt.: Jewish Lights Publishing, 1998.

www.ritualwell.org, for information on innovative Jewish rituals, including welcoming ceremonies for girls and for boys.

www.beritmila.org, or call 1-800-899-0925 x4291, for information about the Reform *mohel* program, including local listings.

Jewish Parenting

Abramowitz, Yosef, and Susan Silverman. *Jewish Family and Life: Traditions, Holidays, and Values for Today's Parents and Children*. New York: Golden Books, 1998.

Dardashti, Danielle, and Roni Sarig. *The Jewish Family Fun Book: Holiday Projects, Everyday Activities, and Travel Ideas with Jewish Themes*. 2nd ed. Woodstock, Vt.: Jewish Lights Publishing, 2008.

Diamant, Anita, and Howard Cooper. *Living a Jewish Life: Jewish Traditions, Customs and Values for Today's Families.* New York: HarperCollins, 1996.

Diamant, Anita, with Karen Kushner. *How to Be a Jewish Parent: A Practical Handbook for Family Life.* New York: Schocken Books, 2000.

Fuchs-Kreimer, Rabbi Nancy. *Parenting as a Spiritual Journey: Deepening Ordinary and Extraordinary Events into Sacred Occasions.* Woodstock, Vt.: Jewish Lights Publishing, 1998.

Jewish Lights Publishing, ed. *The New Jewish Baby Album: Creating and Celebrating the Beginning of a Spiritual Life—A Jewish Lights Companion.* Woodstock, Vt.: Jewish Lights Publishing, 2003.

Mogul, Wendy. *The Blessing of a Skinned Knee: Using Jewish Teachings to Raise Self-Reliant Children.* New York: Penguin Compass, 2001.

www.dannysiegel.com, for books by Danny Siegel about teaching *tzedakah* to kids of all ages.

Interfaith and New-Tradition Families

Cowan, Paul, and Rachel Cowan. *Mixed Blessings: Overcoming the Stumbling Blocks in an Interfaith Marriage.* New York: Doubleday, 1989.

Diamant, Anita. *Choosing a Jewish Life: A Handbook for People Converting to Judaism and for Their Families and Friends.* New York: Schocken Books, 1998.

Friedland, Ronnie, and Edmund Case. *The Guide to Jewish Interfaith Family Life: An InterfaithFamily.com Handbook.* Woodstock, Vt.: Jewish Lights Publishing, 2001.

Gillman, Rabbi Neil. *The Jewish Approach to God: A Brief Introduction for Christians.* Woodstock, Vt.: Jewish Lights Publishing, 2004.

Kushner, Rabbi Lawrence. *Jewish Spirituality: A Brief Introduction for Christians.* Woodstock, Vt.: Jewish Lights Publishing, 2001.

Olitzky, Rabbi Kerry M. *Introducing My Faith and My Community: The Jewish Outreach Institute Guide for the Christian in a Jewish Interfaith Relationship.* Woodstock, Vt.: Jewish Lights Publishing, 2004.

Olitzky, Rabbi Kerry M., and Rabbi Daniel Judson. *Jewish Ritual: A Brief Introduction for Christians.* Woodstock, Vt.: Jewish Lights Publishing, 2005.

Olitzky, Rabbi Kerry M., with Joan Peterson Littman. *Making a Successful Jewish Interfaith Marriage: The Jewish Outreach Institute Guide to Opportunities, Challenges and Resources.* Woodstock, Vt.: Jewish Lights Publishing, 2003.

www.interfaithfamily.com: Interfaith Family.com.

www.joi.org: Jewish Outreach Institute.

www.starsofdavid.org, 800-STAR-349: Stars of David International: A Jewish Adoption Information & Support Network. Adoption information and education for prospective parents, adoptive families, adult adoptees, birth families, and the Jewish community.

www.jewishmultiracialnetwork.org: The Jewish Multiracial Network brings Jewish multiracial families and individuals together to learn about and celebrate their Judaism.

Notes

Part 1: *Chai*—Life

1. For a fuller explanation of the bridal *mikveh,* see Anita Diamant, *The New Jewish Wedding* (New York: Simon & Schuster, 2001), pp. 149–156.

2. Written in 2003 by the ritual creation team of Mayyim Hayyim Living Waters Community Mikveh and Education Center in Newton, Massachusetts, www.mayyimhayyim.org.

3. This prayer comes from a *mikveh* celebration entitled "The Voice of God Echoes Across the Waters" by Rabbi Barbara Penzner and Rabbi Amy Small. (Originally published in *Reconstructionist* magazine, September, 1986, pp. 25–28.) Used with permission of the authors.

4. *Eshet chayil,* "a woman of valor," is the phrase that begins a set of the verses from the Book of Proverbs, a list of praises for a good woman's virtues, that is traditionally recited by husbands to wives on Friday night. For a beautiful rendition, see "*Eshet Chayil,* A New Version" by Susan Grossman, which includes blessings from wife to husband, in Diamant, *New Jewish Wedding,* pp. 229–30.

5. Mark Zborowski and Elizabeth Herzog, *Life Is with People* (New York: Schocken Books, 1952), p. 312.

6. Thanks to Ilana Garber.

7. Zborowski and Herzog, *Life Is with People*, pp. 313–17. According to Jewish folklore, Lilith, Adam's first wife, was punished for her behavior with the awful fate of having to give birth to multitudes of demon babies, who were then murdered. Lilith took a grisly revenge by killing Jewish newborns.

8. Rabbi David Simcha Rosenthal, *A Joyful Mother of Children* (Jerusalem: Feldheim Publishers, 1982).

9. Nina Beth Cardin, *Out of the Depths I Call to You: A Book of Prayers for the Married Jewish Woman* (Northvale, N.J.: Jason Aronson, 1992), pp. 72–77.

10. Rabbi Judy Shanks, © 1983. Recited as part of the *Sh'ma al Ha-Mitah*. Reprinted with permission of the author.

11. Shoshana Zonderman, "Spiritual Preparation for Parenthood," *Response* 14, no. 4 (Spring 1985): 29–39.

12. For more about Rosh Hodesh groups, see Carol Diament, *Moonbeams: A Hadassah Rosh Hodesh Guide* (Woodstock, Vt.: Jewish Lights Publishing, 2000) and Penina V. Adelman, *Miriam's Well: Rituals for Jewish Women around the Year* (New York: Holmes and Meier Publishers, 1996).

13. *Kol Haneshamah, Shirim Uvrahot—Songs, Blessings and Rituals for the Home* (Wyncote, Penn.: The Reconstructionist Press, 1991), pp. 114–15. Used with permission of the publisher. According to the authors of this new blessing, Seth Riemer, Betsy Platkin Teutsch, and David Teutsch, "While it is crafted from biblical verses and rabbinic prayer forms, the synthesis that it embodies is something new. It emerges from a recognition that, because of our distinct gender roles, generally women were excluded from the prayer-house and men from the birthing room. Both were shortchanged. Today we are enriched by the possibility of sharing in both experiences. This affords an opportunity for new words of prayer. These express the joy and wonder of birth."

Part 2: A Jewish Name

1. Nathan Gottlieb, *A Jewish Child Is Born* (New York: Bloch Publishing Co., 1976), p. 111.

2. Alfred Kolatch, *The Complete Dictionary of Hebrew and English First Names* (Middle Village, N.Y.: Jonathan David Publishers, 1984), p. xi.

3. Benzion C. Kaganoff, *A Dictionary of Jewish Names and Their History* (Northvale, N.J.: Jason Aronson, 1996), p. 49.

4. Rabbi Herbert C. Dobrinsky, *A Treasury of Sephardic Laws and Customs* (New York: Yeshiva University; Hoboken, N.J.: Ktav, 1986), p. 4.

5. Kaganoff, *Dictionary of Jewish Names,* p. 53.

6. Dobrinsky, *Sephardic Laws and Customs,* p. 61. The history of Jewish surnames is another fascinating story. It was not until the Middle Ages that European Jews added family names, mostly to facilitate dealings with the non-Jewish world. In Northern Europe, Jews did not take family names until the nineteenth century, and then usually under compulsion by Christian governments.

7. Ibid., p. 4.

8. According to Rabbi David Kline: "Clearly the name is not from the canon, i.e., from Bible or other classic literature. Kolatch defines 'Liana:' from the French, meaning, 'to bind, wrap around.' Akin to the Latin form, meaning 'a tree with creeping vines.' The Hebrew 'li' certainly means 'to me' or 'my.' 'Ana' (with ayin) has one fairly rare and specialized meaning: 'sing loudly, joyfully,' as in 'Sing thanks joyfully to the Lord' (Ps. 147:7); 'Miriam sang loudly to them …' (Exod. 15:21); 'I hear loud singing …' (Exod. 32:18); 'In that day they shall sing joyfully …' (Isa. 27:2). Understanding Liane as 'my joy' is a bit of a stretch, but stretching is healthy."

9. *The New Jewish Baby Album* (Woodstock, Vt.: Jewish Lights Publishing, 2003) is especially appropriate.

10. In the past, Jews tended to adopt Jewish children, which made family status an issue. The ancient ritual statuses of *kohane* and Levite (groups for whom certain special laws and privileges are in effect) are inherited from one's biological parents only. Thus, the adoptive child of Cohen or Levine parents would be called to the Torah as "son of Abraham and Sarah," the generic convert's name. Because the vast majority of children adopted by Jewish parents today are not born Jews, this is rarely a consideration.

Part 3: *Brit*—Covenant

Brit Milah—The Covenant of Curcumcision

1. Lawrence K. Altman, "Pediatricians Find Medical Benefit to Circumcision," *The New York Times*, March 6, 1989.

2. The Internet is full of anti-circumcision websites. Most critics do make a distinction between circumcision for religious reasons and medical removal of the foreskin. For a thoughtful consideration of the Jewish practice, see Elizabeth Wyner Mark, *The Covenant of Circumcision: New Perspectives on an Ancient Jewish Rite* (Hanover, N.H.: University Press of New England, 2003), a collection of essays from a variety of perspectives.

3. Moses Maimonides, *Guide for the Perplexed,* trans. M. Friedlander (New York: Dover, 1956), p. 378.

4. American Academy of Pediatrics Task Force on Circumcision, "Circumcision Policy Statement," *Pediatrics* 103, no. 3 (1999): 686–93.

5. A survey of adult males using self-report suggests more varied sexual practice and less sexual dysfunction in circumcised adult men. There are anecdotal reports that penile sensation and sexual satisfaction are decreased for circumcised males. Masters and Johnson noted no difference in exteroceptive and light tactile discrimination on the ventral or dorsal surfaces of the glans penis between circumcised and uncircumcised men.

Notes
bla
Notes

6. "Sucrose on a pacifier has been demonstrated to be more effective than water for decreasing cries during circumcision" (American Academy of Pediatrics). See also Samuel A. Kunin, *Circumcision: Its Place in Judaism Past and Present* (Los Angeles: Isaac Nathan Publishing, 1998), pp. 29–30.
8. For information about the Reform *mohel* program, including listings, see www.beritmila.org or call 800-899-0925 x4291.
9. The traditional practice of circumcision was even more dramatically sexual. The halachicly prescribed practice of *metitzah*—the drawing of blood away from the wound—was, for centuries, accomplished by the *mohel* with his lips. The erotic and homoerotic suggestions in that act are clearly disturbing. *Mohalim* now either omit *metitzah* or use a pipette to remove the blood ritually.
10. Exodus 4:24–26.
11. Theodore H. Gaster, *The Holy and the Profane: Evolution of Jewish Folkways* (New York: UAHC Press, 1998), pp. 53–54.
12. Rabbi Paysach J. Krohn, *Bris Milah: Circumcision—The Covenant of Abraham* (Brooklyn: Mesorah Publications, 1969), pp. 62–63.
14. Hayyim Schauss, *The Lifetime of a Jew throughout the Ages of Jewish History* (New York: UAHC Press, 1998), p. 33.
16. Charles Weiss, "A Worldwide Survey of the Current Practice of *Milah*," *Jewish Social Studies*, no. 24 (1962), p. 43. The United Kingdom is one of few places with a system for training and regulating of *milah*, begun in 1745 in London. *Mohalim* must pass both a medical examination and a test given by a religious court.
17. Isserles, *Shulchan Aruch, Yore Deah* 264:1: "A man should seek around to find the best and most pious *mohel* and *sandek*."

18. Nathan Ausubel, *The Book of Jewish Knowledge* (New York: Crown Publishers, 1962), p. 114.

19. Krohn, *Bris Milah*, p. 98.

20. Elijah's chair may be a vestigial link to the very ancient custom of leaving out food, tables, and chairs to appease pagan household gods (Schauss, *Lifetime of a Jew,* pp. 36–37).

21. Krohn, *Bris Milah*, pp. 131–32. This passage is often left untranslated and, in some revised ceremonies, even replaced with other citations from Torah and Talmud. The line "I saw you wallowing in your blood" invites all kinds of interpretation. The mention of blood, forbidden by Jewish law in so many other contexts, seems to affirm the physical reality of human life, which includes danger, dread, and death, as well as spiritual aspirations. According to tradition, this passage connects the covenant of *milah* with the covenant of the Hebrew people forged by the physical suffering during the Egyptian captivity. Similarly, the repeated line "because of your blood you shall live" is linked to two signs of Jewish peoplehood: the blood of *milah* and the blood of the paschal offering.

22. Ibid., p. 125.

23. From a ceremony by Rabbi Edward Treister and Rochelle Treister, June 17, 1986, Houston, Texas. Text © Rabbi Edward S. Treister, used with permission.

24. Based on the ceremony by Rabbi Sandy Eisenberg Sasso. The same introductory reading (changed for gender) is used in her *Brit B'not Yisrael* ceremony.

25. Based on a ceremony compiled from many sources, by Rabbi Elaine Zecher and David Eisenberg, for the birth of their son, Jacob Zecher Eisenberg.

Brit Bat—Welcoming Our Daughters

I have tried to give credit to everyone whose words appear in this chapter. However, because of the amount of sharing, copying, and rewriting that typify *brit bat,* someone may find his or her words uncredited or miscredited. For this, I apologize.

I must acknowledge the pioneering work of the Jewish Women's Resource Center, a project of the National Council of Jewish Women, New York section, for their library, which produced the pamphlet "Birth Ceremonies," a groundbreaking source.

Thanks to all the parents and rabbis who shared insights and ceremonies with me. Among them are Fern Amper and Eli Schaap, Aliza Arzt, Rabbi Albert Axelrad, Naomi Bar-Yam, Judith Baskin, Rabbi Gordon Freeman, Randee Rosenberg Freidman, Stanley H. Hellman, Rabbi Rebecca Jacobs, Carol and Michael Katzman, Judith May, Rabbi Barbara Penzner, Rabbi Jeffrey A. Perry-Marx, Rabbi Sandy Eisenberg Sasso, Rabbi Daniel Siegel and Hannah Tiferet Siegel, Rabbi Paul Swerdlow, Rabbi Edward Treister and Rochelle Treister, and Rabbi Elaine Zecher.

26. Raba, son of Rabbi Hana, said to Abaye, "Go forth and see how the public are accustomed to act" (*Seder Zeraim, Brachot* 45b).

27. One revisionist reading attributes the longer period of ritual impurity for the mothers of daughters to the fact that giving birth to a birth-giver represents a more powerful encounter with the source of life, which requires a longer separation from the mundane.

28. Jewish Women's Resource Center, "Birth Ceremonies, *Brit Banot*; Covenant of Our Daughters" (New York, 1985), p. 2.

29. Blu Greenberg, *How to Run a Traditional Jewish Household* (New York: Simon and Schuster, 1983), p. 248.

30. Dobrinsky, *Sephardic Laws and Customs,* pp. 3–25.

31. Toby Fishbein Reifman with Ezrat Nashim, *Blessing the Birth of a Daughter: Jewish Naming Ceremonies for Girls* (Englewood, N.J.: Ezrat Nashim, 1978), p. 27, quoting an unpublished paper by Rabbi Marc Angel of the Spanish and Portuguese Synagogue in New York.

32. Ibid., pp. 26–27. From the ceremony that appears in the *Daily and Sabbath Prayer Book,* ed. Dr. David de Sola Pool (New York: Union of Sephardic Congregations).

33. Debra Cantor and Rebecca Jacobs, "Brit Banot," *Kerem: Creative Explorations in Judaism* (Winter 1992–93), p. 47. This article includes a *brit bat* ceremony with choices for three different covenant "actions." This work was produced at the behest of the Rabbinical Assembly, the association of Conservative movement rabbis, in preparation for a new rabbi's manual. All citations from this article are protected by the copyright of the Rabbinical Assembly, © 1998. The author would like to thank the Rabbinical Assembly for giving permission to quote from this work.

34. *Shir HaShirim Rabbah* 1:24.

35. Sasso. This is one of the earliest covenantal blessings, first used in the early 1970s, written by Rabbi Sandy Eisenberg Sasso and Rabbi Dennis Sasso.

36. Proposals for a ritual drawing of blood to parallel *brit milah* have been suggested but have never met with any enthusiasm.

37. *Brit rehitzah* was written by Rabbis Rebecca Alpert, Nancy Fuchs-Kreimer, Linda Holtzman, Sandy Levine, Joy Levitt, Debbie Prinz, Ruth Sohn, Marjorie Yudkin, and Debbie Zecher. The ceremony was first published in *Menorah,* 1983. A long excerpt from the ceremony appears in Susan Weidman Schneider, *Jewish and Female* (New York: Simon and Schuster, 1983), pp. 124–27. *Brit mikvah,* a ceremony by Sharon and Michael Strassfeld, includes the immersion of the baby in a tiny *mikveh.* It can be found in Reifman, *Blessing the Birth of a Daughter,* pp. 16–22.

38. Cantor and Jacobs, "Brit Banot," pp. 49–50. Reprinted by permission of the Rabbinical Assembly, © 1998.

39. Ibid., pp. 50–52. Reprinted by permission of the Rabbinical Assembly, © 1998.

40. Pamphlet from the Eleanor Leff Jewish Women's Resource Center, a project of the National Council of Jewish Women New York section.

41. Excerpted from a ceremony by Judith Baskin and Warren Ginsberg, written for their daughter and celebrated on October 13, 1985.

42. Excerpted from a ceremony for Rivka Yael by Rabbi Edward S. Treister, © 1986. Reprinted with permission.

43. Excerpted from a ceremony by Rabbi Jeffrey Marx, written for his daughter, Sarah Beth, and celebrated on September 18, 1983. Rabbi Marx credits the following sources: *brit banot* by Janet Ross Marder; *brit habat* by Sue and Stephen Elwell, *brit rehitzah,* and *Gates of the House,* a publication of the Central Conference of American Rabbis. The grandparents' prayer was written by Rabbi Sandy Eisenberg Sasso.

44. For Shabbat ceremonies, the Siegels suggest lighting two 24-hour candles on Friday afternoon, holding the baby up to the lights, and saying, "May her eyes be enlightened by Torah."

45. By Ronald Laye, at the naming of his daughter, Devora. Used with permission.

46. Adapted from the Sephardic prayer book.

47. Excerpted from a ceremony by Hanna Tiferet Siegel and Rabbi Daniel Siegel.

48. Selections by Rabbi Debra Cantor and Rebbeca Jacobs on *simhat bat* adapted from *Moreh Derekh,* the Rabbinical Assembly's Rabbi's Manual, edited by Rabbis Perry R. Rank and Gordon M. Freeman, © 1998 by the Rabbinical Assembly, page 228.

Hiddur Mitzvah—Beautiful Touches

49. Krohn, *Brit Milah,* p. 96.

50. Ibid., p. 96.

51. Rabbi Fred V. Davidow, "Blessing of a Newborn-Child." Rabbi Davidow suggests the parents alternate lines and read the last one together.

52. Use a piece of cotton, silk, linen, or wool as a swaddling blanket or as a covering for a table or pillow used at the *brit*. Later, create a strip seven to eight inches wide and nine to twelve feet long and decorate it as you wish, noting the child's name and birth date. For ideas, consult books and stores that sell Jewish needlepoint kits, and look at patterns used on challah covers, tablecloths, and the like.

53. Thanks to Cantor Robert Scherr, of Temple Israel in Natick, Massachusetts, for his assistance.

54. Danny Siegel, originally published in *Unlocked Doors* (Spring Valley, NY: Town House Press), © 1983. Reprinted with the permission of the author. Danny Siegel, who wrote this and other poems that appear in this book, is also a *tzedakah* teacher and the founder and prime mover behind the Ziv Tzedakah Fund, a nonprofit organization that from 1981 to 2009 collected and distributed funds to various little-known grassroots projects in Israel and in the United States. Ziv ("radiance") provided money and support for individuals and programs providing direct services to the needy. Ziv has supported an Israeli woman who cares for children with Down syndrome, a Philadelphia teenager who single-handedly began a campaign to help homeless people, and a synagogue shelter in North Carolina. Siegel is also involved in bringing the message of *tzedakah* to communities and schools throughout the United States, Canada, and Israel.

55. Danny Siegel, originally published in *Unlocked Doors*, © 1983. Reprinted with the permission of the author.

56. Danny Siegel, originally published in *Unlocked Doors*, © 1983. Reprinted with the permission of the author.

57. Danny Siegel, originally published in *A Hearing Heart* (Pittsboro, NC: Town House Press), © 1992. Reprinted with the permission of the author.

58. Sandy Eisenberg Sasso, © 1988. Reprinted with the permission of the author.

59. Stephanie Loo, © 1985/29 Heshvan 5746. Reprinted with the permission of the author.

60. Joel Rosenberg, © 1979. Written for Benjamin Yosef Novak, on the eighth day of his life, August 8, 1979/15 Av 5739. Reprinted with the permission of the author.

61. Joel Rosenberg, © 1987. Written in honor of Sara Henna Wolf Pollen's birth. Reprinted with the permission of the author.

62. Hanna Tiferet Siegel, © 1985. Reprinted with the permission of the author.

63. Reprinted with permission of the authors.

64. Translation from *Vitaher Libenu,* the prayer book of Congregation Beth El of the Sudbury River Valley, Sudbury, Massachusetts.

65. Original source unknown.

66. Original source unknown.

Part 4: *Simcha*—Joy

1. Dobrinsky, *Sephardic Laws and Customs,* p. 6.

2. A full version of the special *Birkat Hamazon* to follow a *bris* is given in Krohn, *Bris Milah,* pp. 141–60. For a short, English version, see Anita Diamant and Howard Cooper, *Living a Jewish Life* (New York: HarperCollins, 1991), pp. 53–54.

3. Krohn, *Bris Milah,* p. 5.

4. Thirty days was the biblical measure of a child's viability. Babies younger than a month old often died, and it was considered inappropriate to dedicate to God anything or anyone so vulnerable. If the thirty-first day falls on Shabbat or a holiday, the ceremony is postponed until the following day.

5. *Pidyon haben* is not required for firstborn sons whose fathers are either *kohanes* or Levites, or whose mother is the daughter of a *kohane* or Levite father.

6. Rabbi Marc S. Golub and Rabbi Norman Cohen, *"Kiddush Petter Rechem:* An Alternative to *Pidyon Haben," CCAR Journal* (Winter l973), p. 72.

7. Sasso, pp. 23–24.

8. This ceremony is based on one written by Rabbi Sandy Sasso. Also see the ritual by Daniel I. Leifer and Myra Leifer, published in Elizabeth Koltun, *The Jewish Woman: New Perspectives* (New York: Schocken Books, 1976), pp. 26–29.

9. Krohn, *Bris Milah,* p. 73.

10. Ibid., p. 95.

11. Schauss, *Lifetime of a Jew,* p. 46.

12. Leo Trepp, *The Complete Book of Jewish Observance* (New York: Behrman House, 1980), p. 226.

13. For more about Lilith, see Schauss, *Lifetime of a Jew,* pp. 67–74.

14. Rabbi Sandy Eisenberg Sasso, © 1993. Reprinted by permission of the author.

Part 5: The Changing Jewish Family

1. Rabbi Aryeh Kaplan. *Waters of Eden: The Mystery of the Mikveh* (New York: National Conference of Synagogue Youth/Union of Orthodox Jewish Congregations, 1976), p. 35.

2. Janelle Bohrod, "Janelle Bohrod's Story," *Startracks* (Spring 1986), pp. 5–7.

3. The right of renunciation is based on a child's knowledge of his or her origins. Thus, if the adoption has been kept a secret, he or she cannot make an informed decision, and thus his or her Jewish status cannot be settled.

4. Since ritual statuses—like that of *kohane* and Levite—are inherited biologically, the rabbis wanted to be certain there would be no confusion if a Jewish child took the last name of his adoptive Cohen or Levinson parents.

5. See Anita Diamant, *Choosing a Jewish Life* (New York: Schocken Books, 1997), for a fuller discussion of this issue.

6. Converts and immigrants find ways around the law. Many go to Cyprus for a wedding that the Israeli government will then recognize. Russian immigrants in Israel face the same difficulties, and legal experts predict that their numbers will eventually cause a change in the laws. The situation in Israel is fluid and ever-changing. For up-to-date details about this unfolding story, consult the website of the Reform movement's Israel Religious Action Center: www.irac.org. Thanks to Brian Rosman for exploring and explaining the complexities of the Israeli situation.

7. Used by permission of the author.

8. Adapted from a ceremony by Rabbi Daniel Shevitz and Susan Shevitz.

Part 6: The First Year

1. *The New Jewish Baby Album* (Woodstock Vt.: Jewish Lights Publishing, 2003).

2. *Pesikta de Rav Kahana* 12:2.

3. From a ceremony written by Fern Amper and Eli Schaap for their daughter.

Glossary

aleph-bet. Name of the Hebrew alphabet; also, its first two letters.

aliyah. Literally, "to go up." In the synagogue, to be called to the Torah. "Making *aliyah*" refers to moving to the Land of Israel.

Apochrypha. Fourteen "chapters," including the Book of Esther, that were not included in the final version of the Bible, but which are, nevertheless, important Jewish texts.

Aramaic. Ancient Semitic language closely related to Hebrew. The Talmud was written in Aramaic.

Ashkenazic. Jews and Jewish culture of eastern and central Europe.

Baal Shem Tov. Israel ben Eliezer, the founder of Hasidism, the eighteenth-century mystical revival movement.

Baruch ata Adonai. Words that begin Hebrew blessings, most commonly rendered in English as "Blessed art Thou, Lord our God." This book contains a number of alternatives to that translation.

bat. Daughter, or daughter of, as in bat mitzvah, daughter of the commandment. Pronounced "baht."

B.C.E. Before the Common Era. Jews avoid the Christian designation B.C., which stands for "before Christ."

bet din. A court (literally a house of law) of three rabbis that is convened to witness and give communal sanction to events such as conversions to Judaism.

bracha (pl., *brachot*). Blessing(s).

bris. Yiddish for *brit,* the most common way of referring to the covenant of circumcision.

brit. Covenant. In this book, the term applies to covenant ceremonies.

brit milah. The covenant of circumcision.

bubbe. Yiddish word for grandma.

C.E. Common Era. Jews avoid A.D., which stands for *anno domini,* or "the year of our lord."

chai. Life.

challah. Braided loaf of egg bread, traditional for Shabbat, the holidays, and festive occasions.

Conservative. A movement begun in the United States as a more traditional response to modernity than that offered by Reform.

Diaspora. Exile. The dwelling of Jews outside the Land of Israel.

d'rash. Religious insight, often on a text from the Torah.

draydl. A top used for playing a child's game of chance during the festival of Hanukkah.

d'var Torah. Literally, "words of Torah." An explication of a portion of the Torah.

flayshig. Meat food, which, according to kashrut, or traditional laws governing what Jews eat, may not be mixed with dairy products.

Haggadah. The book containing the liturgy of the Passover Seder.

halachah. Traditional Jewish law, contained in the Talmud and its commentaries.

Hasidism. Eighteenth-century mystical revival, a movement that stressed God's presence in the world and the idea that joy could be seen as a way of communing with God.

havdalah. Separation; also, the Saturday evening ceremony that separates Shabbat from the rest of the week.

huppah. Wedding canopy.

kashrut. Traditional system of laws that govern what Jews eat.

ketubah. Marriage contract.

kiddush. Sanctification; also, the blessing over wine.

kippah. Skullcap, *yarmulke.*

kisei shel Eliyahu. Elijah's chair, a ceremonial chair used at a brit ceremony.

kohane. The biblical social class that comprised the priesthood.

kosher. Foods deemed fit for consumption according to the laws of kashrut.

kvatter, kvatterin. Godfather, godmother.

mazal tov. Literally, "good luck." In common use, it means "congratulations."

mensch. Person; an honorable, decent person.

mezuzah (pl., mezuzot). First two paragraphs of the *Shema,* a Jewish prayer, written on a parchment scroll and encased in a small container, affixed to the doorposts of a home.

milah. Circumcision. *Brit milah* is the covenant of circumcision.

milchig. Dairy foods, which, according to kashrut, may not be mixed with meat.

Midrash. Imaginative exposition of stories based on the Bible. Refers to the entire literature and to individual stories.

mikveh. Ritual bath.

minyan. A prayer quorum of ten adult Jews—for traditional Jews, ten men.

Mi Shebeirach. Blessing for healing.

Mishnah. The first part of the Talmud, comprised of six "orders" of laws regarding everything from agriculture to marriage.

mitzvah (pl., *mitzvot*). A sacred obligation or commandment, mentioned in the Torah.

mohel (pl., *mohalim*). One who is trained in the rituals and procedures of *brit milah,* circumcision. Pronounced mo-hail, in Hebrew; moil, in Yiddish.

Motzi. Blessing over bread recited before meals.

nachas. Special joy from the achievements of one's children.

niggun. A wordless, prayer-like melody

Oneg Shabbat. Literally, joy of the Sabbath. A gathering, for food and fellowship, after Friday night synagogue services.

Orthodox. In general use, the term refers to Jews who follow traditional Jewish law. The modern Orthodox movement developed in the nineteenth century in response to the Enlightenment and Reform Judaism.

Pesach. Passover.

pidyon haben. The ceremony of "redeeming" a firstborn son from the ancient obligation of Temple service.

rabbi. Teacher. A rabbi is a seminary-ordained member of the clergy. "The Rabbis" refers to the men who codified the Talmud.

Reconstructionist. A religious movement begun in the United States in the twentieth century by Mordecai Kaplan, who saw Judaism as an evolving religious civilization.

Reform. A movement begun in nineteenth-century Germany that sought to reconcile Jewish tradition with modernity; the largest of the contemporary denominations.

Rosh Hodesh. First day of every lunar month; the New Moon, a semi-holiday.

sandek. Jewish godfather; the one who holds the baby during a circumcision. *Sandeket* is a new term for Jewish godmother.

Shabbat. Sabbath. In Yiddish, Shabbos.

Shechinah. God's feminine attributes.

Sheheheyanu. A common prayer of thanksgiving for new blessings.

Shema. The Jewish prayer that declares God's unity.

Sheva Brachot. The seven marriage blessings.

shtetl. A general name for the small towns inhabited by Ashkenazic Jews before the Holocaust.

simcha. Joy; also, the celebration of joy.

s'udat mitzvah. A commanded meal; the festive celebration of a milestone.

taharat hamishpahah. Laws of family purity prescribing women's sexual availability and the use of *mikveh.*

tallis, tallit. Prayer shawl. *Tallis* is Yiddish, *tallit* Hebrew.

Talmud. Collection of rabbinic thought and laws, compiled from 200 B.C.E. to 500 C.E.

tikkun olam. Repairing the world. A fundamental Jewish concept of taking responsibility in and improving the temporal world.

Torah. First five books of the Hebrew Bible, divided into fifty-four portions that are read aloud and studied in an annual cycle.

tzedakah. Charity; righteous giving or action toward the poor.

Yiddish. Language spoken by Ashkenazic Jews, a combination of early German and Hebrew.

yichus. Family status. Pride in family members' achievements.

Yom Kippur. Day of Atonement, the holiest of the High Holy Days.

Directory of Artists

Elaine Adler
3 Sunny Knoll Terrace
Lexington, MA 02421
scribe@elaineadler.com
www.elaineadler.com

Mickie Caspi
Caspi Cards & Art
P.O. Box 600220
Newtonville, MA 02460
www.caspicards.com

Peggy H. Davis
Adamsville Road
Colrain, MA 01340
Phone/fax 413-624-3204
www.HebrewLettering.com
phd@ganeydn.com

Jonathan Kremer
610-642-6711
www.kremerdesigns.com

Index

Index

Bible Study / Midrash

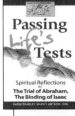

Passing Life's Tests: Spiritual Reflections on the Trial of Abraham, the Binding of Isaac *By Rabbi Bradley Shavit Artson, DHL*
Invites us to use this powerful tale as a tool for our own soul wrestling, to confront our existential sacrifices and enable us to face—and surmount—life's tests.
6 x 9, 176 pp, Quality PB, 978-1-58023-631-7 **$18.99**

The Messiah and the Jews: Three Thousand Years of Tradition, Belief and Hope *By Rabbi Elaine Rose Glickman; Foreword by Rabbi Neil Gillman, PhD; Preface by Rabbi Judith Z. Abrams, PhD*
Explores and explains an astonishing range of primary and secondary sources, infusing them with new meaning for the modern reader.
6 x 9, 192 pp, Quality PB, 978-1-58023-690-4 **$16.99**

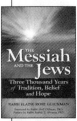

Speaking Torah: Spiritual Teachings from around the Maggid's Table—in Two Volumes *By Arthur Green, with Ebn Leader, Ariel Evan Mayse and Or N. Rose*
The most powerful Hasidic teachings made accessible—from some of the world's preeminent authorities on Jewish thought and spirituality.
Volume 1—6 x 9, 512 pp, Hardcover, 978-1-58023-668-3 **$34.99**
Volume 2—6 x 9, 448 pp, Hardcover, 978-1-58023-694-2 **$34.99**

Masking and Unmasking Ourselves: Interpreting Biblical Texts on Clothing & Identity *By Dr. Norman J. Cohen*
Presents ten Bible stories that involve clothing in an essential way, as a means of learning about the text, its characters and their interactions.
6 x 9, 240 pp, HC, 978-1-58023-461-0 **$24.99**

The Genesis of Leadership: What the Bible Teaches Us about Vision, Values and Leading Change *By Rabbi Nathan Laufer; Foreword by Senator Joseph I. Lieberman*
6 x 9, 288 pp, Quality PB, 978-1-58023-352-1 **$18.99**

Hineini in Our Lives: Learning How to Respond to Others through 14 Biblical Texts and Personal Stories *By Rabbi Norman J. Cohen, PhD* 6 x 9, 240 pp, Quality PB, 978-1-58023-274-6 **$16.99**

The Modern Men's Torah Commentary: New Insights from Jewish Men on the 54 Weekly Torah Portions *Edited by Rabbi Jeffrey K. Salkin*
6 x 9, 368 pp, HC, 978-1-58023-395-8 **$24.99**

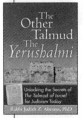

Moses and the Journey to Leadership: Timeless Lessons of Effective Management from the Bible and Today's Leaders *By Rabbi Norman J. Cohen, PhD*
6 x 9, 240 pp, Quality PB, 978-1-58023-351-4 **$18.99**; HC, 978-1-58023-227-2 **$21.99**

The Other Talmud—*The Yerushalmi*: Unlocking the Secrets of The Talmud of Israel for Judaism Today *By Rabbi Judith Z. Abrams, PhD*
6 x 9, 256 pp, HC, 978-1-58023-463-4 **$24.99**

Sage Tales: Wisdom and Wonder from the Rabbis of the Talmud
By Rabbi Burton L. Visotzky 6 x 9, 256 pp, HC, 978-1-58023-456-6 **$24.99**

The Torah Revolution: Fourteen Truths That Changed the World
By Rabbi Reuven Hammer, PhD 6 x 9, 240 pp, HC, 978-1-58023-457-3 **$24.99**

The Wisdom of Judaism: An Introduction to the Values of the Talmud
By Rabbi Dov Peretz Elkins 6 x 9, 192 pp, Quality PB, 978-1-58023-327-9 **$16.99**

Bar / Bat Mitzvah

The Mitzvah Project Book
Making Mitzvah Part of Your Bar/Bat Mitzvah ... and Your Life
By Liz Suneby and Diane Heiman; Foreword by Rabbi Jeffrey K. Salkin; Preface by Rabbi Sharon Brous
The go-to source for Jewish young adults and their families looking to make the world a better place through good deeds—big or small.
6 x 9, 224 pp, Quality PB Original, 978-1-58023-458-0 **$16.99** *For ages 11–13*

The Bar/Bat Mitzvah Memory Book, 2nd Edition: An Album for Treasuring the Spiritual Celebration
By Rabbi Jeffrey K. Salkin and Nina Salkin
8 x 10, 48 pp, 2-color text, Deluxe HC, ribbon marker, 978-1-58023-263-0 **$19.99**

For Kids—Putting God on Your Guest List, 2nd Edition: How to Claim the Spiritual Meaning of Your Bar or Bat Mitzvah *By Rabbi Jeffrey K. Salkin*
6 x 9, 144 pp, Quality PB, 978-1-58023-308-8 **$15.99** *For ages 11–13*

The Jewish Prophet: Visionary Words from Moses and Miriam to Henrietta Szold and A. J. Heschel *By Rabbi Dr. Michael J. Shire*
6½ x 8½, 128 pp, 123 full-color illus., HC, 978-1-58023-168-8 **$14.95**

Putting God on the Guest List, 3rd Edition: How to Reclaim the Spiritual Meaning of Your Child's Bar or Bat Mitzvah *By Rabbi Jeffrey K. Salkin*
6 x 9, 224 pp, Quality PB, 978-1-58023-222-7 **$16.99**
        Teacher's Guide: 8½ x 11, 48 pp, PB, 978-1-58023-226-5 **$8.99**

Teens / Young Adults

Text Messages: A Torah Commentary for Teens
Edited by Rabbi Jeffrey K. Salkin
Shows today's teens how each Torah portion contains worlds of meaning for them, for what they are going through in their lives, and how they can shape their Jewish identity as they enter adulthood.
6 x 9, 304 pp (est), HC, 978-1-58023-507-5 **$24.99**

Hannah Senesh: Her Life and Diary, the First Complete Edition
By Hannah Senesh; Foreword by Marge Piercy; Preface by Eitan Senesh; Afterword by Roberta Grossman
6 x 9, 368 pp, b/w photos, Quality PB, 978-1-58023-342-2 **$19.99**

I Am Jewish: Personal Reflections Inspired by the Last Words of Daniel Pearl
Edited by Judea and Ruth Pearl 6 x 9, 304 pp, Deluxe PB w/ flaps, 978-1-58023-259-3 **$19.99**
Download a free copy of the *I Am Jewish Teacher's Guide* at www.jewishlights.com.

The JGirl's Guide: The Young Jewish Woman's Handbook for Coming of Age
By Penina Adelman, Ali Feldman and Shulamit Reinharz
6 x 9, 240 pp, Quality PB, 978-1-58023-215-9 **$14.99** *For ages 11 & up*
        Teacher's & Parent's Guide: 8½ x 11, 56 pp, PB, 978-1-58023-225-8 **$8.99**

The JGuy's Guide: The GPS for Jewish Teen Guys
By Rabbi Joseph B. Meszler, Dr. Shulamit Reinharz, Liz Suneby and Diane Heiman
6 x 9, 208 pp, Quality PB Original, 978-1-58023-721-5 **$16.99**
        Teacher's Guide: 8½ x 11, 30pp, PB, 978-1-58023-773-4 **$8.99**

Tough Questions Jews Ask, 2nd Edition: A Young Adult's Guide to Building a Jewish Life *By Rabbi Edward Feinstein*
6 x 9, 160 pp, Quality PB, 978-1-58023-454-2 **$16.99** *For ages 11 & up*
        Teacher's Guide: 8½ x 11, 72 pp, PB, 978-1-58023-187-9 **$8.95**

Pre-Teens

Be Like God: God's To-Do List for Kids
By Dr. Ron Wolfson
Encourages kids ages eight through twelve to use their God-given superpowers to find the many ways they can make a difference in the lives of others and find meaning and purpose for their own.
7 x 9, 144 pp, Quality PB, 978-1-58023-510-5 **$15.99** *For ages 8–12*

The Book of Miracles: A Young Person's Guide to Jewish Spiritual Awareness
By Lawrence Kushner, with all-new illustrations by the author.
6 x 9, 96 pp, 2-color illus., HC, 978-1-879045-78-1 **$16.95** *For ages 9–13*

Theology / Philosophy

Believing and Its Tensions: A Personal Conversation about God, Torah, Suffering and Death in Jewish Thought
By Rabbi Neil Gillman, PhD
Explores the changing nature of belief and the complexities of reconciling the intellectual, emotional and moral questions of Gillman's own searching mind and soul.
5½ x 8½, 144 pp, HC, 978-1-58023-669-0 **$19.99**

God of Becoming and Relationship: The Dynamic Nature of Process Theology *By Rabbi Bradley Shavit Artson, DHL*
Explains how Process Theology breaks us free from the strictures of ancient Greek and medieval European philosophy, allowing us to see all creation as related patterns of energy through which we connect to everything.
6 x 9, 208 pp, HC, 978-1-58023-713-0 **$24.99**

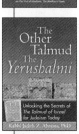

The Other Talmud—*The Yerushalmi*: Unlocking the Secrets of The Talmud of Israel for Judaism Today *By Rabbi Judith Z. Abrams, PhD*
A fascinating—and stimulating—look at "the other Talmud" and the possibilities for Jewish life reflected there. 6 x 9, 256 pp, HC, 978-1-58023-463-4 **$24.99**

The Way of Man: According to Hasidic Teaching
By Martin Buber; New Translation and Introduction by Rabbi Bernard H. Mehlman and Dr. Gabriel E. Padawer; Foreword by Paul Mendes-Flohr
An accessible and engaging new translation of Buber's classic work—*available as an e-book only*. E-book, 978-1-58023-601-0 Digital List Price **$14.99**

The Death of Death: Resurrection and Immortality in Jewish Thought
By Rabbi Neil Gillman, PhD 6 x 9, 336 pp, Quality PB, 978-1-58023-081-0 **$18.95**

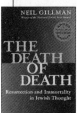

Doing Jewish Theology: God, Torah & Israel in Modern Judaism *By Rabbi Neil Gillman, PhD*
6 x 9, 304 pp, Quality PB, 978-1-58023-439-9 **$18.99**; HC, 978-1-58023-322-4 **$24.99**

From Defender to Critic: The Search for a New Jewish Self
By Dr. David Hartman 6 x 9, 336 pp, HC, 978-1-58023-515-0 **$35.00**

The God Who Hates Lies: Confronting & Rethinking Jewish Tradition
By Dr. David Hartman with Charlie Buckholtz 6 x 9, 208 pp, HC, 978-1-58023-455-9 **$24.99**

A Heart of Many Rooms: Celebrating the Many Voices within Judaism
By Dr. David Hartman 6 x 9, 352 pp, Quality PB, 978-1-58023-156-5 **$19.95**

Jewish Theology in Our Time: A New Generation Explores the Foundations and Future of Jewish Belief *Edited by Rabbi Elliot J. Cosgrove, PhD; Foreword by Rabbi David J. Wolpe; Preface by Rabbi Carole B. Balin, PhD* 6 x 9, 240 pp, Quality PB, 978-1-58023-630-1, **$19.99**; HC, 978-1-58023-413-9 **$24.99**

Maimonides—Essential Teachings on Jewish Faith & Ethics: The Book of Knowledge & the Thirteen Principles of Faith—Annotated & Explained
Translation and Annotation by Rabbi Marc D. Angel, PhD
5½ x 8½, 224 pp, Quality PB Original, 978-1-59473-311-6 **$18.99***

Maimonides, Spinoza and Us: Toward an Intellectually Vibrant Judaism
By Rabbi Marc D. Angel, PhD 6 x 9, 224 pp, HC, 978-1-58023-411-5 **$24.99**

Our Religious Brains: What Cognitive Science Reveals about Belief, Morality, Community and Our Relationship with God
By Rabbi Ralph D. Mecklenburger; Foreword by Dr. Howard Kelfer; Preface by Dr. Neil Gillman
6 x 9, 224 pp, HC, 978-1-58023-508-2 **$24.99**

Your Word Is Fire: The Hasidic Masters on Contemplative Prayer
Edited and translated by Rabbi Arthur Green, PhD, and Barry W. Holtz
6 x 9, 160 pp, Quality PB, 978-1-879045-25-5 **$16.99**

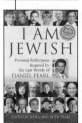

I Am Jewish
Personal Reflections Inspired by the Last Words of Daniel Pearl
Almost 150 Jews—both famous and not—from all walks of life, from all around the world, write about many aspects of their Judaism.
Edited by Judea and Ruth Pearl 6 x 9, 304 pp, Deluxe PB w/ flaps, 978-1-58023-259-3 **$19.99**
Download a free copy of the *I Am Jewish Teacher's Guide* at www.jewishlights.com.

*A book from SkyLight Paths, Jewish Lights' sister imprint

Theology / Philosophy / The Way Into... Series

The Way Into... series offers an accessible and highly usable "guided tour" of the Jewish faith, people, history and beliefs—in total, an introduction to Judaism that will enable you to understand and interact with the sacred texts of the Jewish tradition. Each volume is written by a leading contemporary scholar and teacher, and explores one key aspect of Judaism. The Way Into... series enables all readers to achieve a real sense of Jewish cultural literacy through guided study.

The Way Into Encountering God in Judaism
By Rabbi Neil Gillman, PhD
For everyone who wants to understand how Jews have encountered God throughout history and today.
6 x 9, 240 pp, Quality PB, 978-1-58023-199-2 **$18.99**; HC, 978-1-58023-025-4 **$21.95**
Also Available: **The Jewish Approach to God:** A Brief Introduction for Christians
By Rabbi Neil Gillman, PhD
5½ x 8¼, 192 pp, Quality PB, 978-1-58023-190-9 **$16.95**

The Way Into Jewish Mystical Tradition
By Rabbi Lawrence Kushner
Allows readers to interact directly with the sacred mystical texts of the Jewish tradition. An accessible introduction to the concepts of Jewish mysticism, their religious and spiritual significance, and how they relate to life today.
6 x 9, 224 pp, Quality PB, 978-1-58023-200-5 **$18.99**

The Way Into Jewish Prayer
By Rabbi Lawrence A. Hoffman, PhD
Opens the door to 3,000 years of Jewish prayer, making anyone feel at home in the Jewish way of communicating with God.
6 x 9, 208 pp, Quality PB, 978-1-58023-201-2 **$18.99**

The Way Into Jewish Prayer Teacher's Guide
By Rabbi Jennifer Ossakow Goldsmith
8½ x 11, 42 pp, PB, 978-1-58023-345-3 **$8.99**
Download a free copy at www.jewishlights.com.

The Way Into Judaism and the Environment
By Jeremy Benstein, PhD
Explores the ways in which Judaism contributes to contemporary social-environmental issues, the extent to which Judaism is part of the problem and how it can be part of the solution.
6 x 9, 288 pp, Quality PB, 978-1-58023-368-2 **$18.99**; HC, 978-1-58023-268-5 **$24.99**

The Way Into *Tikkun Olam* (Repairing the World)
By Rabbi Elliot N. Dorff, PhD
An accessible introduction to the Jewish concept of the individual's responsibility to care for others and repair the world.
6 x 9, 304 pp, Quality PB, 978-1-58023-328-6 **$18.99**

The Way Into Torah
By Rabbi Norman J. Cohen, PhD
Helps guide you in the exploration of the origins and development of Torah, explains why it should be studied and how to do it.
6 x 9, 176 pp, Quality PB, 978-1-58023-198-5 **$16.99**

The Way Into the Varieties of Jewishness
By Sylvia Barack Fishman, PhD
Explores the religious and historical understanding of what it has meant to be Jewish from ancient times to the present controversy over "Who is a Jew?"
6 x 9, 288 pp, Quality PB, 978-1-58023-367-5 **$18.99**; HC, 978-1-58023-030-8 **$24.99**

Ecology / Environment

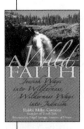

A Wild Faith: Jewish Ways into Wilderness, Wilderness Ways into Judaism
By Rabbi Mike Comins; Foreword by Nigel Savage 6 x 9, 240 pp, Quality PB, 978-1-58023-316-3 **$16.99**

Ecology & the Jewish Spirit: Where Nature & the Sacred Meet
Edited by Ellen Bernstein 6 x 9, 288 pp, Quality PB, 978-1-58023-082-7 **$18.99**

Torah of the Earth: Exploring 4,000 Years of Ecology in Jewish Thought
Vol. 1: Biblical Israel & Rabbinic Judaism; Vol. 2: Zionism & Eco-Judaism
Edited by Rabbi Arthur Waskow Vol. 1: 6 x 9, 272 pp, Quality PB, 978-1-58023-086-5 **$19.95**
Vol. 2: 6 x 9, 336 pp, Quality PB, 978-1-58023-087-2 **$19.95**

The Way Into Judaism and the Environment *By Jeremy Benstein, PhD*
6 x 9, 288 pp, Quality PB, 978-1-58023-368-2 **$18.99**; HC, 978-1-58023-268-5 **$24.99**

Graphic Novels / Graphic History

The Adventures of Rabbi Harvey: A Graphic Novel of Jewish Wisdom and Wit in the
Wild West *By Steve Sheinkin* 6 x 9, 144 pp, Full-color illus., Quality PB, 978-1-58023-310-1 **$16.99**

Rabbi Harvey Rides Again: A Graphic Novel of Jewish Folktales Let Loose in the
Wild West *By Steve Sheinkin* 6 x 9, 144 pp, Full-color illus., Quality PB, 978-1-58023-347-7 **$16.99**

Rabbi Harvey vs. the Wisdom Kid: A Graphic Novel of Dueling Jewish Folktales in
the Wild West *By Steve Sheinkin*
6 x 9, 144 pp, Full-color illus., Quality PB, 978-1-58023-422-1 **$16.99**

The Story of the Jews: A 4,000-Year Adventure—A Graphic History Book
By Stan Mack 6 x 9, 288 pp, Illus., Quality PB, 978-1-58023-155-8 **$16.99**

Grief / Healing

Judaism and Health: A Handbook of Practical, Professional and Scholarly
Resources *Edited by Jeff Levin, PhD, MPH, and Michele F. Prince, LCSW, MAJCS*
Foreword by Rabbi Elliot N. Dorff, PhD
Explores the expressions of health in the form of overviews of research studies,
first-person narratives and advice. 6 x 9, 448 pp, HC, 978-1-58023-714-7 **$50.00**

Facing Illness, Finding God: How Judaism Can Help You and Caregivers Cope
When Body or Spirit Fails *By Rabbi Joseph B. Meszler*
6 x 9, 208 pp, Quality PB, 978-1-58023-423-8 **$16.99**

Grief in Our Seasons: A Mourner's Kaddish Companion *By Rabbi Kerry M. Olitzky*
4½ x 6½, 448 pp, Quality PB, 978-1-879045-55-2 **$15.95**

Healing and the Jewish Imagination: Spiritual and Practical Perspectives on
Judaism and Health *Edited by Rabbi William Cutter, PhD*
6 x 9, 240 pp, Quality PB, 978-1-58023-373-6 **$19.99**

Healing from Despair: Choosing Wholeness in a Broken World
By Rabbi Elie Kaplan Spitz with Erica Shapiro Taylor; Foreword by Abraham J. Twerski, MD
5½ x 8½, 208 pp, Quality PB, 978-1-58023-436-8 **$16.99**

Healing of Soul, Healing of Body: Spiritual Leaders Unfold the Strength & Solace
in Psalms *Edited by Rabbi Simkha Y. Weintraub, LCSW*
6 x 9, 128 pp, 2-color illus. text, Quality PB, 978-1-879045-31-6 **$16.99**

Midrash & Medicine: Healing Body and Soul in the Jewish Interpretive Tradition
Edited by Rabbi William Cutter, PhD; Foreword by Michele F. Prince, LCSW, MAJCS
6 x 9, 352 pp, Quality PB, 978-1-58023-484-9 **$21.99**

Mourning & Mitzvah, 2nd Edition: A Guided Journal for Walking the Mourner's
Path through Grief to Healing *By Rabbi Anne Brener, LCSW*
7½ x 9, 304 pp, Quality PB, 978-1-58023-113-8 **$19.99**

Tears of Sorrow, Seeds of Hope, 2nd Edition: A Jewish Spiritual Companion
for Infertility and Pregnancy Loss *By Rabbi Nina Beth Cardin*
6 x 9, 208 pp, Quality PB, 978-1-58023-233-3 **$18.99**

A Time to Mourn, a Time to Comfort, 2nd Edition: A Guide to Jewish
Bereavement *By Dr. Ron Wolfson; Foreword by Rabbi David J. Wolpe*
7 x 9, 384 pp, Quality PB, 978-1-58023-253-1 **$21.99**

When a Grandparent Dies: A Kid's Own Remembering Workbook for Dealing
with Shiva and the Year Beyond *By Nechama Liss-Levinson, PhD*
8 x 10, 48 pp, 2-color text, HC, 978-1-879045-44-6 **$15.95** *For ages 7–13*

Judaism / Christianity / Interfaith

Christians & Jews—Faith to Faith: Tragic History, Promising Present, Fragile Future *By Rabbi James Rudin*
A probing examination of Christian-Jewish relations that looks at the major issues facing both faith communities.
6 x 9, 288 pp, Quality PB, 978-1-58023-717-8 **$18.99** HC, 978-1-58023-432-0 **$24.99**

Religion Gone Astray: What We Found at the Heart of Interfaith
By Pastor Don Mackenzie, Rabbi Ted Falcon and Imam Jamal Rahman
Probes more deeply into the problem aspects of our religious institutions—specifically exclusivity, violence, inequality of men and women, and homophobia—to provide a profound understanding of the nature of what divides us.
6 x 9, 192 pp, Quality PB, 978-1-59473-317-8 **$16.99***

Getting to the Heart of Interfaith: The Eye-Opening, Hope-Filled Friendship of a Pastor, a Rabbi and an Imam
By Rabbi Ted Falcon, Pastor Don Mackenzie and Imam Jamal Rahman
Presents ways we can work together to transcend the differences that have divided us historically. 6 x 9, 192 pp, Quality PB, 978-1-59473-263-8 **$16.99***

How to Do Good & Avoid Evil: A Global Ethic from the Sources of Judaism
By Hans Küng and Rabbi Walter Homolka 6 x 9, 224 pp, HC, 978-1-59473-255-3 **$19.99***

Claiming Earth as Common Ground: The Ecological Crisis through the Lens of Faith *By Rabbi Andrea Cohen-Kiener* 6 x 9, 192 pp, Quality PB, 978-1-59473-261-4 **$16.99***

Modern Jews Engage the New Testament: Enhancing Jewish Well-Being in a Christian Environment *By Rabbi Michael J. Cook, PhD* 6 x 9, 416 pp, HC, 978-1-58023-313-2 **$29.99**

The Changing Christian World: A Brief Introduction for Jews
By Rabbi Leonard A. Schoolman 5½ x 8½, 176 pp, Quality PB, 978-1-58023-344-6 **$16.99**

Christians & Jews in Dialogue: Learning in the Presence of the Other
By Mary C. Boys and Sara S. Lee 6 x 9, 240 pp, Quality PB, 978-1-59473-254-6 **$18.99***

Disaster Spiritual Care: Practical Clergy Responses to Community, Regional and National Tragedy *Edited by Rabbi Stephen B. Roberts, BCJC, and Rev. Willard W. C. Ashley Sr., DMin, DH*
6 x 9, 384 pp, HC, 978-1-59473-240-9 **$40.00***

How to Be a Perfect Stranger, 5th Edition: The Essential Religious Etiquette Handbook *Edited by Stuart M. Matlins and Arthur J. Magida*
6 x 9, 432 pp, Quality PB, 978-1-59473-294-2 **$19.99***

InterActive Faith: The Essential Interreligious Community-Building Handbook
Edited by Rev. Bud Heckman with Rori Picker Neiss
6 x 9, 304 pp, Quality PB, 978-1-59473-273-7 **$16.99**; HC, 978-1-59473-237-9 **$29.99***

Introducing My Faith and My Community
The Jewish Outreach Institute Guide for the Christian in a Jewish Interfaith Relationship
By Rabbi Kerry M. Olitzky 6 x 9, 176 pp, Quality PB, 978-1-58023-192-3 **$16.99**

The Jewish Approach to Repairing the World (*Tikkun Olam*)
A Brief Introduction for Christians *By Rabbi Elliot N. Dorff, PhD, with Rev. Cory Willson*
5½ x 8½, 256 pp, Quality PB, 978-1-58023-349-1 **$16.99**

The Jewish Connection to Israel, the Promised Land: A Brief Introduction for Christians *By Rabbi Eugene Korn, PhD* 5½ x 8½, 192 pp, Quality PB, 978-1-58023-318-7 **$14.99**

Jewish Holidays: A Brief Introduction for Christians *By Rabbi Kerry M. Olitzky and Rabbi Daniel Judson* 5½ x 8½, 176 pp, Quality PB, 978-1-58023-302-6 **$16.99**

Jewish Ritual: A Brief Introduction for Christians *By Rabbi Kerry M. Olitzky and Rabbi Daniel Judson* 5½ x 8½, 144 pp, Quality PB, 978-1-58023-210-4 **$14.99**

A Jewish Understanding of the New Testament *By Rabbi Samuel Sandmel;
Preface by Rabbi David Sandmel* 5½ x 8½, 368 pp, Quality PB, 978-1-59473-048-1 **$19.99***

Righteous Gentiles in the Hebrew Bible: Ancient Role Models for Sacred Relationships *By Rabbi Jeffrey K. Salkin; Foreword by Rabbi Harold M. Schulweis; Preface by Phyllis Tickle*
6 x 9, 192 pp, Quality PB, 978-1-58023-364-4 **$18.99**

We Jews and Jesus: Exploring Theological Differences for Mutual Understanding
By Rabbi Samuel Sandmel; Preface by Rabbi David Sandmel
6 x 9, 192 pp, Quality PB, 978-1-59473-208-9 **$16.99**

*A book from SkyLight Paths, Jewish Lights' sister imprint

Meditation

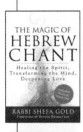

The Magic of Hebrew Chant: Healing the Spirit, Transforming the Mind, Deepening Love
By Rabbi Shefa Gold; Foreword by Sylvia Boorstein
Introduces this transformative spiritual practice as a way to unlock the power of sacred texts and make prayer and meditation the delight of your life. Includes musical notations. 6 x 9, 352 pp, Quality PB, 978-1-58023-671-3 **$24.99**

The Magic of Hebrew Chant Companion—The Big Book of Musical Notations and Incantations
8½ x 11, 154 pp, PB, 978-1-58023-722-2 **$19.99**

Jewish Meditation Practices for Everyday Life
Awakening Your Heart, Connecting with God
By Rabbi Jeff Roth
Offers a fresh take on meditation that draws on life experience and living life with greater clarity as opposed to the traditional method of rigorous study.
6 x 9, 224 pp, Quality PB, 978-1-58023-397-2 **$18.99**

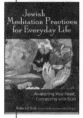

Discovering Jewish Meditation, 2nd Edition
Instruction & Guidance for Learning an Ancient Spiritual Practice
By Nan Fink Gefen, PhD 6 x 9, 208 pp, Quality PB, 978-1-58023-462-7 **$16.99**

The Handbook of Jewish Meditation Practices
A Guide for Enriching the Sabbath and Other Days of Your Life
By Rabbi David A. Cooper 6 x 9, 208 pp, Quality PB, 978-1-58023-102-2 **$16.95**

Meditation from the Heart of Judaism
Today's Teachers Share Their Practices, Techniques, and Faith
Edited by Avram Davis 6 x 9, 256 pp, Quality PB, 978-1-58023-049-0 **$16.95**

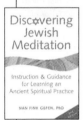

Ritual / Sacred Practices

God in Your Body: Kabbalah, Mindfulness and Embodied Spiritual Practice
By Jay Michaelson
The first comprehensive treatment of the body in Jewish spiritual practice and an essential guide to the sacred. 6 x 9, 272 pp, Quality PB, 978-1-58023-304-0 **$18.99**

The Book of Jewish Sacred Practices: CLAL's Guide to Everyday & Holiday Rituals & Blessings *Edited by Rabbi Irwin Kula and Vanessa L. Ochs, PhD*
6 x 9, 368 pp, Quality PB, 978-1-58023-152-7 **$18.95**

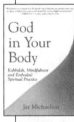

The Jewish Dream Book: The Key to Opening the Inner Meaning of Your Dreams
By Vanessa L. Ochs, PhD, with Elizabeth Ochs; Illus. by Kristina Swarner
8 x 8, 128 pp, Full-color illus., Deluxe PB w/ flaps, 978-1-58023-132-9 $16.95

Jewish Ritual: A Brief Introduction for Christians
By Rabbi Kerry M. Olitzky and Rabbi Daniel Judson
5½ x 8½, 144 pp, Quality PB, 978-1-58023-210-4 **$14.99**

The Rituals & Practices of a Jewish Life: A Handbook for Personal Spiritual Renewal *Edited by Rabbi Kerry M. Olitzky and Rabbi Daniel Judson*
6 x 9, 272 pp, Illus., Quality PB, 978-1-58023-169-5 **$18.95**

The Sacred Art of Lovingkindness: Preparing to Practice
By Rabbi Rami Shapiro 5½ x 8½, 176 pp, Quality PB, 978-1-59473-151-8 **$16.99**
(A book from SkyLight Paths, Jewish Lights' sister imprint)

Mystery & Detective Fiction

Criminal Kabbalah: An Intriguing Anthology of Jewish Mystery & Detective Fiction *Edited by Lawrence W. Raphael; Foreword by Laurie R. King*
All-new stories from twelve of today's masters of mystery and detective fiction—sure to delight mystery buffs of all faith traditions.
6 x 9, 256 pp, Quality PB, 978-1-58023-109-1 **$16.95**

Mystery Midrash: An Anthology of Jewish Mystery & Detective Fiction
Edited by Lawrence W. Raphael; Preface by Joel Siegel
6 x 9, 304 pp, Quality PB, 978-1-58023-055-1 **$16.95**

Spirituality / Prayer

Davening: A Guide to Meaningful Jewish Prayer
By Rabbi Zalman Schachter-Shalomi with Joel Segel; Foreword by Rabbi Lawrence Kushner
A fresh approach to prayer for all who wish to appreciate the power of prayer's poetry, song and ritual, and to join the age-old conversation that Jews have had with God. 6 x 9, 240 pp, Quality PB, 978-1-58023-627-0 **$18.99**

Jewish Men Pray: Words of Yearning, Praise, Petition, Gratitude and Wonder from Traditional and Contemporary Sources
Edited by Rabbi Kerry M. Olitzky and Stuart M. Matlins; Foreword by Rabbi Bradley Shavit Artson, DHL
A celebration of Jewish men's voices in prayer—to strengthen, heal, comfort, and inspire—from the ancient world up to our own day.
5 x 7¼, 400 pp, HC, 978-1-58023-628-7 **$19.99**

Making Prayer Real: Leading Jewish Spiritual Voices on Why Prayer Is Difficult and What to Do about It *By Rabbi Mike Comins* 6 x 9, 320 pp, Quality PB, 978-1-58023-417-7 **$18.99**

Witnesses to the One: The Spiritual History of the *Sh'ma*
By Rabbi Joseph B. Meszler; Foreword by Rabbi Elyse Goldstein
6 x 9, 176 pp, Quality PB, 978-1-58023-400-9 **$16.99**; HC, 978-1-58023-309-5 **$19.99**

My People's Prayer Book Series: Traditional Prayers, Modern Commentaries *Edited by Rabbi Lawrence A. Hoffman, PhD*
Provides diverse and exciting commentary to the traditional liturgy. Will help you find new wisdom in Jewish prayer, and bring liturgy into your life. Each book includes Hebrew text, modern translations and commentaries from all perspectives of the Jewish world.
Vol. 1—The *Sh'ma* and Its Blessings
   7 x 10, 168 pp, HC, 978-1-879045-79-8 **$29.99**
Vol. 2—The *Amidah* 7 x 10, 240 pp, HC, 978-1-879045-80-4 **$24.95**
Vol. 3—*P'sukei D'zimrah* (Morning Psalms)
   7 x 10, 240 pp, HC, 978-1-879045-81-1 **$29.99**
Vol. 4—*Seder K'riat Hatorah* (The Torah Service)
   7 x 10, 264 pp, HC, 978-1-879045-82-8 **$29.99**
Vol. 5—*Birkhot Hashachar* (Morning Blessings)
   7 x 10, 240 pp, HC, 978-1-879045-83-5 **$24.95**
Vol. 6—*Tachanun* and Concluding Prayers
   7 x 10, 240 pp, HC, 978-1-879045-84-2 **$24.95**
Vol. 7—Shabbat at Home 7 x 10, 240 pp, HC, 978-1-879045-85-9 **$24.95**
Vol. 8—*Kabbalat Shabbat* (Welcoming Shabbat in the Synagogue)
   7 x 10, 240 pp, HC, 978-1-58023-121-3 **$24.99**
Vol. 9—Welcoming the Night: *Minchah* and *Ma'ariv* (Afternoon and Evening Prayer) 7 x 10, 272 pp, HC, 978-1-58023-262-3 **$24.99**
Vol. 10—Shabbat Morning: *Shacharit* and *Musaf* (Morning and Additional Services) 7 x 10, 240 pp, HC, 978-1-58023-240-1 **$29.99**

Spirituality / Lawrence Kushner

I'm God; You're Not: Observations on Organized Religion & Other Disguises of the Ego
   6 x 9, 256 pp, Quality PB, 978-1-58023-513-6 **$18.99**; HC, 978-1-58023-441-2 **$21.99**

The Book of Letters: A Mystical Hebrew Alphabet
   Popular HC Edition, 6 x 9, 80 pp, 2-color text, 978-1-879045-00-2 **$24.95**
   Collector's Limited Edition, 9 x 12, 80 pp, gold-foil-embossed pages, w/ limited-edition silkscreened print, 978-1-879045-04-0 **$349.00**

The Book of Miracles: A Young Person's Guide to Jewish Spiritual Awareness
   6 x 9, 96 pp, 2-color illus., HC, 978-1-879045-78-1 **$16.95** For ages 9–13

God Was in This Place & I, i Did Not Know: Finding Self, Spirituality and Ultimate Meaning 6 x 9, 192 pp, Quality PB, 978-1-879045-33-0 **$16.95**

Honey from the Rock: An Introduction to Jewish Mysticism
   6 x 9, 176 pp, Quality PB, 978-1-58023-073-5 **$16.95**

Invisible Lines of Connection: Sacred Stories of the Ordinary
   5½ x 8½, 160 pp, Quality PB, 978-1-879045-98-9 **$16.99**

The Way Into Jewish Mystical Tradition
   6 x 9, 224 pp, Quality PB, 978-1-58023-200-5 **$18.99**; HC, 978-1-58023-029-2 **$21.95**

Spirituality

Amazing Chesed: Living a Grace-Filled Judaism
By Rabbi Rami Shapiro Drawing from ancient and contemporary, traditional and non-traditional Jewish wisdom, reclaims the idea of grace in Judaism.
6 x 9, 176 pp, Quality PB, 978-1-58023-624-9 **$16.99**

Jewish with Feeling: A Guide to Meaningful Jewish Practice
By Rabbi Zalman Schachter-Shalomi with Joel Segel
Takes off from basic questions like "Why be Jewish?" and whether the word God still speaks to us today and lays out a vision for a whole-person Judaism.
5½ x 8½, 288 pp, Quality PB, 978-1-58023-691-1 **$19.99**

Perennial Wisdom for the Spiritually Independent: Sacred Teachings—Annotated & Explained *Annotation by Rami Shapiro; Foreword by Richard Rohr*
Weaves sacred texts and teachings from the world's major religions into a coherent exploration of the five core questions at the heart of every religion's search.
5½ x 8½, 336 pp, Quality PB Original, 978-1-59473-515-8 **$16.99**

Aleph-Bet Yoga: Embodying the Hebrew Letters for Physical and Spiritual Well-Being
By Steven A. Rapp; Foreword by Tamar Frankiel, PhD, and Judy Greenfeld; Preface by Hart Lazer
7 x 10, 128 pp, b/w photos, Quality PB, Lay-flat binding, 978-1-58023-162-6 **$16.95**

A Book of Life: Embracing Judaism as a Spiritual Practice
By Rabbi Michael Strassfeld 6 x 9, 544 pp, Quality PB, 978-1-58023-247-0 **$19.99**

Bringing the Psalms to Life: How to Understand and Use the Book of Psalms
By Rabbi Daniel F. Polish, PhD 6 x 9, 208 pp, Quality PB, 978-1-58023-157-2 **$16.95**

Does the Soul Survive? A Jewish Journey to Belief in Afterlife, Past Lives & Living with Purpose *By Rabbi Elie Kaplan Spitz; Foreword by Brian L. Weiss, MD*
6 x 9, 288 pp, Quality PB, 978-1-58023-165-7 **$18.99**

Entering the Temple of Dreams: Jewish Prayers, Movements and Meditations for the End of the Day *By Tamar Frankiel, PhD, and Judy Greenfeld*
7 x 10, 192 pp, illus., Quality PB, 978-1-58023-079-7 **$16.95**

First Steps to a New Jewish Spirit: Reb Zalman's Guide to Recapturing the Intimacy & Ecstasy in Your Relationship with God *By Rabbi Zalman M. Schachter-Shalomi with Donald Gropman* 6 x 9, 144 pp, Quality PB, 978-1-58023-182-4 **$16.95**

Foundations of Sephardic Spirituality: The Inner Life of Jews of the Ottoman Empire
By Rabbi Marc D. Angel, PhD 6 x 9, 224 pp, Quality PB, 978-1-58023-341-5 **$18.99**

God & the Big Bang: Discovering Harmony between Science & Spirituality
By Dr. Daniel C. Matt 6 x 9, 216 pp, Quality PB, 978-1-879045-89-7 **$18.99**

God in Our Relationships: Spirituality between People from the Teachings of Martin Buber *By Rabbi Dennis S. Ross* 5½ x 8½, 160 pp, Quality PB, 978-1-58023-147-3 **$16.95**

The Jewish Lights Spirituality Handbook: A Guide to Understanding, Exploring & Living a Spiritual Life *Edited by Stuart M. Matlins*
6 x 9, 456 pp, Quality PB, 978-1-58023-093-3 **$19.99**

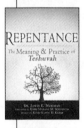

Judaism, Physics and God: Searching for Sacred Metaphors in a Post-Einstein World
By Rabbi David W. Nelson 6 x 9, 352 pp, Quality PB, inc. reader's discussion guide,
978-1-58023-306-4 **$18.99**; HC, 352 pp, 978-1-58023-252-4 **$24.99**

Meaning & Mitzvah: Daily Practices for Reclaiming Judaism through Prayer, God, Torah, Hebrew, Mitzvot and Peoplehood *By Rabbi Goldie Milgram*
7 x 9, 336 pp, Quality PB, 978-1-58023-256-2 **$19.99**

Repentance: The Meaning and Practice of Teshuvah
By Dr. Louis E. Newman; Foreword by Rabbi Harold M. Schulweis; Preface by Rabbi Karyn D. Kedar
6 x 9, 256 pp, HC, 978-1-58023-426-9 **$24.99** Quality PB, 978-1-58023-718-5 **$18.99**

The Sabbath Soul: Mystical Reflections on the Transformative Power of Holy Time
Selection, Translation and Commentary by Eitan Fishbane, PhD
6 x 9, 208 pp, Quality PB, 978-1-58023-459-7 **$18.99**

Tanya, the Masterpiece of Hasidic Wisdom: Selections Annotated & Explained
Translation & Annotation by Rabbi Rami Shapiro; Foreword by Rabbi Zalman M. Schachter-Shalomi
5½ x 8½, 240 pp, Quality PB, 978-1-59473-275-1 **$16.99**

These Are the Words, 2nd Edition: A Vocabulary of Jewish Spiritual Life
By Rabbi Arthur Green, PhD 6 x 9, 320 pp, Quality PB, 978-1-58023-494-8 **$19.99**

Inspiration

Into the Fullness of the Void: A Spiritual Autobiography By Dov Elbaum
The spiritual autobiography of one of Israel's leading cultural figures that provides
insights and guidance for all of us. 6 x 9, 288 pp, Quality PB Original, 978-1-58023-715-4 **$18.99**

Saying No and Letting Go: Jewish Wisdom on Making Room for What Matters Most
By Rabbi Edwin Goldberg, DHL; Foreword by Rabbi Naomi Levy
Taps into timeless Jewish wisdom that teaches how to "hold on tightly" to the
things that matter most while learning to "let go lightly" of the demands and worries that do not ultimately matter. 6 x 9, 192 pp, Quality PB, 978-1-58023-670-6 **$16.99**

The Bridge to Forgiveness: Stories and Prayers for Finding God and Restoring
Wholeness By Rabbi Karyn D. Kedar 6 x 9, 176 pp, Quality PB, 978-1-58023-451-1 **$16.99**

The Empty Chair: Finding Hope and Joy—Timeless Wisdom from a Hasidic Master,
Rebbe Nachman of Breslov Adapted by Moshe Mykoff and the Breslov Research Institute
4 x 6, 128 pp, Deluxe PB w/ flaps, 978-1-879045-67-5 **$9.99**

A Formula for Proper Living: Practical Lessons from Life and Torah
By Rabbi Abraham J. Twerski, MD 6 x 9, 144 pp, HC, 978-1-58023-402-3 **$19.99**

The Gentle Weapon: Prayers for Everyday and Not-So-Everyday Moments—
Timeless Wisdom from the Teachings of the Hasidic Master, Rebbe Nachman of Breslov
Adapted by Moshe Mykoff and S. C. Mizrahi, together with the Breslov Research Institute
4 x 6, 144 pp, Deluxe PB w/ flaps, 978-1-58023-022-3 **$9.99**

The God Upgrade: Finding Your 21st-Century Spirituality in Judaism's 5,000-Year-
Old Tradition By Rabbi Jamie Korngold; Foreword by Rabbi Harold M. Schulweis
6 x 9, 176 pp, Quality PB, 978-1-58023-443-6 $15.99

God Whispers: Stories of the Soul, Lessons of the Heart By Rabbi Karyn D. Kedar
6 x 9, 176 pp, Quality PB, 978-1-58023-088-9 **$15.95**

God's To-Do List: 103 Ways to Be an Angel and Do God's Work on Earth
By Dr. Ron Wolfson 6 x 9, 144 pp, Quality PB, 978-1-58023-301-9 **$16.99**

Happiness and the Human Spirit: The Spirituality of Becoming the Best You Can Be
By Rabbi Abraham J. Twerski, MD
6 x 9, 176 pp, Quality PB, 978-1-58023-404-7 **$16.99**; HC, 978-1-58023-343-9 **$19.99**

Life's Daily Blessings: Inspiring Reflections on Gratitude and Joy for Every Day, Based
on Jewish Wisdom By Rabbi Kerry M. Olitzky 4½ x 6½, 368 pp, Quality PB, 978-1-58023-396-5 **$16.99**

The Magic of Hebrew Chant: Healing the Spirit, Transforming the Mind,
Deepening Love By Rabbi Shefa Gold; Foreword by Sylvia Boorstein
6 x 9, 352 pp, Quality PB, 978-1-58023-671-3 **$24.99**

Restful Reflections: Nighttime Inspiration to Calm the Soul, Based on Jewish Wisdom
By Rabbi Kerry M. Olitzky and Rabbi Lori Forman-Jacobi 5 x 8, 352 pp, Quality PB, 978-1-58023-091-9 **$16.99**

Sacred Intentions: Morning Inspiration to Strengthen the Spirit, Based on Jewish Wisdom
By Rabbi Kerry M. Olitzky and Rabbi Lori Forman-Jacobi 4½ x 6½, 448 pp, Quality PB, 978-1-58023-061-2 **$16.99**

The Seven Questions You're Asked in Heaven: Reviewing and Renewing Your
Life on Earth By Dr. Ron Wolfson 6 x 9, 176 pp, Quality PB, 978-1-58023-407-8 **$16.99**

Kabbalah / Mysticism

Ehyeh: A Kabbalah for Tomorrow
By Rabbi Arthur Green, PhD 6 x 9, 224 pp, Quality PB, 978-1-58023-213-5 **$18.99**

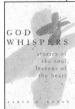

The Gift of Kabbalah: Discovering the Secrets of Heaven, Renewing Your Life on Earth
By Tamar Frankiel, PhD 6 x 9, 256 pp, Quality PB, 978-1-58023-141-1 **$16.95**

Jewish Mysticism and the Spiritual Life: Classical Texts, Contemporary
Reflections Edited by Dr. Lawrence Fine, Dr. Eitan Fishbane and Rabbi Or N. Rose
6 x 9, 256 pp, HC, 978-1-58023-434-4 **$24.99**; Quality PB, 978-1-58023-719-2 **$18.99**

Seek My Face: A Jewish Mystical Theology By Rabbi Arthur Green, PhD
6 x 9, 304 pp, Quality PB, 978-1-58023-130-5 **$19.95**

Zohar: Annotated & Explained Translation & Annotation by Dr. Daniel C. Matt; Foreword by
Andrew Harvey 5½ x 8½, 176 pp, Quality PB, 978-1-893361-51-5 **$16.99**
(A book from SkyLight Paths, Jewish Lights' sister imprint)

See also *The Way Into Jewish Mystical Tradition* in The Way Into... Series.

Holidays / Holy Days

Prayers of Awe Series

An exciting new series that examines the High Holy Day liturgy to enrich the praying experience of everyone—whether experienced worshipers or guests who encounter Jewish prayer for the very first time.

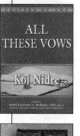

May God Remember: Memory and Memorializing in Judaism—*Yizkor*
Edited by Rabbi Lawrence A. Hoffman, PhD
Examines the history and ideas behind *Yizkor*, the Jewish memorial service, and this fascinating chapter in Jewish piety.
6 x 9, 304 pp, HC, 978-1-58023-689-8 **$24.99**

We Have Sinned—Sin and Confession in Judaism: *Ashamnu* and *Al Chet*
Edited by Rabbi Lawrence A. Hoffman, PhD 6 x 9, 304 pp, HC, 978-1-58023-612-6 **$24.99**

Who by Fire, Who by Water—*Un'taneh Tokef*
Edited by Rabbi Lawrence A. Hoffman, PhD
6 x 9, 272 pp, Quality PB, 978-1-58023-672-0 **$19.99**; HC, 978-1-58023-424-5 **$24.99**

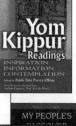

All These Vows—*Kol Nidre*
Edited by Rabbi Lawrence A. Hoffman, PhD 6 x 9, 288 pp, HC, 978-1-58023-430-6 **$24.99**

Rosh Hashanah Readings: Inspiration, Information and Contemplation
Yom Kippur Readings: Inspiration, Information and Contemplation
Edited by Rabbi Dov Peretz Elkins; Section Introductions from Arthur Green's These Are the Words
Rosh Hashanah: 6 x 9, 400 pp, Quality PB, 978-1-58023-437-5 **$19.99**
Yom Kippur: 6 x 9, 368 pp, Quality PB, 978-1-58023-438-2 **$19.99**; HC, 978-1-58023-271-5 **$24.99**

Reclaiming Judaism as a Spiritual Practice: Holy Days and Shabbat
By Rabbi Goldie Milgram 7 x 9, 272 pp, Quality PB, 978-1-58023-205-0 **$19.99**

The Sabbath Soul: Mystical Reflections on the Transformative Power of Holy Time
Selection, Translation and Commentary by Eitan Fishbane, PhD
6 x 9, 208 pp, Quality PB, 978-1-58023-459-7 **$18.99**

Shabbat, 2nd Edition: The Family Guide to Preparing for and Celebrating the Sabbath
By Dr. Ron Wolfson 7 x 9, 320 pp, Illus., Quality PB, 978-1-58023-164-0 **$19.99**

Hanukkah, 2nd Edition: The Family Guide to Spiritual Celebration
By Dr. Ron Wolfson 7 x 9, 240 pp, Illus., Quality PB, 978-1-58023-122-0 **$18.95**

Passover

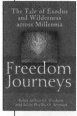

My People's Passover Haggadah
Traditional Texts, Modern Commentaries
Edited by Rabbi Lawrence A. Hoffman, PhD, and David Arnow, PhD
A diverse and exciting collection of commentaries on the traditional Passover Haggadah—in two volumes!
Vol. 1: 7 x 10, 304 pp, HC, 978-1-58023-354-5 **$24.99**
Vol. 2: 7 x 10, 320 pp, HC, 978-1-58023-346-0 **$24.99**

Creating Lively Passover Seders, 2nd Edition: A Sourcebook of Engaging Tales,
Texts & Activities *By David Arnow, PhD* 7 x 9, 464 pp, Quality PB, 978-1-58023-444-3 **$24.99**

Freedom Journeys: The Tale of Exodus and Wilderness across Millennia
By Rabbi Arthur O. Waskow and Rabbi Phyllis O. Berman
6 x 9, 288 pp, HC, 978-1-58023-445-0 **$24.99**

Leading the Passover Journey: The Seder's Meaning Revealed, the Haggadah's
Story Retold *By Rabbi Nathan Laufer*
6 x 9, 224 pp, Quality PB, 978-1-58023-399-6 **$18.99**

Passover, 2nd Edition: The Family Guide to Spiritual Celebration
By Dr. Ron Wolfson with Joel Lurie Grishaver 7 x 9, 416 pp, Quality PB, 978-1-58023-174-9 **$19.95**

The Women's Passover Companion: Women's Reflections on the Festival of Freedom
Edited by Rabbi Sharon Cohen Anisfeld, Tara Mohr and Catherine Spector; Foreword by Paula E. Hyman
6 x 9, 352 pp, Quality PB, 978-1-58023-231-9 **$19.99**; HC, 978-1-58023-128-2 **$24.95**

The Women's Seder Sourcebook: Rituals & Readings for Use at the Passover Seder
Edited by Rabbi Sharon Cohen Anisfeld, Tara Mohr and Catherine Spector
6 x 9, 384 pp, Quality PB, 978-1-58023-232-6 **$19.99**

Spirituality / Crafts

Jewish Threads: A Hands-On Guide to Stitching Spiritual Intention into Jewish Fabric Crafts *By Diana Drew with Robert Grayson*
Learn how to make your own Jewish fabric crafts with spiritual intention—a journey of creativity, imagination and inspiration. Thirty projects.
7 x 9, 288 pp, 8-page color insert, b/w illus., Quality PB Original, 978-1-58023-442-9 **$19.99**

Beading—The Creative Spirit: Finding Your Sacred Center through the Art of Beadwork *By Wendy Ellsworth*
Invites you on a spiritual pilgrimage into the kaleidoscope world of glass and color.
7 x 9, 240 pp, 8-page full-color insert, b/w photos and diagrams, Quality PB, 978-1-59473-267-6 **$18.99***

Contemplative Crochet: A Hands-On Guide for Interlocking Faith and Craft *By Cindy Crandall-Frazier; Foreword by Linda Skolnik*
Will take you on a path deeper into your crocheting and your spiritual awareness.
7 x 9, 208 pp, b/w photos, Quality PB, 978-1-59473-238-6 **$16.99***

The Knitting Way: A Guide to Spiritual Self-Discovery
By Linda Skolnik and Janice MacDaniels
Shows how to use knitting to strengthen your spiritual self.
7 x 9, 240 pp, b/w photos, Quality PB, 978-1-59473-079-5 **$16.99***

The Painting Path: Embodying Spiritual Discovery through Yoga, Brush and Color *By Linda Novick; Foreword by Richard Segalman*
Explores the divine connection you can experience through art.
7 x 9, 208 pp, 8-page full-color insert, b/w photos, Quality PB, 978-1-59473-226-3 **$18.99***

The Quilting Path: A Guide to Spiritual Self-Discovery through Fabric, Thread and Kabbalah *By Louise Silk* Explores how to cultivate personal growth through quilt making. 7 x 9, 192 pp, b/w photos, Quality PB, 978-1-59473-206-5 **$16.99***

Travel / History

Israel—A Spiritual Travel Guide, 2nd Edition: A Companion for the Modern Jewish Pilgrim *By Rabbi Lawrence A. Hoffman, PhD*
Helps today's pilgrim tap into the deep spiritual meaning of the ancient—and modern—sites of the Holy Land.
4¾ x 10, 256 pp, Illus., Quality PB, 978-1-58023-261-6 **$18.99**
Also Available: **The Israel Mission Leader's Guide** 5½ x 8½, 16 pp, PB, 978-1-58023-085-8 **$4.95**

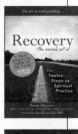

On the Chocolate Trail: A Delicious Adventure Connecting Jews, Religions, History, Travel, Rituals and Recipes to the Magic of Cacao
By Rabbi Deborah R. Prinz
Take a delectable journey through the religious history of chocolate—a real treat!
6 x 9, 272 pp w/ 20+ b/w photographs, Quality PB, 978-1-58023-487-0 **$18.99**

Twelve Steps

Recovery—The Sacred Art: The Twelve Steps as Spiritual Practice
By Rami Shapiro; Foreword by Joan Borysenko, PhD
Draws on insights and practices of different religious traditions to help you move more deeply into the universal spirituality of the Twelve Step system.
5½ x 8½, 240 pp, Quality PB Original, 978-1-59473-259-1 **$16.99***

100 Blessings Every Day: Daily Twelve Step Recovery Affirmations, Exercises for Personal Growth & Renewal Reflecting Seasons of the Jewish Year *By Rabbi Kerry M. Olitzky; Foreword by Rabbi Neil Gillman, PhD* 4½ x 6½, 432 pp, Quality PB, 978-1-879045-30-9 **$16.99**

Recovery from Codependence: A Jewish Twelve Steps Guide to Healing Your Soul
By Rabbi Kerry M. Olitzky 6 x 9, 160 pp, Quality PB, 978-1-879045-32-3 **$13.95**

Twelve Jewish Steps to Recovery, 2nd Edition: A Personal Guide to Turning from Alcoholism & Other Addictions—Drugs, Food, Gambling, Sex...
By Rabbi Kerry M. Olitzky and Stuart A. Copans, MD; Preface by Abraham J. Twerski, MD
6 x 9, 160 pp, Quality PB, 978-1-58023-409-2 **$16.99**

*A book from SkyLight Paths, Jewish Lights' sister imprint

Children's Books

Around the World in One Shabbat
Jewish People Celebrate the Sabbath Together
By Durga Yael Bernhard
Takes your child on a colorful adventure to share the many ways Jewish people celebrate Shabbat around the world.
11 x 8½, 32 pp, Full-color illus., HC, 978-1-58023-433-7 **$18.99** *For ages 3–6*

It's a ... It's a ... It's a Mitzvah
By Liz Suneby and Diane Heiman; Full-color Illus. by Laurel Molk
Join Mitzvah Meerkat and friends as they introduce children to the everyday kindnesses that mark the beginning of a Jewish journey and a lifetime commitment to *tikkun olam* (repairing the world). 9 x 12, 32 pp, Full-color illus., HC, 978-1-58023-509-9 **$18.99** *For ages 3–6*

What You Will See Inside a Synagogue
By Rabbi Lawrence A. Hoffman, PhD, and Dr. Ron Wolfson; Full-color photos by Bill Aron
A colorful, fun-to-read introduction that explains the ways and whys of Jewish worship and religious life. 8½ x 10¼, 32 pp, Full-color photos, Quality PB, 978-1-59473-256-0 **$8.99** *For ages 6 & up*
(A book from SkyLight Paths, Jewish Lights' sister imprint)

Because Nothing Looks Like God
By Lawrence Kushner and Karen Kushner
Real-life examples of happiness and sadness—from goodnight stories, to the hope and fear felt the first time at bat, to the closing moments of someone's life—invite parents and children to explore, together, the questions we all have about God, no matter what our age. 11 x 8½, 32 pp, Full-color illus., HC, 978-1-58023-092-6 **$18.99** *For ages 4 & up*

The Book of Miracles: A Young Person's Guide to Jewish Spiritual Awareness
Written and illus. by Lawrence Kushner
Easy-to-read, imaginatively illustrated book encourages kids' awareness of their own spirituality. Revealing the essence of Judaism in a language they can understand and enjoy. 6 x 9, 96 pp, 2-color illus., HC, 978-1-879045-78-1 **$16.95** *For ages 9–13*

In God's Hands   *By Lawrence Kushner and Gary Schmidt*
Brings new life to a traditional Jewish folktale, reminding parents and kids of all faiths and all backgrounds that each of us has the power to make the world a better place—working ordinary miracles with our everyday deeds.
9 x 12, 32 pp, Full-color illus., HC, 978-1-58023-224-1 **$16.99** *For ages 5 & up*

In Our Image: God's First Creatures
By Nancy Sohn Swartz
A playful new twist to the Genesis story, God asks all of nature to offer gifts to humankind—with a promise that the humans would care for creation in return. 9 x 12, 32 pp, Full-color illus., HC, 978-1-879045-99-6 **$16.95** *For ages 4 & up*
Animated app available on Apple App Store and The Google Play Marketplace **$9.99**

The Jewish Family Fun Book, 2nd Ed.
Holiday Projects, Everyday Activities, and Travel Ideas with Jewish Themes
By Danielle Dardashti and Roni Sarig
The complete sourcebook for families wanting to put a new spin on activities for Jewish holidays, holy days and the everyday. It offers dozens of easy-to-do activities that bring Jewish tradition to life for kids of all ages.
6 x 9, 304 pp, w/ 70+ b/w illus., Quality PB, 978-1-58023-333-0 **$18.99**

What Makes Someone a Jew?   *By Lauren Seidman*
Reflects the changing face of American Judaism. Helps preschoolers and young readers (ages 3–6) understand that you don't have to look a certain way to be Jewish.
10 x 8½, 32 pp, Full-color photos, Quality PB, 978-1-58023-321-7 **$8.99** *For ages 3–6*

When a Grandparent Dies: A Kid's Own Remembering Workbook for
Dealing with Shiva and the Year Beyond   *By Nechama Liss-Levinson*
8 x 10, 48 pp, 2-color text, HC, 978-1-879045-44-6 **$15.95** *For ages 7–13*

Children's Books by Sandy Eisenberg Sasso

The *Shema* in the Mezuzah: Listening to Each Other
Introduces children ages 3 to 6 to the words of the *Shema* and the custom of putting up the mezuzah. Winner, National Jewish Book Award
9 x 12, 32 pp, Full-color illus., HC, 978-1-58023-506-8 **$18.99**

Adam & Eve's First Sunset: God's New Day
Explores fear and hope, faith and gratitude in ways that will delight kids and adults—inspiring us to bless each of God's days and nights.
9 x 12, 32 pp, Full-color illus., HC, 978-1-58023-177-0 **$17.95** *For ages 4 & up*

Also Available as a Board Book: **Adam and Eve's New Day**
5 x 5, 24 pp, Full-color illus., Board Book, 978-1-59473-205-8 **$7.99** *For ages 0–4*
(A book from SkyLight Paths, Jewish Lights' sister imprint)

But God Remembered: Stories of Women from Creation to the
Promised Land   Four different stories of women—Lilith, Serach, Bityah and the Daughters of Z—teach us important values through their faith and actions.
9 x 12, 32 pp, Full-color illus., Quality PB, 978-1-58023-372-9 **$8.99** *For ages 8 & up*

For Heaven's Sake
Heaven is often found where you least expect it.
9 x 12, 32 pp, Full-color illus., HC, 978-1-58023-054-4 **$16.95** *For ages 4 & up*

God in Between
If you wanted to find God, where would you look? This magical, mythical tale teaches that God can be found where we are: within all of us and the relationships between us. 9 x 12, 32 pp, Full-color illus., HC, 978-1-879045-86-6 **$16.95** *For ages 4 & up*

God Said Amen
An inspiring story about hearing the answers to our prayers.
9 x 12, 32 pp, Full-color illus., HC, 978-1-58023-080-3 **$16.95** *For ages 4 & up*

God's Paintbrush: Special 10th Anniversary Edition
Wonderfully interactive, invites children of all faiths and backgrounds to encounter God through moments in their own lives. Provides questions adult and child can explore together. 11 x 8¼, 32 pp, Full-color illus., HC, 978-1-58023-195-4 **$17.95** *For ages 4 & up*

Also Available as a Board Book: **I Am God's Paintbrush**
5 x 5, 24 pp, Full-color illus., Board Book, 978-1-59473-265-2 **$7.99** *For ages 0–4*
(A book from SkyLight Paths, Jewish Lights' sister imprint)

Also Available: **God's Paintbrush Teacher's Guide**
8½ x 11, 32 pp, PB, 978-1-879045-57-6 **$8.95**

God's Paintbrush Celebration Kit
A Spiritual Activity Kit for Teachers and Students of All Faiths, All Backgrounds
9½ x 12, 40 Full-color Activity Sheets & Teacher Folder w/ complete instructions
HC, 978-1-58023-050-6 **$21.95**
8-Student Activity Sheet Pack (40 sheets/5 sessions), 978-1-58023-058-2 **$19.95**

In God's Name
Like an ancient myth in its poetic text and vibrant illustrations, this award-winning modern fable about the search for God's name celebrates the diversity and, at the same time, the unity of all people.
9 x 12, 32 pp, Full-color illus., HC, 978-1-879045-26-2 **$16.99** *For ages 4 & up*

Also Available as a Board Book: **What Is God's Name?**
5 x 5, 24 pp, Full-color illus., Board Book, 978-1-893361-10-2 **$7.99** *For ages 0–4*
(A book from SkyLight Paths, Jewish Lights' sister imprint)

Also Available in Spanish: **El nombre de Dios**
9 x 12, 32 pp, Full-color illus., HC, 978-1-893361-63-8 **$16.95** *For ages 4 & up*

Noah's Wife: The Story of Naamah
9 x 12, 32 pp, Full-color illus., HC, 978-1-58023-134-3 **$16.95** *For ages 4 & up*

Also Available as a Board Book: **Naamah, Noah's Wife**
5 x 5, 24 pp, Full-color illus., Board Book, 978-1-893361-56-0 **$7.95** *For ages 0–4*
(A book from SkyLight Paths, Jewish Lights' sister imprint)

Social Justice

Where Justice Dwells
A Hands-On Guide to Doing Social Justice in Your Jewish Community
By Rabbi Jill Jacobs; Foreword by Rabbi David Saperstein
Provides ways to envision and act on your own ideals of social justice.
7 x 9, 288 pp, Quality PB Original, 978-1-58023-453-5 **$24.99**

There Shall Be No Needy
Pursuing Social Justice through Jewish Law and Tradition
By Rabbi Jill Jacobs; Foreword by Rabbi Elliot N. Dorff, PhD; Preface by Simon Greer
Confronts the most pressing issues of twenty-first-century America from a deeply Jewish perspective. 6 x 9, 288 pp, Quality PB, 978-1-58023-425-2 **$16.99**
There Shall Be No Needy Teacher's Guide 8½ x 11, 56 pp, PB, 978-1-58023-429-0 **$8.99**

Conscience
The Duty to Obey and the Duty to Disobey
By Rabbi Harold M. Schulweis
Examines the idea of conscience and the role conscience plays in our relationships to government, law, ethics, religion, human nature, God—and to each other.
6 x 9, 160 pp, Quality PB, 978-1-58023-419-1 **$16.99**; HC, 978-1-58023-375-0 **$19.99**

Judaism and Justice
The Jewish Passion to Repair the World
By Rabbi Sidney Schwarz; Foreword by Ruth Messinger
Explores the relationship between Judaism, social justice and the Jewish identity of American Jews. 6 x 9, 352 pp, Quality PB, 978-1-58023-353-8 **$19.99**

Spirituality / Women's Interest

New Jewish Feminism
Probing the Past, Forging the Future
Edited by Rabbi Elyse Goldstein; Foreword by Anita Diamant
Looks at the growth and accomplishments of Jewish feminism and what they mean for Jewish women today and tomorrow.
6 x 9, 480 pp, HC, 978-1-58023-359-0 **$24.99**

The Divine Feminine in Biblical Wisdom Literature
Selections Annotated & Explained
Translation & Annotation by Rabbi Rami Shapiro
5½ x 8½, 240 pp, Quality PB, 978-1-59473-109-9 **$16.99**
(A book from SkyLight Paths, Jewish Lights' sister imprint)

The Quotable Jewish Woman
Wisdom, Inspiration & Humor from the Mind & Heart
Edited by Elaine Bernstein Partnow
6 x 9, 496 pp, Quality PB, 978-1-58023-236-4 **$19.99**

The Women's Haftarah Commentary
New Insights from Women Rabbis on the 54 Weekly Haftarah Portions, the 5 Megillot & Special Shabbatot
Edited by Rabbi Elyse Goldstein
Illuminates the historical significance of female portrayals in the Haftarah and the Five Megillot. 6 x 9, 560 pp, Quality PB, 978-1-58023-371-2 **$19.99**

The Women's Torah Commentary
New Insights from Women Rabbis on the 54 Weekly Torah Portions
Edited by Rabbi Elyse Goldstein
Over fifty women rabbis offer inspiring insights on the Torah, in a week-by-week format.
6 x 9, 496 pp, Quality PB, 978-1-58023-370-5 **$19.99**; HC, 978-1-58023-076-6 **$34.95**

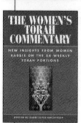

See Passover for *The Women's Passover Companion: Women's Reflections on the Festival of Freedom* and *The Women's Seder Sourcebook: Rituals & Readings for Use at the Passover Seder.*

Life Cycle
Marriage / Parenting / Family / Aging

The New Jewish Baby Album: Creating and Celebrating the Beginning of a Spiritual Life—A Jewish Lights Companion
By the Editors at Jewish Lights; Foreword by Anita Diamant; Preface by Rabbi Sandy Eisenberg Sasso
A spiritual keepsake that will be treasured for generations. More than just a memory book, *shows you how—and why it's important—*to create a Jewish home and a Jewish life. 8 x 10, 64 pp, Deluxe Padded HC, Full-color illus., 978-1-58023-138-1 **$19.95**

The Jewish Pregnancy Book: A Resource for the Soul, Body & Mind during Pregnancy, Birth & the First Three Months *By Sandy Falk, MD, and Rabbi Daniel Judson, with Steven A. Rapp* Medical information, prayers and rituals for each stage of pregnancy. 7 x 10, 208 pp, b/w photos, Quality PB, 978-1-58023-178-7 **$16.95**

Celebrating Your New Jewish Daughter: Creating Jewish Ways to Welcome Baby Girls into the Covenant—New and Traditional Ceremonies *By Debra Nussbaum Cohen; Foreword by Rabbi Sandy Eisenberg Sasso* 6 x 9, 272 pp, Quality PB, 978-1-58023-090-2 **$18.95**

The New Jewish Baby Book, 2nd Edition: Names, Ceremonies & Customs—A Guide for Today's Families *By Anita Diamant* 6 x 9, 320 pp, Quality PB, 978-1-58023-251-7 **$19.99**

Parenting as a Spiritual Journey: Deepening Ordinary and Extraordinary Events into Sacred Occasions *By Rabbi Nancy Fuchs-Kreimer, PhD*
6 x 9, 224 pp, Quality PB, 978-1-58023-016-2 **$17.99**

Parenting Jewish Teens: A Guide for the Perplexed
By Joanne Doades Explores the questions and issues that shape the world in which today's Jewish teenagers live and offers constructive advice to parents.
6 x 9, 176 pp, Quality PB, 978-1-58023-305-7 **$16.99**

Judaism for Two: A Spiritual Guide for Strengthening and Celebrating Your Loving Relationship *By Rabbi Nancy Fuchs-Kreimer, PhD, and Rabbi Nancy H. Wiener, DMin; Foreword by Rabbi Elliot N. Dorff, PhD*
Addresses the ways Jewish teachings can enhance and strengthen committed relationships. 6 x 9, 224 pp, Quality PB, 978-1-58023-254-8 **$16.99**

The Creative Jewish Wedding Book, 2nd Edition: A Hands-On Guide to New & Old Traditions, Ceremonies & Celebrations *By Gabrielle Kaplan-Mayer*
9 x 9, 288 pp, b/w photos, Quality PB, 978-1-58023-398-9 **$19.99**

Divorce Is a Mitzvah: A Practical Guide to Finding Wholeness and Holiness When Your Marriage Dies *By Rabbi Perry Netter; Afterword by Rabbi Laura Geller*
6 x 9, 224 pp, Quality PB, 978-1-58023-172-5 **$16.95**

Embracing the Covenant: Converts to Judaism Talk About Why & How
By Rabbi Allan Berkowitz and Patti Moskovitz 6 x 9, 192 pp, Quality PB, 978-1-879045-50-7 **$16.95**

The Guide to Jewish Interfaith Family Life: An InterfaithFamily.com Handbook
Edited by Ronnie Friedland and Edmund Case
6 x 9, 384 pp, Quality PB, 978-1-58023-153-4 **$18.95**

A Heart of Wisdom: Making the Jewish Journey from Midlife through the Elder Years
Edited by Susan Berrin; Foreword by Rabbi Harold Kushner
6 x 9, 384 pp, Quality PB, 978-1-58023-051-3 **$18.95**

Introducing My Faith and My Community: The Jewish Outreach Institute Guide for the Christian in a Jewish Interfaith Relationship
By Rabbi Kerry M. Olitzky 6 x 9, 176 pp, Quality PB, 978-1-58023-192-3 **$16.99**

Making a Successful Jewish Interfaith Marriage: The Jewish Outreach Institute Guide to Opportunities, Challenges and Resources *By Rabbi Kerry M. Olitzky with Joan Peterson Littman*
6 x 9, 176 pp, Quality PB, 978-1-58023-170-1 **$16.95**

A Man's Responsibility: A Jewish Guide to Being a Son, a Partner in Marriage, a Father and a Community Leader *By Rabbi Joseph B. Meszler*
6 x 9, 192 pp, Quality PB, 978-1-58023-435-1 **$16.99**

So That Your Values Live On: Ethical Wills and How to Prepare Them
Edited by Rabbi Jack Riemer and Rabbi Nathaniel Stampfer
6 x 9, 272 pp, Quality PB, 978-1-879045-34-7 **$18.99**

About Jewish Lights

People of all faiths and backgrounds yearn for books that attract, engage, educate, and spiritually inspire.

Our principal goal is to stimulate thought and help all people learn about who the Jewish People are, where they come from, and what the future can be made to hold. While people of our diverse Jewish heritage are the primary audience, our books speak to people in the Christian world as well and will broaden their understanding of Judaism and the roots of their own faith.

We bring to you authors who are at the forefront of spiritual thought and experience. While each has something different to say, they all say it in a voice that you can hear.

Our books are designed to welcome you and then to engage, stimulate, and inspire. We judge our success not only by whether or not our books are beautiful and commercially successful, but by whether or not they make a difference in your life.

For your information and convenience, at the back of this book we have provided a list of other Jewish Lights books you might find interesting and useful. They cover all the categories of your life:

Bar/Bat Mitzvah	Life Cycle
Bible Study / Midrash	Meditation
Children's Books	Men's Interest
Congregation Resources	Parenting
Current Events / History	Prayer / Ritual / Sacred Practice
Ecology / Environment	Social Justice
Fiction: Mystery, Science Fiction	Spirituality
Grief / Healing	Theology / Philosophy
Holidays / Holy Days	Travel
Inspiration	12-Step
Kabbalah / Mysticism / Enneagram	Women's Interest

Stuart M. Matlins, Publisher

Or phone, fax, mail or e-mail to: **JEWISH LIGHTS Publishing**
Sunset Farm Offices, Route 4 • P.O. Box 237 • Woodstock, Vermont 05091
Tel: (802) 457-4000 • Fax: (802) 457-4004 • www.jewishlights.com
Credit card orders: (800) 962-4544 (8:30AM–5:30PM ET Monday–Friday)
Generous discounts on quantity orders. SATISFACTION GUARANTEED. Prices subject to change.

For more information about each book, visit our website at www.jewishlights.com